Ailsa, Inc., 2005 reprint edition of "Golf: A Royal and Ancient Game," originally published by Macmillan, London, 1893. Privately published for author in 1875.
ISBN: 0-940889-66-8

FLAGSTICK BOOKS

Edition of

GOLF: A ROYAL AND ANCIENT GAME

By

Robert Clark

Foreword by William Gifford

FOREWORD
by
William Gifford

Here is the second edition (the first edition was privately printed and not for sale) of *Golf: A Royal and Ancient Game*, which Edinburgher Robert Clark compiled and edited in 1875, just as golf's popularity was beginning to explode all over the world outside Scotland. His explicit goal was "to gather together all that has been said and sung in praise of the Royal game," and he delved into old records of every sort to extract the best of the art, history, and literature of golf in Scotland through the 19th century, all in original text and (thankfully) with some helpful explanatory notes. The result was a prize: Joseph S.F. Murdoch has characterized it as "one of the masterpieces of golf literature. It is also one of the most important contributions to the library of golf and one of the most handsomely produced of all golf books . . . ."

I am writing this note on a dreary cold and golfless November Saturday afternoon at the Chicago Golf Club, out in Wheaton, Illinois. Even in this historic setting — founded in 1892 by C.B. Macdonald, Chicago Golf was, in turn, a founder of the United States Golf Association (along with Shinnecock, Newport, The Country Club and St. Andrew's) — the question weighing on me was how Clark's collection of some 50 pieces of poetry, song, and prose, and appurtenant illustrations would have much meaning for golfers today, well over a century later. I mean serious golfers today, of course, in the sense of loving the game and understanding how powerfully history and tradition have shaped the evolution of our rules, etiquette and enjoyment of the game. (For reasons that will become clear, I might even limit this audience of "serious golfers" to those who have received a note from, or who have sent one to, a fellow golfer signed "Far and sure.")

For any serious golfer who loves golf *and* literature and the other arts, *Golf* will reward every foray. That *Golf* is a collection of relatively short pieces is another positive attribute. The prospective reader doesn't need to commit to reading the whole book through without interruption. Rather, the individual pieces are quite discrete and can be savored one by one in virtually any order, as time permits and fancy inspires.

Let's start with history and tradition. Clark's own introduction compresses lots of (purely Scottish, perhaps understandably) golf history into just a few pages — from the famous 1457 decree of Parliament forbidding football and golf in favor of archery up through to the great portrait-worthy figures of the 19th century done by Sir Henry Raeburn. Looking out at the flag of Chicago Golf flapping violently in the breeze, with its motto "Far and Sure," however, I enjoyed discovering the apparent origin and real significance of that phrase in Clark's first entry, a "Historical Account of the Game of Golf," taken from some notes of one John Cundell privately printed in Edinburgh in 1824. This piece offers the reader short descriptions of a number of ball games that might lay claim to being the precursor of golf as we know it and, what was new and startling to me, a drawing showing a couple of players of a club-and-ball game taken from a 14th century manuscript book of prayer, with one player poised at the top of a backswing not too different from what appears in golfing art and photographs through the end of the 19th century. The best part of Cundell's piece for me, however, was the charming story of how a lowly Edinburgh shoemaker, John Patersone, teamed up with the Duke of York in 1682 on the links of Leith to defeat a couple of visiting English noblemen for a stake such that Patersone's winnings enabled him to build an enormous house in the Canongate (No. 77) in Edinburgh's Old Town. The Duke affixed a tablet on the house bearing the Patersone family coat of arms and the motto "Far and Sure." Since then numerous golf clubs have adopted "Far and Sure" as their motto, including the Royal Burgess Golfing Society of Edinburgh, Royal Liverpool (Hoylake) and, indeed, Chicago Golf Club. I exchange lots of notes with golfing friends signed off "Far and sure" and thereby take some satisfaction in perpetuating a great tradition.

Another important match at Leith in all probability between two members of The Gentlemen Golfers (the club that now plays at Muirfield), is presented in a distinctly alternative medium: "an heroic-comical poem in three cantos," a classic by Thomas Mathison that is said to be the first book devoted entirely to golf. Notwithstanding its many allusions to classical figures and contemporary (18th century) golfers, the poem is an eminently readable story of a tight match, between David ("Pygmalion") and Goliath ("Castalio"), that Castalio wins by holing an improbable 15 yard pitch over a cart-road.

Another way Clark presents golf history is to take extensive extracts from the record books of the Honourable Company of Edinburgh Golfers, the Royal and Ancient Golf Club of St. Andrews, the Musselburgh Golf Club, and the Burgess Golfing Society. The minutes are serious in part — the Honourable Company's beginning with the competition for the silver club trophy put forth by the Edinburgh Council in 1744 and ending with the opening of the club's new green and clubhouse at Muirfield in 1891, with numerous reports of the club's annual competitions in between and of course, lots of club rules — but there are some humorous entries:

"The Club met according to adjournment. The meeting was so merry it was agreed that matching and every other business should be delayed till next month. (1793)

"Captain Hope challenges Mr. Sanderson for a match to be played on Saturday, 1st Nov., at 2 o'clock — the Captain to shoot with a bow and arrow, and Mr. Sanderson to use a Club and ball, he being allowed to tee the ball at every stroke. (1828) [Captain Hope won "with great ease."]

"Captain Kilgour informed the meeting that Mr. Williamson had sent a small case of spirits of his own manufacturer as a present to the Club. The Secretary was ordered to transmit the thanks of the Society to Mr. Williamson, and to inform him that he was unanimously elected an Honorary Member. (1822)

"Mr. Brown betted with Mr. Spalding one gallon of whisky that he would drive a ball over Arthur Seat [an enormous hill in the center of Edinburgh] in 45 strokes. Mr. Spalding lost . . . . (1815)

There follow selections of poetry, including the longish "Golfiana," a Virgilian tale of St. Andrews, and a number of short poems or songs, with plenty of irony in the vein of those of our Californian contemporaries Fred and Pete Shoemaker (makers of a marvelous CD, "Extraordinary Golf: Songs of a Wonderful Game") and even one celebrating "Far and Sure!" as a cry passed down for generations that should "for ever endure" as a guide to life and golf. The poetry is interspersed with conventional prose essays from 19th century magazines and a short story of a match in rural Fife full of heckling, fisticuffs and other hostilities visited upon a presumptuous visitor from Edinburgh. The last being a tradition that has not — yet? — had much influence on our modern game!

The book is full of golfing treasures of the written word. But for me, the richest medium represented in the book is the visual art — a few full-page copies of historic scenes (including the procession of the silver club in Edinburgh) and portraits (Montrose, Forbes, Raeburn, Balfour), but far rarer, literally *dozens* of charming little cartoons and drawings of every conceivable aspect of golf and golfers. No instructionals, thankfully, but many great graphic inspirations. I'm going to acquire my copy of *Golf* so that I can scan its wonderful images into my computer for a lifetime supply of stationery, bookplates, dinner programs and wherever else an historic, stylish, or humorous golfing image is called for! (The publisher hereby grants each purchaser permission to do the same.)

                                            Far and sure.

Golf : a Royal and Ancient Game

CHARLES I. WHILE PLAYING GOLF ON LEITH LINKS RECEIVES NEWS OF THE BREAKING OUT OF THE IRISH REBELLION.

GOLF: A ROYAL & ANCIENT GAME

EDITED BY ROBERT CLARK
F.R.S.E. F.S.A. Scot.

'Sport Royal, I warrant you.
'I'll give thee leave to play till doomsday.'

Golf in the Olden Time.

	PAGE
Historical Account of the Game of Golf . . .	1
The Goff: An Heroi-Comical Poem in Three Cantos .	23
The Honourable The Edinburgh Company of Golfers .	39
The Royal and Ancient Golf Club of St. Andrews .	64
The Royal Musselburgh Golf Club	88
The Bruntsfield Links Golf Club	95
Edinburgh Burgess Golfing Society	109
Act of Parliament of King James II. 1457 . . .	116
Act of Parliament of King James III. 1471 . .	117
Act of Parliament of King James IV. 1491 . . .	118
The Kings Majesties Declaration to his Subjects concerning lawfull Sports to be used. 1618 . .	118
Declaration concerning lawfull Sports. 1633 . .	121
Early Notices of Golf from Burgh and Parish Records	123
Extracts from the Note-Books of Sir John Foulis .	133
Extracts from Accounts of the Lords High Treasurers of Scotland, 1503	135
Scrap relative to Golf, 1671	135
The Cock o' the Green	137
Sanctandrews	142
The Links of St. Rule	144
Golfiana	155
Address to St. Andrews	157
The Golfiad	158
The First Hole at St. Andrews on a Crowded Day .	163
Another Peep at the Links	168
The Golfer at Home	177

b

Contents

	PAGE
THE NINE HOLES OF THE LINKS OF ST. ANDREWS	194
A GOLF SONG	203
A TALE OF GOLF	206
THE LINKS O' INNERLEVEN	213
IN PRAISE OF GUTTA PERCHA	215
FAR AND SURE	218
A CHAPTER ON GOLF	220
BALLADE OF THE ROYAL GAME OF GOLF	227
SONG—A HUNDRED GOLFERS	228
A GOLFING SONG	230
SONG FOR THE FIRST MUSICAL MEETING OF THE WARRENDER GOLF CLUB	232
DUFFERS YET!	234
ST. ANDREWS	236
TO ST. ANDREW	242
AMONG THE ST. ANDREWS GOLFERS	244
ADDRESS BY THE CAPTAIN OF THE ROYAL AND ANCIENT GOLF CLUB OF ST. ANDREWS TO HIS CREW	253
SUTHERLANDIA	255
THE MORNING ROUND	261
MEDAL DAY AT ST. ANDREWS	263
A VOICE FROM THE RHINE	271
MEDAL DAY AT BLACKHEATH	275
THE GOLFER'S GARLAND	282

APPENDIX

ALLAN ROBERTSON	285
TOM MORRIS JUN.	291
RULES FOR THE GAME OF GOLF AS IT IS PLAYED BY THE ROYAL AND ANCIENT GOLF CLUB OF ST. ANDREWS	294
INDEX	301

PLATES

GOLF IN THE OLDEN TIME	HUGH THOMSON	*Title-page*
THE MARQUIS OF MONTROSE		*To face page* xix
THE EDITOR		,, xxviii
HON. DUNCAN FORBES OF CULLODEN		,, 41
SIR HENRY RAEBURN, R.A.		,, 52
JAMES BALFOUR, ESQ.		,, 56

WOOD ENGRAVINGS

CHARLES I. WHILE PLAYING GOLF ON LEITH LINKS RECEIVES NEWS OF THE IRISH REBELLION	SIR JOHN GILBERT	*Frontispiece*
THE GOLFER'S LAND	JAMES DRUMMOND	16
EDINA'S TOWERS	BIRKET FOSTER	24
VI ET ARTE	DAVID ALLAN	39
PROCESSION OF THE SILVER CLUB	DAVID ALLAN	43
PORTRAIT OF WILLIAM ST. CLAIR		48
ROSLIN CHAPEL	BIRKET FOSTER	49
KING WILLIAM THE FOURTH MEDAL		85
SILVER CROSS OF ST. ANDREW		87
PROFANING THE LORD'S SABBATH	G. AIKMAN	123
COCK O' THE GREEN	JOHN KAY	136
NINE HOLES OF ST. ANDREWS	THOMAS HODGE	194
A HUNDRED GOLFERS	C. A. DOYLE	228
ST. ANDREWS CATHEDRAL	W. BALLINGALL	239
ST. ANDREWS SHORE	BIRKET FOSTER	243
MEDAL DAY AT BLACKHEATH	F. GILBERT	276

And numerous Head and Tail Pieces and Initial Letters
By Clark Stanton and C. A. Doyle.

NOTE TO SECOND EDITION

IT is eighteen years since the first edition of *Golf: a Royal and Ancient Game* was privately printed. The impression was small, and the work has been long out of print. Since its publication, Golf has advanced by leaps and bounds : it is now as popular in England as it is in Scotland ; and it has taken deep root in Ireland.

After all, this volume is but a collection of Scraps and Patches. Many of them, however, have a historico-antiquarian interest.

At one time I contemplated giving some of my own experiences of the Game, but my friends Sir Walter G. Simpson, Bart., Horace Hutchinson, Esq., and others, have so exhaustively treated the subject that no opening is left. A few additions have been made here and there, which will be found in the "Early Notices of Golf," and in Footnotes, but it is disappointing to find that the first edition of the book exhausted nearly all that had been written about the Royal and Ancient Game.

EDINBURGH, *November* 1893.

INTRODUCTION

GOLF is a game peculiar to the Scots, and may indeed be called *par excellence* the national game of Scotland. Its fascinations have always been gratefully acknowledged, and not a few of its worthier practitioners have from time to time, in prose and verse, rehearsed its praises. Golf has, in fact, at once a history and a literature. Both of these the Editor believes must be interesting to Golfers. Hence this volume.

It is strange, considering its antiquity, and the number of its votaries, that hitherto no attempt has been made to gather together all that has been said and sung in praise of the Royal game. Beyond endeavouring to accomplish this—by diving into old records, extracting from them what seemed interesting, and adding such explanatory notes as appeared to be necessary—the Editor claims no merit. He trusts, however, that the gratification which this compilation has

Introduction

afforded him, may in some degree be shared by the reader.

Golf (Goff, Gowff) may literally be said to be in Scotland a game of immemorial antiquity. There is evidence that early in the fifteenth century it was *popular* in such a sense as it can scarcely at this day claim to be; and the obvious inference from this is that its *origin* lies very much further back—perhaps in some prehistoric period. Indeed, so popular had it then become, that the Legislature found it necessary to fulminate repeated statutes against it, as unprofitable, interfering with the more important accomplishment of Archery, and thus tending to impair the military efficiency of the people.

In March 1457 Parliament "decreeted and ordained " that wapinschawingis be halden be the Lordis and " Baronis spirituale and temporale, foure times in the zeir, "*and that the Fute-ball and Golf be utterly cryit doune*, " and nocht usit; and that the bowe merkis be maid " at ilk paroche kirk a pair of buttis, and schutting be " usit *ilk Sunday*."[1] In May 1471 an Act was passed " anent wapinshawings"; and for opposing "our auld enimies of England" it was thought expedient that

---

[1] It is perhaps worth noting that the words "*ilk Sunday*" have been omitted in the editions of the Acts of Parliament printed in 1597, 1681, and 1682. They were, however, restored in the edition printed by the Record Commission, vol. ii. 1814.

Introduction

"ilk yeman that can nocht deil with the bow, that he "haf a gude ax and a targe of leddir, to resist the shot "of Ingland, quhilk is na cost bot the valew of a hide ; ". . . and that the *Fute-ball and Golfe be abusit in tyme* "*cuming*, and the buttis maid up, and schuting usit." In May 1491 it is ordained, "That in na place of the "realme there be usit *Fute-ball, Golfe, or uther sik unpro-* "*fitabill sportis*, but for the commoun gude of the realme, "and defence thairof, and that bowis and schutting be "hantit, and bow-markes maid therefore ordained in "ilk parochin, under the pain of fourtie shillinges, to "be raised be the schireffe and baillies foresaid."

But Archery, to which the people were averse, could not be made popular by Acts of Parliament, and the parish butts were accordingly neglected, whilst the "unprofitabill sportis" still retained their hold. Erelong indeed we find the King himself breaking his own behest, as witness the following entries in the Accounts of the Lords High Treasurers of Scotland :—

1503-4, Feb. 3. Item to the King *to play at the Golf* with the Erle of Bothuile . . . . . . xlij s̃
Item *to Golf Clubbis and Ballis* to the King that he playit with . . . . . ix s̃
1505-6, Feb. 22. Item for xij Golf Ballis to the King . . iiij s̃
1506, July 18. Item the xviij day of Julij for ij Golf Clubbes to the King . . . . . . ij s̃

A century later, we find it sufficiently obvious that

Introduction

these statutes had been little respected, and that the Game continued to be as popular as before. It was not now, however, Scottish valour that was imperilled, but a much more serious matter—Scottish piety.

In 1592 the Town Council of Edinburgh "ordanis "proclamatioun to be maid threw this burgh, that see-"ing the Sabboth day being the Lord's day it becumis "everie christiane to dedicat himselff to the service of "God, thairfore commanding and chairgeing in our "Soverane lord's name, and in name of the provest "and baillies, that na inhabitants of the samyn be sene "at ony pastymes or gammis within or without the "toun upoun the Sabboth day, *sic as Golf*, etc.; and "also that thair dochteris and wemen servands be nocht "fund playing at the ball, nor singing of profayne sangs, "upoun the sam day, under sic paynis as the magestrates "sall lay to thair chairge"; and again, in 1593, the Town Council finding that "dyvers inhabitants of this "burgh repaires upoun the Sabboth day to the toun of "Leyth, and *in tyme of sermonis* are sene vagant athort "the streets, drynking in tavernis, or otherwayes at *Golf*, "aircherie, or other pastymes upoun the Links, thairby "profaning the Sabboth day," warned them to desist, "under the payne of wairding thair persounis quhill "thai pay ane unlaw of fourty shillings, and otherwayes "be punist in thair persouns at the discretioun of the "Magestrates."

Introduction

Ignoring these proclamations, John Henrie, Pat. Bogie, and others, were, in the year 1608, "accusit for "playing of the Gowff on the Links of Leith everie "Sabboth *the tyme of the sermonnes*, notwithstanding "oft admonitioun past befoir ; were convict of xx. lib. "ilk ane of them, and ordainit to be wardet [put in "prison] until the same wer payit, and to find cautioun "not to do the lyke again at na tyme heirefter, under "the paine of c. lib."

In 1604 Robert Robertson and others "were con-"victed of profaning the Lord's Sabbath, by absenting "themselves from hearing of the Word, and playing at "the *Gowf* on the North Inch, Perth, *in time of preach-*"*ing*"; and Robertson, the ringleader, was fined "ane "merk to the poor," and with the others had "to "compear the next Sabbath into the place of public "repentance, in presence of the whole congregation."

In 1621 David Hairt, "prenteis to Gilbert Bauhop, "wrycht, confest prophanatione of the Sabboth in play-"ing at the *Goff* in the park of Stirling on the Sabboth "aftirnone *in tyme of preaching ;*[1] and therfor is ordenit "to pay *ad pios usus* vj s̃ viij d̃."

---

[1] The inference from all this is curious enough. In 1457 it is expressly enacted by the Scottish "Lordis and Baronis spirituale and temporale," that "*schutting be usit ilk Sunday.*" In the century following, it is plain from the terms of the Edicts that the practice of Golf, though held sacrilegious on Sunday in *tyme of preaching—the tyme of the sermonnes—* was at other times of that day at least tolerated. The rigid Sabbatarianism

Introduction

In 1651 the Kirk Session of Humbie, Berwickshire, ordain James Rodger, Johne Howdan, and others "to "mak their publick repentance, having confessed thair "prophaning of the Lord's day by playing at the *Golf*," and Howdan, "being ane deacon," is deposed from his office.

King James VI. in 1618, on his return from Scotland, "when (says he) with our owne eares wee heard "the generall complaint of our people, that they were "barred from all lawfull recreation and exercise upon "the Sundayes afternoone, *after the ending of all Divine* "*service*, for when shal the common people have leave "to exercise, if not upon the Sundayes and holydayes, "seeing they must apply their labour, and winne their "living in all working dayes?" rebuked the "precise "people," and declared his pleasure to be, "that *after the* "*end of divine service*, our good people be not disturbed, "letted, or discouraged from any lawfull recreation— "such as dauncing, either men or women, archerie for "men, leaping, vaulting, or any other such harmless "recreation," but prohibiting "the said recreations *to* "*any that are not present in the church at the service of* "*God before their going to the said recreations.*"

King Charles I. in 1633, "out of a like pious care

---

of Scotland—now much modified, and in course of being more so—is thus plainly of comparatively modern growth. John Knox and the early Reformers knew nothing of it.

Introduction

" for the service of God, and for suppressing of any
" humors that oppose trueth, and for the ease, comfort,
" and recreation of our well deserving people," ratifies
and anew publishes " this our blessed father's declaration," and commands our justices of assize " to see that
" no man doe trouble or molest any of our loyall and
" duetifull people, in or for their lawfull recreations,
" *having first done their duetie to God.*"

To retrace our steps a little, we find that on 4th
April 1603, King James VI. appointed William Mayne,
" bower burges of Edinburgh, during all the dayis of his
" lyif-tyme, clubmaker to his Hienes," and most likely
his handiwork gave satisfaction ; but it would appear
that the golf balls of national manufacture were not up
to the mark, and the golfers of the day were unpatriotic
enough to import them from Holland. James, though
now in England, was determined to do " Justice to
Scotland " ; and in a letter from Salisbury, dated 5th
August 1618, he states, by way of preamble, that
whereas " no small quantitie of gold and siluer is trans-
" ported zeirlie out of his Hienes kingdome of Scotland
" for bying of *golf ballis* "; therefore, to stop this iniquity,
his Majesty confers a monopoly of ball-manufacture on
James Melvill " for the spaice of tuentie-ane zeiris " ;
but lest the said James Melvill should become an
extortioner, it was provided that the cost · of each ball
" exceid not the pryce of four schillingis money of this

Introduction

"realm." Besides fixing the price, precautions were also taken for the identification of the balls—the said James Melvill being ordained "to have ane particular "stamp of his awin, and that all ballis maid within the "kingdome found to be vtherwayis stamped sall be "escheated."

Prince Henry, eldest son of James VI., as we learn from a person who was present,[1] occasionally engaged in the game:—"At another time playing at Goff, "a play not unlike to Pale-maille, whilst his school-"master stood talking with another, and marked not "His Highness warning him to stand further off, the "Prince, thinking he had gone aside, lifted up his Goff-"club to strike the ball ; mean tyme one standing by "said to him,—' Beware that you hit not Master "Newton,' wherewith the Prince, drawing back his hand, "said,—' Had I done so, I had but paid my debts.'"

Many notable scenes and figures in Scottish history are associated with Golf.

Mary, Queen of Scots, her adversaries affirmed, as an instance of her indifference to Darnley's fate, a few days after his murder, "was seen playing Golf and Pallmall in the fields beside Seton."[2]

Halbert Logan of Restalrig, one of the last of his imperious race, while golfing at Lochend, near

---

[1] The anonymous author of a MS. in the Harleian Library.
[2] *Inventories of Mary Queen of Scots*, Preface, p. lxx. 1863.

Introduction

Edinburgh, was summoned to attend the Privy Council. Absorbed in his game, he disregarded the message, and used despiteful language to the officer. A warrant was therefore at once issued for his apprehension on a charge of high treason (as being an accessory to the Gowrie conspiracy), but throwing down his club, he mounted a fleet horse, and fled to England.[1]

In his *Historie of the Kirk of Scotland*,[2] John Row, Minister of Carnock, in mentioning "the apostasie" of some of the newly made Bishops in 1610, states, concerning the Bishop of Galloway, that "being at

---

[1] Chambers's *Traditions of Edinburgh*.

The Logans of Restalrig were the original feudal superiors of Leith, and they ruled the unfortunate burghers with a rod of iron. The representative of the family at the end of the sixteenth century was a man of expensive habits, full of ambitious projects, and one who permitted no obstacle to stand in the way of his desires. During his supremacy the inhabitants of Leith were subject to constant spoliation and robbery. It was not only in matters of property that the unfortunate feudatories were made to feel the power of this "bold bad man." The wives and daughters of the burghers were not unfrequently seduced away or forcibly carried off to his castle of Lochend, and retained there so long as it suited the pleasure or caprice of its haughty lord. He was deeply implicated in the Gowrie conspiracy, but died before his share in it was fully disclosed. His eldest son, Robert, and all others concerned, were cited to appear before the King and the Estates of Parliament on the 15th of July 1609. It was on this occasion that the bones of Logan were dug up and carried into the Parliament House to receive judgment. Having been adjudged guilty of treason, the family of Logan were stripped of all their property.—*Tales and Traditions of Leith*.

[2] *Wodrow Society*, Edinburgh, 1842, p. 259. Row has confounded the two Bishops of Galloway, Gavin Hamilton, 1610-1612, and William Cowper, 1612-1619. It is the earlier of the two to whom the above passage relates. But this is of no moment for our purpose.

Introduction

"his pastime [Golf], (for he loved that all his life-
"tyme verie much, so that that part of the Bishops'
"Verses, '*Ludos Gallowa*,' is his share), in the Links of
"Leith, he was terrified with a vision, or an apprehen-
"sion; for he said to his play-fellows, after he had, in
"ane affrighted and commoved way, cast away his play-
"instruments (*arma campestria*), 'I vow to be about
"with these two men who hes now come upon me with
"drawen swords!' When his play-fellowes replyed,
"'My Lord, it is a dreame! We saw no such thing;
"these men hes been invisible.' He was silent, went
"home trembling, tooke bed instantlie, and died, not
"giving any token of repentance for that wicked course
"he had embraced."

The great Montrose we find, in May 1628, ere "the Troubles" began, "hard at golf on the Links of St. Andrews." In the following year, returning to St. Andrews from Edinburgh, he tarries a day at Leith, expending ten shillings "for two golf balls, my Lord going to the golf there"; and there is a further payment "to the boy who carried my Lord's clubbes to the field." Again, on the 9th Nov. we discover him at Montrose purchasing golf balls in order to play a match with his brother-in-law, Sir John Colquhoun. Having finished his match with the Laird of Luss, he becomes mindful of his match with "sweet Mistress Magdalene Carnegie"; so, having "taken a drink at

From the original in possesion of Sir James Carnegie, Bar^t of Southesk.

Introduction

John Garn's," he mounts for Kinnaird to salute the young lady who was next day to be his wife. He was married in the parish church, on Tuesday, 10th Nov. 1629; but scarcely had the minstrels ceased to serenade them, when we find Montrose at his clubs and balls again. On the ninth day after his marriage there is a sum paid " to ane going to St. Andrews for clubs and balls to my Lord"; and also for "sax new clubs, and dressing some auld anes, and for balls." Immediately follows another payment, "my Lord being in Montrose at golf, for stabling the horse."[1]

---

[1] The Portrait of Montrose by George Jameson, Aberdeen, anno 1629, ætatis 17, was a marriage present from Graham of Morphie to the young Countess. It was painted on 4th and 5th November 1629, and is still in the possession of the Earl of Southesk, at Kinnaird Castle.

John, fourth Earl of Montrose, the father of the great Marquis, was conspicuous in public life, but after the death of his Countess he lived the retired life of a country gentleman, devoted to his children. Montrose was his only son. The factor's books prove that the Earl consumed many puncheons of wine, and tobacco to a great extent. The smaller articles which compete with the above are *golf-balls* and *bowstrings*. "Six bowstrings to my Lord" cost nine shillings, and "ane dozen goiff-balls" three pounds. This last was an expensive indulgence, as the tailor that made "ane *stand of claiths* to my Lord" is only paid four pounds. The Earl died on 14th November 1626. The funeral ceremonies give a curious picture of the age. They lasted for one month and nineteen days. The consumption of claret wine and white wine is reckoned by puncheons; and there could hardly have been a single tear for every bucket of Easter Ale with which the stately castle of Kincardine appears to have been inundated when the last Earl of Montrose who bore that title at his decease was gathered to his fathers in the mausoleum of Aberuthven.—*Memoirs of the Marquis of Montrose.* By Mark Napier. Edinburgh: T. G. Stevenson, 1856.

Introduction

Michael Bruce, an Irish minister who preached in Scotland during the persecution, in a sermon at Cambusnethan in Clydesdale, spoke as follows:—" O sirs, "there is much of childish humors among us, but any "of you that has win to soul-confirmation, ye have win "beyond the reach of them. The more soul-confirma-"tion he has, he puts the Devil to the loss of two: he "losseth his pains and his profit. The Devil has the "Ministers and Professors of Scotland now in a sive, "and O as he sifts, and O as he riddles, and O as he "rattles, and O the chaff he gets! and I fear there be "more chaff nor there be good corn, and that will be "found among us or all be done; but the soul-con-"firmed man leaves ever the Devil at two moe, and he "has ay the matter gadged, and leaves ay the Devil in "the lee side. Sirs, O work in the day of the Cross!"[1]

Charles I. was so passionately fond of the game, that he is said to have practised it at Newcastle during his confinement there;[2] and it was whilst engaged at Golf on the Links of Leith that that ill-fated monarch first received intelligence of the breaking out of the Irish

---

[1] Kirkton's *History*, p. 273. This seems to prove not only that the people of Cambusnethan understood the game of Golf, but that one of the terms at least was the same then as now. The idea of the Devil having to play "two more" was surely a very happy and striking illustration.

[2] The King was nowhere treated with more honour than at Newcastle, as himself confessed, both he and his train having liberty to go abroad and play at *Goff* in the Shield Field, without the walls.—*Local Records of Northumberland.* By John Sykes. Newcastle, 1833.

Introduction

Rebellion in 1642. The evil tidings affected Charles so deeply, that he instantly broke up the match and drove to Holyrood.[1]

The Duke of York, afterwards James II., was frequently to be seen on the green,—"Andrew Dickson"[2] acting as "fore-caddie" to announce where the balls fell. Two English noblemen, having acquired during their attendance at the Scottish Court some knowledge of the game, challenged the Duke and any Scotsman he could find, to play a match for a large stake. The Duke accepted the challenge, and selected as his partner John Patersone, a shoemaker. Winning easily, his Highness dismissed the shoemaker with half the stake, and with the money Patersone built for himself a house in the Canongate.[3]

In 1672 Golf was still the fashionable amusement of

---

[1] *The History of Leith.* By A. Campbell, 1827.

[2] In the copy of the Solemn League and Covenant signed at St. Andrews in 1643, one of the signatories is "Androw Dicksone, balmaker." Presumably he was a golf-ball maker.

James Dickson, servitor to the Master of Orkney, writing to Andrew Martin from Kirkwall, on the 23rd of November 1585, says: "Ye will remember to bring with you ane dossen of commoun golf ballis to me and David Moncreiff."—*Correspondence of Sir Pat. Waus*, 1882, p. 341.

In 1642 the Town Council of Aberdeen granted "licence and tolerance to John Dickson to use and exercise his trade of making gowff ballis within this burgh in respect ther is not sich ane tradisman in this burgh."

[3] After the Restoration, the Duke of York was sent to Edinburgh, and his favourite pastimes appear to have been the torturing of the adherents to the Covenant, and the playing of Golf on the Links of Leith.—Robertson's *Historical Notices of Leith.*

Introduction

the Edinburgh aristocracy, as the Note-Book of Sir John Foulis, Bart., of Ravelstoun, amusingly instructs:—

1672.

Jan. 13. Lost at Golfe with Pittarro and Comissar Munro	0 13 0
Lost at Golfe with Lyon and Harry Hay	1 4 0
Feb. 14. Spent at Leith at Golfe	2 0 0
Mar. 2. Lost at Golfe at Mussleboorgh with Gosfoord, Lyon, etc.	3 5 0
Nov. 19. Lost at Golfe with the Chancellour, Lyon, Master of Saltoune, etc.	5 10 0
30. Lost at Golfe with the Chancellour, Duke Hamilton, etc.	4 15 0
Dec. 7. For a Golfe Club to Archie	0 6 0

In 1724 Alexander Elphinstone (the immediate younger brother of Arthur, who perished so nobly on Tower Hill in 1746) engaged on the Links of Leith in what a newspaper of the day called "a solemn match at golf" with the afterwards notorious Captain Porteous of the Edinburgh City Guard, for Twenty guineas—a stake so remarkable that the match was "attended by "the Duke of Hamilton, the Earl of Morton, and a vast "mob of the great and little besides,"—Alexander Elphinstone ending as the winner. Both players, not many years afterwards, had blood upon their hands.

Duncan Forbes of Culloden, President of the Court of Session, was such an ardent lover of the national amusement, that when the Links of Leith were covered with snow, he played on the Sands. Again, we find him playing golf with his son on the Links of Musselburgh:—

Introduction

" This day (Nov. 1, 1728), after a very hard pull, I got
" the better of my son at the Gouf. If he was as good
" at any other thing as he is at that, there might be some
" hopes of him." This great and patriotic Scotsman
competed in 1745 for the Silver Club presented in the
previous year to the Gentlemen Golfers of Leith by the
Good Town of Edinburgh. That was probably his last
round, as the rising of the Clans compelled him to set off
for the North, where he used all his influence to prevent
them from joining the cause of the young Pretender.

The Rev. Dr. Alexander Carlyle, minister of Inveresk, near Musselburgh, was a "mighty swiper." In
1758, while in London, he was invited to dine with
Garrick at his house in Hampton, along with John
Home, the author of *Douglas*, Dr. Robertson the
Historian, Parson Black from Aberdeen, and others.
Garrick had " told us to bring golf clubs and balls,
" that we might play at the Golf on Molesly Hurst.
" We accordingly set out in good time, six of us, in
" a landau. As we passed through Kensington, the
" Coldstream regiment were changing guard, and, on
" seeing our clubs, they gave us three cheers in honour
" of a diversion peculiar to Scotland—so much does the
" remembrance of one's native country dilate the heart,
" when one has been some time absent. The same
" sentiment made us open our purses, and give our
" countrymen wherewithal to drink the ' Land o' Cakes.'

Introduction

"Garrick met us by the way, so impatient he seemed
" to be for his company. Immediately after we arrived,
" we crossed the river to the golfing ground, which was
" very good. None of the company could play but
" Home and myself, and Parson Black. We returned
" and dined sumptuously, Mrs. Garrick, the only lady,
" now grown fat, though still very lively, being a woman
" of uncommon good sense, and now mistress of English,
" was in all respects most agreeable company. She did
" not seem at all to recognise me, which was no wonder,
" at the end of twelve years, having thrown away my
" bag-wig and sword, and appearing in my own grisly
" hairs, and in parson's clothes; nor was I likely to
" remind her of her former state.[1] After dinner, Garrick

---

[1] Carlyle first made the acquaintance of Mrs. Garrick in 1746 on the passage from Helvoet to Harwich, on his return from Holland :—We had one cabin passenger who was afterwards much celebrated. When we were on the quarterdeck in the morning we observed three foreigners, of different ages, who had under their care a young person of about sixteen, very handsome indeed, whom we took for a Hanoverian baron coming to Britain to pay his court at St. James's. The gale freshened so soon, that we had not an opportunity of conversing with those foreigners when we were obliged to take to our beds in the cabin. The young person was the only one of the strangers who had a berth there, because, as we supposed, it occasioned an additional freight. My bed was directly opposite to that of the stranger, but we were so sick that there was no conversation among us till the young foreigner became very frightened in spite of the sickness, and called out to me in French if we were not in danger. The voice betrayed her sex at once, no less than her fears. I consoled her as well as I could, and soon brought her above the fear of danger. This beautiful person was Violetti the dancer, who was engaged to the opera in the Haymarket. There she maintained her ground as first dancer, till Garrick married her.—*Autobiography of Rev. Dr. Carlyle.*

Introduction

"ordered the wine to be carried to a temple in the "garden. Having observed a green mount opposite "the archway, I said to our landlord I would surprise "him with a stroke at the golf, as I should drive a ball "through his archway into the Thames, once in three "strokes. I had measured the distance with my eye "in walking about the garden, and accordingly, at the "second stroke, made the ball alight in the mouth of "the gateway, and roll down the green slope into the "river. This was so dexterous, that he was quite "surprised, and begged the club of me by which such "a feat had been performed."

William St. Clair of Roslin was so uniformly successful at golf and archery that the common people ascribed to him a knowledge of *The Black Art*. Sir Walter Scott describes St. Clair as "a man considerably above six feet, "with dark-grey locks, a form upright, but gracefully so, "thin-flanked and broad-shouldered, built it would seem "for the business of war or the chase, a noble eye of "chastened pride and undoubted authority, and features "handsome and striking in their general effect. As "schoolboys we crowded to see him perform feats of "strength and skill in the old Scottish games of Golf "and Archery." His portrait by Sir George Chalmers, in the attitude of striking a ball from the *tee*, was painted for the Gentlemen Golfers in 1771.

Sir Henry Raeburn, although he worked hard in his

Introduction

studio all the other days of the week, devoted the Saturday afternoon to the practice of golf. Dr. Andrew Duncan senior, in a Tribute of Regard to his memory, says—" While, however, he was distinguished in literary
" institutions, he was also conspicuous in companies for
" healthful and manly exercise; and I am proud to say,
" that, even in the 80th year of my age, I was his
" antagonist on the Links. I was his opponent in the
" last game at Golf he ever played. On Saturday, the
" 7th of June 1823, I called at his painting rooms, after
" concluding the business I had allotted for the day.
" After he had also finished his business, we walked
" together to Leith Links. There, removed from the
" smoke of the city of Edinburgh, we conjoined, with
" pleasing conversation, a trial of skill at a salutary and
" interesting exercise, to which we had both a strong
" attachment. After dedicating the Saturday afternoon
" to healthful amusement, we enjoyed a temperate meal
" in the Golfers' Hall. That Hall is already ornamented
" with several good portraits. It contains, among others,
" two from the pencil of Sir Henry, of men, now dead,
" who were once very conspicuous ornaments of that
" Society, both as excellent golfers, and as possessing
" uncommon social powers—the portraits of John Gray,
" Esq., a social spirit, and of James Balfour, Esq., whose
" musical talents and amiable temper could not fail to
" support the hilarity and harmony of every company

Introduction

" in which he was present. Indeed, Sir Henry's picture
" of Balfour, drawn in the character of singing a joyous
" song, is thought by many to be one of the best he
" ever painted. At that meeting it was agreed that a
" full-length picture of one of the most distinguished
" members of the Company of Golfers, Mr. John Taylor
" of the Exchequer, who has at present the character of
" being one of the best golfers in Scotland, should be
" drawn by Sir Henry, to afford an additional ornament
" to the Hall, as soon as the convenience of both would
" permit. After partaking of a sober, but social glass,
" we returned to Edinburgh in the same carriage. We
" then separated, in the confident hope that we might
" soon meet again on a similar party of pleasure.
" But, alas! the will of Heaven had otherwise deter-
" mined: for in little more than the short space of a
" single month, I had to perform the melancholy duty
" of accompanying his dead body to the grave." [1]

Alexander M'Kellar, "The Cock o' the Green,"
rendered famous by Kay, spent his life on Bruntsfield
Links, playing by himself when unable to procure an
opponent, and was not unfrequently found practising
" putting" at the " short holes" by lamp-light. His
golf-hating wife, annoyed by his all-absorbing passion,
on one occasion carried his dinner and his nightcap to

---

[1] *A Tribute of Regard to the Memory of Sir Henry Raeburn, R.A.* Edinburgh, 1824.

Introduction

the Links; but M'Kellar, blind to the satire, good-humouredly observed to his better half that she "cou'd "wait if she likit till the game was dune, but at present "he had no time for refreshment."

Scotland, which, though probably not the birthplace, is yet the chosen Home of Golf, may well be proud of her ancient game, by the spell of which king and cobbler alike are led captive; and although her hardy sons, in search of fame or fortune, carry their favourite game South, East, and West,—" far as the breeze can bear, the billows foam,"—still they never forget their native greens, and gladly return to the happy golfing-grounds of their youth, where every hole seems eloquent with recollections of famous putts and glorious drives! Pastime passing excellent! we owe thee much.

To authors and publishers for permission to reprint —to artists for kindly help in rendering the book attractive—to antiquaries for valuable notes and extracts— the Editor returns his warmest thanks.

EDINBURGH, *September* 1875.

FROM A MS. BOOK OF PRAYERS OF THE FOURTEENTH CENTURY

HISTORICAL ACCOUNT OF THE GAME OF GOLF[1]

BEING about to reprint a set of Rules formerly drawn up for regulating the concerns of their fraternity, the Council of the THISTLE GOLF CLUB have conceived that a short Historical Account of their favourite amusement would prove not altogether unacceptable to the lovers of a game at once so ancient and so national. With this view, they have collected whatever notices they could find which seemed calculated to throw any light on the origin and history of Golf, and, at the same time, to preserve from oblivion some of those names which, either from rank, or from distinguished proficiency in the game itself, have entitled themselves to a place in its annals. The in-

---

[1] *Some Historical Notices relative to the Progress of the Game of Golf in Scotland.* By Mr. John Cundell. Privately printed at Edinburgh, 1824, 8vo.

Historical Account

formation which they have obtained is indeed neither very various nor important. If the origin of the most valuable institutions of civilised life, the laws and usages of the most enlightened nations, are lost in the mist of antiquity, eluding the researches of the philosopher and historian, it was not to be expected that any distinct record would be found, setting forth the invention and progress of a mere popular recreation.

The etymology of the word *golf* has been traced, with much appearance of probability, to the Teutonic term, from which the Germans have their noun *kolbe*, a club, and whence springs the Low Dutch *kolf*, a sound which very closely resembles that of golf, the exchange of the labial letter *b* for *lf* being very common in that language. If this derivation be correct, it follows that the game of Golf is strictly synonymous with the "game of Club."

By most authorities this amusement is regarded as being not only very ancient, but also as peculiar to the natives of North Britain. It will be seen, by the extracts about to be introduced from Strutt's *Sports and Pastimes of the People of England*, that the latter opinion is not quite incontrovertible; whilst, in regard to the precise period at which the game of Golf became common in Scotland, our best antiquaries supply no facts upon which we can arrive at a satisfactory determination. That it is of considerable antiquity, however, there is no reasonable ground to doubt; and as the best proof of this, it may be mentioned that there are statutes of so early a date as the year 1457, prohibiting the exercise of Golf, lest it should interfere with the more important accomplishment of archery. In those times the bow was the principal instrument of war among all the nations of Europe,

of the Game

and a weapon, too, in the use of which the English, from whom our Scottish ancestors had most to fear, had attained a noted superiority. In one of the Acts alluded to,[1] it is "decreeted and ordained, that the weaponschawinges be halden be the Lordes and Barronnes Spirituel and Temporel foure times in the zeir, and that the fute-ball and golfe be vtterly cryit downe, and not to be vsed."

This prohibition shows clearly that, in the time of James the Second, the game of Golf had already become a very general amusement in Scotland; and as, in the former reign, there is a similar Act of Parliament, anno 1424,[2] discouraging the exercise of football, without any mention being made of Golf, it seems probable that the latter pastime was introduced into the northern parts of Britain about the beginning of the fifteenth century.

In both the subsequent reigns of James the Third and James the Fourth, there are similar Acts of Parliament against Football and Golf. Under the former of these monarchs, anno 1471,[3] it is enacted that "the fute-ball and golfe be abused in time cumming, and that the buttes be maid up and schutting used, after the tenour of the Acte of Parliament maid thereupon." In the reign of James the Fourth, anno 1491,[4] it is statute and ordained, "That in na place of the realme there be vsit futte-ballis, golfe, or uther sik unprofitabill sportis, for the commoun gude of the realme, and defence thairof, and that bowis and schutting be hantit, and bow-markes maid therefore ordained in ilk parochin, under the

---

[1] James II. Parl. 14, cap. 64.
[2] James I. Parl. 1, cap. 17.   [3] James III. Parl. 6, cap. 44.
[4] James IV. Parl. 3, cap. 32.

Historical Account

pain of fourtie shillinges, to be raised be the schireffe and baillies foresaid."

The reader, by perusing the following extracts from the volume of Strutt, will be enabled to determine whether any of the various games at ball, in which the English at that period indulged, are to be classed with the game of Golf.

I. The Ball has given origin to many popular pastimes, and I have appropriated this chapter to such of them as are or have been usually practised in the fields and other open places. The most ancient amusement of this kind is distinguished with us by the name of Hand-ball, and is, if Homer may be accredited, coeval at least with the destruction of Troy. Herodotus attributes the invention of the ball to the Lydians;[1] succeeding writers have affirmed that a female of distinction named Anagalla, a native of Corcyra, was the first who made a ball for the purpose of pastime, which she presented to Nausicaa, the daughter of Alcinous, King of Phæacia, and at the same time taught her how to use it.[2] This piece of history is partly derived from Homer, who introduces the Princess of Corcyra, with her maidens, amusing themselves at hand-ball.

> ' O'er the green mead the sporting virgins play,
> Their shining veils unbound ; along the skies,
> Tost and retost, the ball incessant flies.'[3]

Homer has restricted this pastime to the young maidens of Corcyra, at least he has not mentioned its being practised by the men. In times posterior to the poet, the game of hand-ball was indiscriminately played by both sexes.

II. It is altogether uncertain at what period the ball was brought into England. The author of a manuscript, written in the fourteenth century, and containing the Life of St. Cuthbert,[4] says of him, that when he was young, "he pleyde atte balle with the children that his fellowes were." On what authority this information is established, I cannot tell. The

---

[1] Lib. i. [2] Ælian, lib. ii. Volaterranus, lib. xxix.
[3] *Odyssey*, lib. vi. Pope's translation.
[4] Trinity College Library, Oxford, marked lvii.

of the Game

Venerable Bede, who also wrote the Life of that saint, makes no mention of ball-play, but tells us he excelled in jumping, running, wrestling, and such exercises as required great muscular exertion;[1] and among them, indeed, it is highly probable that of the ball might be included.

III. Fitzstephen, who wrote in the thirteenth century, speaking of the London schoolboys, says, "Annually upon Shrove Tuesday, they go into the fields immediately after dinner, and play at the celebrated game of ball;[2] every party of boys carrying their own ball"; for it does not appear that those belonging to one school contended with those of another, but that the youth of each school diverted themselves apart. Some difficulty has been started by those who have translated this passage, respecting the nature of the game at ball here mentioned. Stowe, considering it as a kind of Goff or bandy-ball, has, without the least sanction from the Latin, added the word bastion,[3] meaning a bat or cudgel; others again have taken it for football,[4] which pastime, though probably known at the time, does not seem to be a very proper one for children: and indeed, as there is not any just authority to support an argument on either side, I see no reason why it should not be rendered hand-ball.[5]

IV. The game of hand-ball is called by the French palm-play,[6] because, says a modern author, originally "this exercise consisted in receiving the ball and driving it back again with the palm of the hand. In former times they played with the naked hand, then with a glove, which in some instances was lined; afterwards they bound cords and tendons round their hands, to make the ball rebound more forcibly, and hence the racket derived its origin."[7] During the reign of Charles the Fifth, palm-play, which may properly enough be denominated hand-tennis, was exceedingly fashionable in France, being played by the nobility for large sums of money: and when they had lost all that they had about them, they would

---

[1] "Sive enim saltu, sive cursu, sive luctatu," etc. *Vita Sancti Cudbercti*, c. i. [2] "Lusum pilæ celebrem," Stephanides *de ludis*.

[3] "The scholars of every school have their ball or bastion in their hands."—*Survey of London*.

[4] Lord Lyttelton, *History of Henry the Second*, vol. iii. p. 275, and the anonymous translator of Fitzstephen, published by Mr. White, A.D. 1772.

[5] By the word *celebrem*, the author might advert to the antiquity of the pastime. [6] *Jeu de paume*, and in Latin *pila palmaria*.

[7] *Essais Historiques sur Paris*, par Saint Foix, vol. i. p. 160.

Historical Account

sometimes pledge a part of their wearing apparel rather than give up the pursuit of the game. The Duke of Burgundy, according to an old historian,[1] having lost sixty franks at palm-play with the Duke of Bourbon, Messire William de Lyon, and Messire Guy de la Trimouille, and not having money enough to pay them, gave his girdle as a pledge for the remainder, and shortly afterwards he left the same girdle with the Comte D'Eu for eighty franks, which he also lost at tennis.

V. At the time when tennis-play was taken up seriously by the nobility, new regulations were made in the game, and covered courts erected, wherein it might be practised without any interruption from the weather. In the sixteenth century tennis-courts were common in England, and the establishment of such places countenanced by the example of the monarchs. In the Vocabulary of Commenius,[2] we see a rude representation of a tennis-court, divided by a line stretched in the middle, and the players standing on either side with their rackets ready to receive and return the ball, which the rules of the game required to be stricken over the line.[3]

VI. We have undoubted authority to prove that Henry the Seventh was a tennis-player,[4] and his son Henry, who succeeded him, in the early part of his reign was much attached to this diversion; which propensity, as Hall assures us, being perceived by "certayne craftie persons aboute him, they brought in Frenchmen and Lombards to make wagers with hym, and so he lost muche money; but when he perceyved theyr crafte, he eschued the company and let them goe."[5] He did not, however, give up the amusement, for we find him, according to the same historian, in the thirteenth year of his reign, playing at tennis with the Emperor Maximilian for his partner, against the Prince of Orange and the Marquis of Brandenborow; "the Earl of Devonshire stopped on the Prince's side,"

---

[1] Laboureur. Sub an. 1368.

[2] *Orbis sensualium pictus*, published by Hoole, A.D. 1658.

[3] Hence the propriety of Heywoode's proverb, "thou hast stricken the ball under the line," meaning he had failed in his purpose.—John Heywoode's Works, London, 1566.

[4] In a MS. register of his expenditures, made in the thirteenth year of his reign, and preserved in the Remembrancer's Office, this entry occurs: "Item, for the King's loss at tennis, twelvepence, for the loss of balls, threepence." Hence one may infer the game was played abroad, for the loss of balls would hardly have happened in a tennis-court.

[5] In the *Life of Henry VIII.* the second year of his reign, fol. 11.

of the Game

says my author, "and the Lord Edmond on the other side, and they departed even handes on both sides after eleven games fully played."[1] Among the additions that King Henry made to Whitehall, if Stowe be correct, were "divers fair tennis-courts, bowling-allies, and a cock-pit."[2]

James the First, if not himself a tennis-player, speaks of the pastime with commendation, and recommends it to his son as a species of exercise becoming a Prince.[3] Charles the Second frequently diverted himself with playing at tennis, and had particular kind of dresses made for that purpose.[4]

VII. A French writer speaks of a damsel named Margot, who resided at Paris, and played at hand-tennis with the palm, and also with the back of her hand, better than any man; and what is most surprising, adds my author, at that time the game was played with the naked hand, or at best with a double glove.[5]

VIII. Hand-ball was formerly a favourite pastime among the young persons of both sexes, and in many parts of the kingdom it was customary for them to play at this game during the Easter holidays for tansy cakes; but why, says Bourne, they should prefer hand-ball at this time to any other pastime, or play it particularly for a tansy cake, I have not been able to find out.[6] The learned Selden conceives the institution of this reward to have originated from the Jewish custom of eating bitter herbs at the time of the Passover.[7]

Anciently, the mayor, aldermen, and sheriff of Newcastle, accompanied with a great number of burgesses, used to go every year, at the feasts of Easter and Whitsuntide, to the Forth,[8] with the mace, the sword, and the cap of maintenance carried before them. The young people still continue to assemble there at those seasons particularly, and play at hand-ball, or dance, but are no longer countenanced by the presence of their governors.[9]

---

[1] In the *Life of Henry VIII.* the second year of his reign, fol. 98.
[2] *Survey of London*, p. 496.   [3] *Basilicon Doron*, lib. iii.
[4] So had Henry VIII. In the wardrobe rolls we meet with tenes-cotes for the King, also tennis-drawers and tennis-slippers. — MSS. Harl. 2248 and 6271.
[5] A.D. 1424. Saint Foix, *Essais Historiques sur Paris*, vol. i. p. 160.
[6] *Antiquities of the Common People*, chapter xxiv.
[7] *Table Talk*, under the article "Christmas."
[8] The little mall of the town.
[9] Mr. Brand in his additions to Bourne.

Historical Account

Fuller mentions the following proverbial saying used by the citizens of Chester, "When the daughter is stolen, shut Pepper Gate," which he thus explains: "The mayor of the city had his daughter, as she was playing at ball with other maidens in Pepper-street, stolen away by a young man through the same gate, whereupon he caused it to be shut up."[1]

IX. Hand-tennis still continues to be played, though under a different name, and probably a different modification of the game; it is now called Fives, which denomination, perhaps, it might receive from having five competitors on each side, as the succeeding passage seems to indicate: When Queen Elizabeth was entertained at Elvetham, in Hampshire, by the Earl of Hertford, "after dinner, about three o'clock, ten of his lordship's servants, all Somersetshire men, in a square greene court before her Majesties windowe, did hang up lines, squaring out the forme of a tennis-court, and making a crosse line in the middle; in this square they[2] played five to five, with hand-ball at bord and cord, as they tearme it, to the great liking of her highness."[3]

XIV. There are many games played with the ball that require the assistance of a club or bat, and probably the most ancient among them is the pastime now distinguished by the name of Goff. In the northern parts of the kingdom, Goff is much practised. It requires much room to perform this game with propriety, and therefore I presume it is rarely seen at present in the vicinity of the metropolis. It answers to a rustic pastime of the Romans, which they played with a ball of leather stuffed with feathers, called Paganica,[4] and the goff-ball is composed of the same materials to this day.[5] In the reign of Edward the Third the Latin name, Cambuca,[6] was applied to this pastime, and it derived the denomination,

---

[1] Fuller's *Worthies*, published 1662, p. 188.

[2] "Being stript out of their dublets."

[3] *Progresses of Queen Elizabeth*, published by Mr. Nichols, vol. ii. p. 19. This circumstance occurred A.D. 1591.

[4] Because it was used by the country people.

[5] I have been told it is sometimes stuffed with cotton.

[6] *Cambuta vel cambuca. Baculus incurvatus,* a crooked club or staff; the word *cambuca* was also used for the *virga episcoporum*, or episcopal crosier, because it was curved at the top.—Du Cange, *Glossary* in voce "Cambuta."

of the Game

no doubt, from the crooked club or bat with which it was played; the bat was also called a bandy, from its being bent, and hence the game itself is frequently written in English bandy-ball. At the bottom of the seventh plate the reader will find two figures engaged at bandy-ball, and the form of the bandy as it was used early in the fourteenth century.[1]

Goff, according to the present modification of the game, is performed with a bat not much unlike the bandy: the handle of this instrument is straight, and usually made of ash, about four feet and a half in length; the curvature is affixed to the bottom, faced with horn, and backed with lead; the ball is a little one, but exceedingly hard, being made with leather, and, as before observed, stuffed with feathers. There are generally two players, who have each of them his bat and ball. The game consists in driving the ball into certain holes made in the ground, which he who achieves the soonest, or in the fewest number of strokes, obtains the victory. The Goff lengths, or the spaces between the first and last holes, are sometimes extended to the distance of two or three miles; the number of intervening holes appears to be optional, but the balls must be struck into the holes, and not beyond them; when four persons play, two of them are sometimes partners, and have but one ball, which they strike alternately, but every man has his own bandy.

It should seem that Goff was a fashionable game among the nobility at the commencement of the seventeenth century, and it was one of the exercises with which Prince Henry, eldest son to James the First, occasionally amused himself, as we learn from the following anecdote recorded by a person who was present.[2] "At another time playing at Goff, a play not unlike to Pale-maille, whilst his schoolmaster stood talking with another, and marked not his highness warning him to stand further off, the prince, thinking he had gone aside, lifted up his goff-club to strike the ball; mean tyme one standing by said to him, beware that you hit not Master Newton, wherewith he, drawing back his hand, said, Had I done so, I had but paid my debts."

XV. A pastime called Stow-ball is frequently mentioned by the writers of the sixteenth and seventeenth centuries, which, I presume, was a species

---

[1] Taken from a MS. Book of Prayers, beautifully illuminated, in the possession of Francis Douce, Esq., and now, with the rest of his books, in the Bodleian Library, Oxford (see p. 1).

[2] An anonymous author of a MS. in the Harleian Library, marked 6391.

Historical Account

of Goff, at least it appears to have been played with the same kind of ball.[1]

XVI. According to the author just now quoted, Pall-mall was a pastime not unlike Goff; but if the definition of the former, given by Cotgrave, be correct, it will be found to differ materially from the latter, at least as it was played in modern times. "Pale-maille," says he, "is a game wherein a round box-ball is struck with a mallet through a high arch of iron, which he that can do at the fewest blows, or at the number agreed upon, wins." It is to be observed that there are two of these arches, that is, "one at either end of the alley."[2] The game of Mall was a fashionable amusement in the reign of Charles the Second, and the walk in St. James's Park, now called the Mall, received its name from having been appropriated to the purpose of playing at Mall, where Charles himself and his courtiers frequently exercised themselves in the practice of this pastime. The denomination Mall, given to the game, is evidently derived from the mallet, or wooden hammer, used by the players to strike the ball.

XVII. Commenius[3] mentions a game, which he attributes, indeed, to the children, and tells us it consisted in striking a ball with a bandy through a ring fastened into the ground: a similar kind of pastime, I am informed, exists to this day in the north of England; it is played in a ground or alley appropriated to the purpose, and a ball is to be driven from one end of it to the other with a mallet, the handle of which is about three feet three or four inches in length, and so far it resembles Pall-mall; but there is the addition of a ring,[4] which is placed at an equal distance from the sides of the alley, but much nearer to the bottom than the top of the ground, and through this ring it is necessary for the ball to be passed in its progress; the ring is made to turn with great facility upon a swivel, and the two flat sides are distinguished from each other; if the ball passes through the one, it is said to be lawful, and the player goes on; but if through the other, it is declared to be unlawful, and he is obliged to beat the ball back, and drive it through again, until such time

---

[1] In Littleton's *Latin and English Dictionary*, the Golf-ball and the Stow-ball are the same. See his explanation of the Latin word *Paganica*.

[2] *French and English Dictionary*, under "Pale-maille."

[3] *Orbis sensualium pictus*, chap. cxxxvi.

[4] The ring is not mentioned by Cotgrave. I have, however, been told that it was sometimes used in the game of mall.

of the Game

as he causes it to pass on the lawful side; this done, he proceeds to the bottom of the ground, where there is an arch of iron, through which it is also necessary for the ball to be passed, and then the game is completed. The contest is decided by the blows given to the ball in the performance, and he who executes his task with the smallest number is the victor.

XVIII. Club-ball is a pastime clearly distinguished from Cambuc, or Goff, in the edict above-mentioned, established by Edward the Third, and the difference seems to have consisted in the one being played with a curved bat, and the other with a straight one. Upon the eighth plate are two specimens of club-ball; the first exhibits a female figure in the action of throwing the ball to a man who elevates his bat to strike it;[1] behind the woman, at a little distance, appear, in the original delineation, several other figures of both sexes, waiting attentively to catch or stop the ball when returned by the batsman; these figures have been damaged, and are very indistinct in many parts, for which reason I did not think it proper to insert them upon the plate. The second specimen of Club-ball, which, indeed, is taken from a drawing more ancient than the former,[2] presents to us two players only, and he who is possessed of the bat holds the ball also, which he either threw into the air, and struck with his bat as it descended, or cast forcibly upon the ground, and beat it away when it rebounded; the attention of his antagonists to catch the ball need not be remarked.[3]

XIX. From the Club-ball originated, I doubt not, that pleasant and manly exercise, distinguished, in modern times, by the name of Cricket; I say in modern times, because I cannot trace the appellation beyond the commencement of the last century, where it occurs in one of the songs[4] published by D'Urfey; the first four lines run thus:

> Her was the prettiest fellow
> At foot-ball or at cricket;
> At hunting chace, or nimble race,
> How featly her could prick it.

---

[1] From a MS. in the Bodleian Library at Oxford, dated 1344, and marked Bodl. 264.

[2] From a genealogical roll of the Kings of England, to the time of Henry III., in the Royal Library, British Museum, marked 14. B. v.

[3] It does not appear in either of these instances how the game was determined.

[4] "Of a noble race was Shenkin." *Pills to purge Melancholy*, vol. ii. p. 172, the fourth edition, published 1719.

Historical Account

Cricket, of late years, is become exceedingly fashionable, being much countenanced by the nobility and gentlemen of fortune, who frequently join in the diversion.

When, by the invention of gunpowder, the use of the bow, as a military weapon, was superseded in Scotland, the sundry statutes which had been enacted against the use of Golf, were permitted to fall into desuetude; upon which this popular game was once more practised without any restraint, and soon became the favourite amusement of the nobility and gentry in all parts of the country. Even kings themselves did not decline this manly exercise; and it will not be displeasing to the golfers of the present day to be informed, in the words of the *Scots Magazine*, for May 1792, "That the two last crowned heads that ever visited this country, used to practise the Golf in the Links of Leith."

King Charles I. was extremely fond of this exercise; and it is said that, when he was engaged in a party at Golf, on the Links of Leith, a letter was delivered into his hands, which gave him the first account of the insurrection and rebellion in Ireland.[1] On reading which he suddenly called for his coach, and leaning on one of his attendants, and in great agitation, drove to the Palace of Holyrood House, from whence next day he set out for London.[2]

---

[1] See *Transactions of the Society of Antiquaries of Scotland*, p. 504.

[2] In the above article Charles is said to have set off from Holyrood House for London, the day after he received intelligence of the Irish Rebellion. This appears to be a mistake, but in so far as the King's love for Golf is concerned, it is of no importance.

The Irish Rebellion broke out under Sir Phelim O'Neale, on the 23rd of October, and Charles received intelligence of it from Lord Chichester and others on the 28th. He immediately communicated this to the Scottish Parliament, and despatched a messenger to the English; but far from setting

of the Game

James, Duke of York, afterwards James II., was not less attached to this elegant diversion. In the years 1681 and 1682, being then commissioner from the King to Parliament, while the Duke resided at Edinburgh with his Duchess, and his daughter the Princess Anne (afterwards Queen Anne), a splendid court was kept at the Palace of Holyrood House, to which the principal nobility and gentry resorted.[1] The Duke, though a bigot in his principles, was no cynic in his manners and pleasures. At that time he seemed to have studied to make himself popular among all ranks of men. Balls, plays, and masquerades, were introduced for the entertainment of both sexes; and tea, for the first time heard of in Scotland, was given as a treat by the Princesses to the Scottish ladies who visited at the Abbey. The Duke, however, did not confine himself to diversions within doors. On the contrary, he was frequently seen in a party at Golf, on the Links of Leith, with some of the nobility and gentry. "I remember," says Mr. Tytler of Woodhouselee,[2] "in my youth, to have often conversed with an old man, named Andrew Dickson, a golf-club maker, who said that, when a boy, he used to carry the Duke's golf-clubs, and to run before him and announce where the balls fell." Dickson was then performing the duty of what is now commonly called a fore-caddie.

---

off next day himself, he stayed in Edinburgh till the Scottish Parliament was dissolved, which occurred on the 17th of November. He was present that day himself, as appears by the minutes. He probably left Scotland soon after; for he tarried at York a day or two, which occasioned alarm, and yet reached London on the 25th.

[1] See *Transactions of the Society of Antiquaries of Scotland*, p. 504.
[2] *Ibid.*

Historical Account

From that time till the present the game of Golf has continued to be a fashionable amusement in Scotland, particularly at Musselburgh and St. Andrews.

In connection with the anecdotes related above, there is a traditionary narrative on the same subject, which tends to illustrate the history of Golf as a royal amusement, as well as to throw some light on a heraldic device and inscription which have of late attracted considerable notice.

In the Canongate of Edinburgh, on the wall of a very ancient-looking house[1] (No. 77) is a tablet, bearing the following coat-armorial:—Three pelicans vulned:—on a chief three mullets. Crest—a dexter hand grasping a golf-club—Motto, "Far and sure."

There are several stories connected with this achievement, which, though they all obviously relate to the same occurrence, embrace a considerable variety of circumstances, and require no small latitude in respect of chronology. According to one account, the important match at Golf, which it was no doubt meant to commemorate, is said to have taken place in the reign of James the Fifth; and it is added that the monarch himself bore a part in it. The following notice is perhaps better entitled to the confidence of the reader, inasmuch as the date of the match, in the time of James, Duke of York (who, from what has been said, appears to have been a noted golfer), corresponds with the apparent age of the house, much more closely than would any similar event, supposed to have taken place in the reign of so remote an ancestor:

---

[1] This house is situated on the north side of the Canongate, a little above Queensberry House.

of the Game

"Two English noblemen, who, during their attendance at the Scottish Court, had, among other fashionable amusements of the period, occasionally practised Golf, were one day debating the question with his Highness the Duke of York, whether that amusement were peculiar to Scotland or England; and having some difficulty in coming to an issue on the subject, it was proposed to decide the question by an appeal to the game itself; the Englishmen agreeing to rest the legitimacy of their national pretensions as golfers, together with a large sum of money, on the result of a match, to be played with his Highness and any Scotchman he could bring forward. The Duke, whose great aim at that time was popularity, thinking this no bad opportunity both for asserting his claim to the character of a Scotchman, and for flattering a national prejudice, immediately accepted the challenge; and, in the meantime, caused diligent inquiry to be made as to where the most efficient partner was to be found. The person recommended to him for this purpose was a poor man, named John Patersone, a shoemaker, who was not only reputed the best golf-player of his day, but whose ancestors had been equally celebrated from time immemorial.

"On the matter being explained to him, Patersone was not quite satisfied as to how he should be able to acquit himself in such great company; but on the Duke encouraging him, he said he would do his best.

"The match was played, in which the Duke was, of course, completely victorious; and the shoemaker was dismissed with a reward corresponding to the importance of his service; being an equal share of the stake played for.

Historical Account

"With this money he immediately built himself a comfortable house in the Canongate, upon the wall of which the Duke

FROM A PEN-AND-INK SKETCH BY JAMES DRUMMOND, R.S.A.

caused an escutcheon to be affixed, bearing the arms of the family of Patersone,[1] surmounted by the above crest and motto."

---

[1] "The name of Paterson bears Argent, three pelicans feeding their young, or, in nests vert."—Mack. *Her.*

"The Patersons, designed of Dalkeith of old, carried the same with a

of the Game

The inscription alluded to consists of four elegiac verses in Latin, written by the celebrated Doctor Pitcairne, and which is to be found in a collection of *jeux d'esprit*, entitled "Selecta Poemata Archibaldi Pitcairn, Med. Doctoris, Gulielmi Scot a Thirlstane, Equitis, Thomæ Kincadii, Civis Edinburgensis, et Aliorum. Edinburgi Excusa anno MDCCXXVII."

> cum victor ludo fcotis qui proprius effet
> ter tres victores poft redimitus avos
> paterfonus humo tunc educebat in altum
> hanc quæ victores tot tulit una domum
> I hate no perfon

The motto, "I hate no person," being an anagrammatical transposition of the letters contained in the words "John Patersone," leaves no room for doubt as to the name of the hero who figures in the several legends to which the fact in question has given rise.

It must have been remarked that the scene of all the exploits performed by the golfers of the "olden time," was the Links of Leith.[1]

---

chief azure, charged with three mollets argent. (Pont's MS.)"—Nisbet's *Scottish Heraldry*, Edin. MDCCXXII. p. 362.

[1] John, fifth Lord Balmerino, a descendant of the lord who had been the subject of a notable prosecution under the tyrannical government of Charles I., was residing (24th Dec. 1729) in advanced age at his house in Coatfield Lane, in Leith. One of his younger sons, named Alexander (the immediate younger brother of Arthur, who made so gallant a death on Tower Hill in 1746), was

Historical Account

In a spirited poem entitled *The Goff*, composed by Mr. Thomas Mathison, originally a writer in Edinburgh, and afterwards minister of Brechin, there is the following allusion to the locality which we have just specified :—

> North from Edina eight furlongs and more
> Lies that fam'd field, on Fortha's sounding shore.

leading a life of idleness and pleasure at the same place. As this young gentleman was now to be involved in a bloody affair which took place in Leith Links, it may be worth while to recall that, five years back, he was engaged on the same ground in an affair of gaiety and sport, which yet had some ominous associations about it. It was what a newspaper of the day calls "a solemn match at golf" played by him for twenty guineas with Captain Porteous[1] of the Edinburgh Town-guard ; an affair so remarkable on account of the stake, that it was attended by the Duke of Hamilton, the Earl of Morton, and a vast mob of the great and little besides—Alexander Elphinstone ending as the winner. No one could well have imagined, as that cheerful game was going on, that both the players were, not many years after, to have blood upon their hands, one of them to take on the murderer's mark upon this very field.

On the 23rd of December 1729, the Honourable Alexander Elphinstone met a Lieutenant Swift, of Cadogan's regiment, at the house of Mr. Michael Watson, merchant in Leith. Some hot words having risen between them, Elphinstone rose to depart, but before he went, he touched Swift on the shoulder with his sword, and dropped a hint that he would expect to receive satisfaction next morning on the Links. Next day, accordingly, the two gentlemen met at eleven in the forenoon in that comparatively public place (as

---

[1] John Porteous was the son of a tailor in Edinburgh. His father intended to breed him up to his own trade, but the youthful profligacy of the son defeated the parent's prudent intention, and he enlisted into the Scotch corps at that time in the service of the States of Holland. There he learned military discipline, and on his return to his own country in 1715, he was engaged by the Magistrates of Edinburgh to discipline the City Guard. For such a task he was eminently qualified, not only by his military education, but by his natural activity and resolution ; and, in spite of the profligacy of his character, he received a captain's commission in the corps.

The duty of the Edinburgh City Guard was to preserve the public peace when any tumult was apprehended. At executions they generally surrounded the scaffold, and it was on an occasion of this kind, in 1736, that Porteous, their captain, committed the outrage for which he paid the penalty of his life.

We need hardly remind our readers that a full account of the murder of Captain Porteous is given in the *Heart of Midlothian*, and forms one of the most striking incidents in the novel.

of the Game

    Here, Caledonian chiefs for health resort,
    Confirm their sinews by the manly sport.
    Macdonald and unmatch'd Dalrymple ply
    Their pond'rous weapons, and the green defy :
    Rattray for skill, and Crosse for strength renown'd,
    Stuart and Leslie beat the sandy ground,
    And Brown and Alston, chiefs well known to fame,
    And numbers more the Muse forbears to name.
    Gigantic Biggar here full oft is seen,
    Like huge behemoth on an Indian green ;
    His bulk enormous scarce can 'scape the eyes,
    Amaz'd spectators wonder how he plies.
    Yea, here great Forbes,[1] patron of the just,
    The dread of villains and the good man's trust,

---

it now appears), and fought a single combat with swords, which ended in Swift receiving a mortal wound in the breast.

Elphinstone was indicted for this act before the High Court of Justiciary ; but the case was never brought forward, and the young man died without molestation at Leith three years after.

Chambers's Domestic Annals of Scotland.

    The common called Craigentinny, a piece of waste ground which once skirted the beach opposite Seafield toll-bar, and is now entirely washed away by the sea, was likewise a great resort of golfers during the seventeenth century. The Logans of Restalrig had a piece of ground near their seat at Lochend, appropriated to their own amusement ; to which the inhabitants of Canongate, and the courtiers in latter times, were in the habit of repairing, after the possessions of the above family were forfeited. There is a tradition preserved among the descendants of the Logans, who are considerable proprietors in Berwickshire, that Halbert Logan, one of the last of the race who resided in the neighbourhood of his ancient patrimonial territory, was one day playing here, when a messenger summoned him to attend the Privy Council. Despising this, and being also heated by his game, he used some despiteful language to the officer, who instantly went to court and reported the same ; and a warrant being then issued by the incensed councillors, on a charge of high treason, he was obliged to throw down his club, mount a fleet horse, and fly to England.   Chambers's *Traditions of Edinburgh.*

[1] Duncan Forbes, Esq., Lord President of the Court of Session in Scotland. It is reported of this great man, that he was so fond of Golf as to play on the sands of Leith when the Links were covered with snow. He died 10th December 1747.

In the *Lives of Simon, Lord Lovat, and Duncan Forbes of Culloden,*

Historical Account

When spent with toils in serving human kind,
His body recreates, and unbends his mind.[1]

Since the preceding sheets were thrown off, copies of two very curious instruments, under the Privy Seal of Scotland, have been obtained from the Public Archives. These throw considerable light on the history of Golf, about the beginning of the seventeenth century, the period when it seems to have been in greatest repute in Scotland.

The first is an appointment by James VI., in favour of William Mayne, to the office of fledger, bower, club-maker, and spear-maker to his Majesty, and is dated at Holyrood House, 4th April 1603; the other is a similar appointment, in favour of James Melvill, and others, to the office of golf-ball makers, and is dated at Salisbury, 5th August 1618.

REGISTRUM SECRETI SIGILLI
LIB. LXXIIJ. 234

ANE Letter maid to Williame Mayne, bower burges of Edinburgh, makand and constituand the said Williame, during all the dayis of his lyif-tyme, Mr. fledger, bower, club-maker, and speir-maker to his Hienes, alsweill for gayme as weir, and gevand to him the offices thairof, with all feyis and casualities apperteining and belanging thairto, and quhairof onie vtheris persounes quhatsumeuir that hes vseit and exercit the saidis offices of befoir hes beine in vse, with command thairin to his Hienes thesaurer, present and to cum, to reddelie ansuer and mak payment to the said Williame Mayne, of the zeirlie fie and dewtie vsit, and wount to be payit for the

---

we find the following notice of his playing Golf with his son on the links of Musselburgh :—"This day (1st Nov. 1728), after a very hard pull, I got the better of my son at the gouf in Musselburgh links. If he was as good at any other thing as he is at that, there might be some hopes of him."—*MS. at Culloden House.*

[1] The names of the players, left blank in first edition of Mathison's poem, are supplied from the Record Book of the Honourable Company of Golfers, all of whom were Members of the Club.

of the Game

dischargeing of the saidis offices, to onie persoun or persounes in onie tyme bigane, induring all the dayis of the said Williames lyfetime, etc. At Halirudhous, the fourt day of Aprile, IM. sex hundrethe thrie zeiris.

Per Signaturam.

REGISTRUM SECRETI SIGILLI

LIB. LXXXVIJ. 169

ANE Letter maid makand mentioun that our Souerane Lord vnderstanding that thair is no small quantitie of gold and siluer transported zeirlie out of his Hienes kingdome of Scotland for bying of *golf ballis*, vsit in that kingdome for recreatioun of his Majesties subjectis, and his Hienes being earnestlie dealt with by James Melvill, in favors of Williame Bervick and his associate, who onlie makis, or can mak golf ballis within the said kingdome for the present, and were the inbringeris off the said trade thair : The said James Melvill vndertaking by them, and vther puir peopill (who now for laik of calling wantis mantenance), whome he sall adjoyne to the said Williame Bervick and his associate, to furnische the said kingdome with better golf ballis, and at ane moir easie rate then have beine sauld there these manie zeiris bypast : In consideratioun quhairof, his Majestie, bothe tendring the generall weill of his subjectis and increase of vertew within his said kingdome, geving and granting vnto the said James Melvill, with Williame Bervick and his said associate, and sik vtheris as the said James Melvill sall adjoyne to them, onlie libertie to mak golf ballis within the said kingdome for the spaice of tuentie ane zeiris allanerlie, dischairging all vtheris alsweill of making as selling any golf ballis maid within the kingdome bot those that ar maid by the said James, his servantis, and Williame Bervick and his associate : Provyding allwayis, that the (said) merchandis sall not be restranit from importing and selling the said golfe ballis so brocht home or maid by the saidis patentis : Provyding lykwayis, that the saidis patentaris exceid not the pryce of four schillingis money of this realme for everie ane of the saidis golfe ballis as for the pryce thairof : And to the effect the said James and his associates may have the benefite of his Majestie's grant, his Hienes by these presentis dothe expresslie prohibite and dischairge and forbid all and sindrie his Majesties subjectis, and vther persounes quhatsumever, that nane of them presume, nor tak vpone hand, to mak or sell anie golf ballis maid within the said kingdome,

Historical Account

vtheris then the said James Melvill and his deputies, with the said Williame Bervick and his associate, for the spaice foirsaid, or to utter or sell the samyne to his Hienes subjectis vpone quhatsumever collour or pretence, vnder the paine of escheitting of all suche ballis so to be maid or sauld ; the ane halff of the benefite aryssing thairby to come to our Souerane Lordis use, and the vther half to the use of the said James Melvill and his assignayis onlie : And that the said letter be extendit in the best form, with all clauses neidfull, with power in the samyn to the said James, by himself, his deputies, and servantis, in his name, to seirche, seik, and apprehend all sik golf ballis as sal be maid or sauld within his Hienes said kingdome vtherways then according to the trew meaning of his Majesties grant, and to escheit the samyn in maner aboue specifeit. And for the better tryell heirof, his Majestie ordanes the said James Melvill to have ane particular stamp of his awin, and to cause mark and stamp all suche ballis maid be him and his foirsaidis thairwith ; and that all ballis maid within the kingdome found to be vtherwayis stamped sall be escheated in maner foirsaid. Gevin at our Court of Sallisbery the fyft day of August, the zeir of God IM. VIC. and auchteine zeiris. *Per Signaturam.*

YE GOLFER AND YE CADDIE OF YE PERIOD

The Goff

AN HEROI-COMICAL POEM IN THREE CANTOS

*Cætera, quæ vacuas tenuissent carmina mentes,
Omnia jam volgata.*—VIRG.

Edinburgh : J. Cochran & Co., 1743, 8vo.
Second Edition.—Edinburgh : Printed for James Reid,
Bookseller in Leith, 1763.
Third Edition.—Peter Hill, Edinburgh, 1793, 4to.

NOTICE of the Author of the following Poem may not be deemed out of place. THOMAS MATHISON, who was probably a native of Edinburgh, and born before the year 1720, was originally an agent or writer in Edinburgh. At the time when he wrote *The Goff*, which was first published at Edinburgh in 1743, he may have been personally acquainted with President Forbes, mentioned in the Poem as "great Forbes, patron of the just"; and it may have been at his suggestion that he turned his attention to the Church. He was licensed by the Presbytery of Dalkeith, 1st November 1748, and for a time officiated in a Presbyterian congregation in the North of England. In September 1750 he was ordained assistant and successor to William Hepburn, minister of Inverkeilor; and was translated to the second charge of the parish of Brechin in July 1754. He died 19th June 1760. He married Margaret Whyte, who survived him. Publications : *The Goff*, 8vo, Edin. 1743 ; reprinted 1763 and 1793. *A Sacred Ode, occasioned by the late successes attending the British Arms*, Edin. 1760, 8vo.

EDINA'S TOWERS

THE GOFF[1]

Goff, and the *Man*, I sing, who, em'lous, plies
The jointed club; whose balls invade the skies;
Who from *Edina's* tow'rs, his peaceful home,
In quest of fame o'er *Letha's* plains did roam.
Long toil'd the hero, on the verdant field,
Strain'd his stout arm the weighty club to wield;
Such toils it cost, such labours to obtain

---

[1] By Thomas Mathison, originally a writer in Edinburgh, and afterwards minister of Brechin. Reprinted from first edition, 1743.

The Goff

The bays of conquest, and the bowl to gain.
    O thou GOLFINIA, Goddess of these plains!
Great Patroness of GOFF! indulge my strains;
Whether beneath the *thorn-tree* shade you lie,
Or from *Mercerian* tow'rs the game survey,
Or, round the green the flying ball you chase,
Or make your bed in some hot sandy *face :*
Leave your much-lov'd abode, inspire his lays
Who sings of GOFF, and sings thy fav'rite's praise.
    North from *Edina* eight furlongs and more
Lies that fam'd field, on *Fortha's* sounding shore.
Here, *Caledonian* Chiefs for health resort,
Confirm their sinews by the manly sport.
Macdonald and unmatch'd *Dalrymple* ply
Their pond'rous weapons, and the green defy;
Rattray for skill, and *Crosse* for strength renown'd,
Stuart and *Leslie* beat the sandy ground,
And *Brown* and *Alston*, Chiefs well known to fame,
And numbers more the Muse forbears to name.
Gigantic *Biggar* here full oft is seen,
Like huge behemoth on an *Indian* green;
His bulk enormous scarce can 'scape the eyes,
Amaz'd spectators wonder how he plies.
Yea, here great *Forbes*,[1] patron of the just,
The dread of villains and the good man's trust,
When spent with toils in serving human kind,
His body recreates, and unbends his mind.

---

[1] Duncan Forbes (Lord President of the Court of Session in Scotland), Dalrymple, Rattray, Crosse, Leslie, Alston, and Biggar, were all members of the Company of Gentlemen Golfers.

The Goff

Bright *Phœbus* now had measur'd half the day
And warm'd the earth with genial noon-tide ray:
Forth rush'd *Castalio* and his daring foe,
Both arm'd with clubs, and eager for the blow.
Of finest ash *Castalio's* shaft was made,
Pond'rous with lead, and fenc'd with horn the head,
(The work of *Dickson*,[1] who in *Letha* dwells,
And in the art of making clubs excels),
Which late beneath great *Claro's* arm did bend,
But now is wielded by his greater friend.

Not with more fury *Norris* cleav'd the main,
To pour his thund'ring arms on guilty *Spain*;
Nor with more haste brave *Haddock* bent his course,
To guard *Minorca* from *Iberian* force,—
Than thou, intrepid hero, urg'd thy way,
O'er roads and sands, impatient for the fray.

With equal warmth *Pygmalion* fast pursu'd,
(With courage oft are little wights endued),
'Till to GOLFINIA'S downs the heroes came,
The scene of combat, and the field of fame.

Upon a verdant bank, by FLORA grac'd,
Two sister Fairies found the Goddess plac'd;
Propp'd by her snowy hand her head reclin'd,
Her curling locks hung waving in the wind.
She eyes intent the consecrated green,
Crowded with waving clubs and vot'ries keen,
And hears the prayers of youths to her address'd,
And from the hollow face relieves the ball distress'd.

---

[1] Andrew Dickson, clubmaker, who ran fore-caddie to the Duke of York, afterwards James II.

The Goff

On either side the sprightly Dryads sat,
And entertain'd the Goddess with their chat.
     First VERDURILLA, thus: O rural Queen!
What Chiefs are those that drive along the green?
With brandish'd clubs the mighty heroes threat,
Their eager looks foretell a keen debate.
To whom GOLFINIA: Nymph, your eyes behold
Pygmalion stout, *Castalio* brave and bold.
From silver *Ierna's* banks *Castalio* came,
But first on *Andrean* plains he courted fame.
His sire, a Druid, taught (one day of seven)
The paths of virtue, the sure road to heaven.
In *Pictish* capital the good man past
His virtuous life, and there he breath'd his last.
The son now dwells in fair *Edina's* town,
And on our sandy plains pursues renown.
See low *Pygmalion*, skilled in GOFFING art,
Small is his size, but dauntless is his heart:
Fast by a desk in *Edin's* domes he sits,
With *saids* and *sicklikes* length'ning out the writs.
For no mean prize the rival Chiefs contend,
But full rewards the victor's toils attend.
The vanquish'd hero for the victor fills
A mighty bowl containing thirty gills;
With noblest liquor is the bowl replete;
Here sweets and acids, strength and weakness meet.
From *Indian* isles the strength and sweetness flow,
And *Tagus'* banks their golden fruits bestow;
Cold *Caledonia's* lucid streams controul
The fiery spirits, and fulfil the bowl;

The Goff

For *Albion's* peace and *Albion's* friends they pray,
And drown in *punch* the labours of the day.
    The Goddess spoke, and thus GAMBOLIA pray'd:
Permit to join in brave *Pygmalion's* aid,
O'er each deep road the hero to sustain,
And guide his ball to the desired plain.
    To this the Goddess of the manly sport:
Go, and be thou that daring Chief's support.
Let VERDURILLA be *Castalio's* stay:
I from this flow'ry seat will view the fray.
She said: the nymphs trip nimbly o'er the green,
And to the combatants approach unseen.

CANTO II

YE rural powers that on these plains preside,
Ye nymphs that dance on Fortha's flow'ry side,
Assist the Muse that in your fields delights,
And guide her course in these uncommon flights.
But chief, thee, O GOLFINIA! I implore;
High as thy balls instruct my Muse to soar:
So may thy green for ever crowded be,
And balls on balls invade the azure sky.

Now at that hole the Chiefs begin the game,
Which from the neighb'ring *thorn-tree* takes its name;
Ardent they grasp the ball-compelling clubs,
And stretch their arms t' attack the little globes.
Not as our warriors brandish'd dreadful arms,
When fierce *Bellona* sounded war's alarms,
When conqu'ring *Cromwell* stain'd fair *Eska's* flood,
And soak'd her banks with *Caledonian* blood;
Or when our bold ancestors madly fought,
And Clans engag'd for trifles or for nought.
That *Fury* now from our bless'd fields is driv'n,
To scourge unhappy nations doom'd by heav'n.
Let *Kouli Kan* destroy the fertile East,
Victorious *Vernon* thunder in the West;

The Goff

Let horrid war involve perfidious *Spain*,
And GEORGE assert his empire o'er the main:
But on our plains *Britannia's* sons engage,
And void of ire the sportive war they wage.

    Lo, tatter'd *Irus*, who their armour bears,
Upon the green two little pyr'mids rears;
On these they place two balls with careful eye,
That with *Clarinda's* breasts for colour vye,
The work of *Bobson*, who, with matchless art,
Shapes the firm hide, connecting ev'ry part,
Then in a socket sets the well-stitch'd void,
And thro' the eyelet drives the downy tide;
Crowds urging crowds the forceful brogue impels,
The feathers harden and the leather swells;
He crams and sweats, yet crams and urges more,
Till scarce the turgid globe contains its store:
The dreaded falcon's pride here blended lies
With pigeons' glossy down of various dyes;
The lark's small pinions join the common stock,
And yellow glory of the martial cock.

    Soon as *Hyperion* gilds old *Andrea's* spires,
From bed the artist to his cell retires;
With bended back, there plies his steely awls,
And shapes, and stuffs, and finishes the balls.
But when the glorious God of day has driv'n
His flaming chariot down the steep of heav'n,
He ends his labour, and with rural strains
Enchants the lovely maids and weary swains:
As thro' the streets the blythsome piper plays,
In antick dance they answer to his lays;

The Goff

At ev'ry pause the ravish'd crowd acclaim,
And rend the skies with tuneful *Bobson's* name.
Not more rewarded was old *Amphion's* song;
That rear'd a town, and this drags one along.
Such is fam'd *Bobson*, who in *Andrea* thrives,
And such the balls each vig'rous hero drives.

    First, bold *Castalio*, ere he struck the blow,
Lean'd on his club, and thus address'd his foe:
Dares weak *Pygmalion* this stout arm defy,
Which brave *Matthias* doth with terror try?
Strong as he is, *Moravio* owns my might,
Distrusts his vigour, and declines the fight.
Renown'd *Clephanio* I constrain'd to yield,
And drove the haughty vet'ran from the field.
Weak is thine arm, rash youth, thy courage vain;
Vanquish'd with shame you'll curse the fatal plain.
The half-struck balls your weak endeavours mock,
Slowly proceed, and soon forget the stroke.
Not so the orb eludes my thund'ring force;
Thro' fields of air it holds its rapid course;
Swift as the balls from martial engines driv'n,
Streams like a comet thro' the arch of heav'n.

    Vaunter, go on (*Pygmalion* thus replies);
Thine empty boasts with justice I despise.
Hadst thou the strength Goliah's spear to wield,
Like its great master thunder on the field,
And with that strength *Culloden's* matchless art,
Not one unmanly thought should daunt my heart.
He said, and sign'd to *Irus*, who, before,
With frequent warnings fill'd the sounding shore.

The Goff

    Then great *Castalio* his whole force collects,
And on the orb a noble blow directs.
Swift as a thought the ball obedient flies,
Sings high in air, and seems to cleave the skies;
Then on the level plain its fury spends;
And *Irus* to the Chief the welcome tidings sends.
Next in his turn *Pygmalion* strikes the globe:
On th' upper half descends the erring club;
Along the green the ball confounded scours;
No lofty flight the ill-sped stroke impow'rs.

    Thus, when the trembling hare descries the hounds,
She from her whinny mansion swiftly bounds;
O'er hills and fields she scours, outstrips the wind;
The hounds and huntsmen follow far behind.

    GAMBOLIA now afforded timely aid,
She o'er the sand the fainting ball convey'd,
Renew'd its force, and urg'd it on its way,
Till on the summit of the hill it lay.

    Now all on fire the Chiefs their orbs pursue,
With the next stroke the orbs their flight renew;
Thrice round the green they urge the whizzing ball,
And thrice three holes to great *Castalio* fall;
The other six *Pygmalion* bore away,
And sav'd a while the honours of the day.

    Had some brave champion of the sandy field
The Chiefs attended, and the game beheld,
With ev'ry stroke his wonder had increas'd,
And em'lous fires had kindled in his breast.

CANTO III

HARMONIOUS Nine, that from *Parnassus* view
The subject world, and all that's done below;
Who from oblivion snatch the patriot's name,
And to the stars extol the hero's fame,
Bring each your lyre, and to my song repair,
Nor think GOLFINIA's train below the Muses' care.

 Declining *Sol* with milder beams invades
The *Scotian* fields, and lengthens out the shades;
Hastes to survey the conquer'd golden plains,
Where captive *Indians* mourn in *Spanish* chains;
To gild the waves where hapless *Hosier* dy'd,
Where *Vernon* late proud *Bourbon's* force defy'd,
Triumphant rode along the wat'ry plain,
Britannia's glory and the scourge of *Spain*.

 Still from her seat the *Power* of GOFF beheld
Th' unweary'd heroes toiling on the field:
The light-foot Fairies in their labours share,
Each nymph her hero seconds in the war;
Pygmalion and GAMBOLIA there appear,
And VERDURILLA with *Castalio* here.

The Goff

The Goddess saw, and op'd the book of Fate,
To search the issue of the grand debate.
Bright silver plates the sacred leaves infold,
Bound with twelve shining clasps of solid gold.
The wond'rous book contains the fate of all
That lift the club, and strike the missive ball;
Mysterious rhymes, that thro' the pages flow,
The past, the present, and the future show.
GOLFINIA reads the fate-foretelling lines,
And soon the sequel of the war divines;
Sees conquest doom'd *Castalio's* toils to crown,
Pygmalion doom'd superior might to own.
Then at her side VICTORIA straight appears,
Her sister Goddess, arbitress of wars.
Upon her head a wreath of bays she wore,
And in her hand a laurel sceptre bore;
Anxious to know the will of Fate, she stands,
And waits obsequious on the Queen's commands.

  To whom GOLFINIA: Fate-fulfilling maid,
Hear the Fates' will, and be their will obey'd:
Straight to the field of fight thyself convey,
Where brave *Castalio* and *Pygmalion* stray;
There bid the long-protracted combat cease,
And with thy bays *Castalio's* temples grace.
She said; and swift, as *Hermes* from above
Shoots to perform the high behests of JOVE,
VICTORIA from her sister's presence flies,
Pleas'd to bestow the long-disputed prize.

  Meanwhile the Chiefs for the last hole contend,
The last great hole, which should their labours end;

The Goff

For this the Chiefs exert their skill and might,
To drive the balls, and to direct their flight.
Thus two fleet coursers for the Royal plate,
(The others distanc'd) run the final heat;
With all his might each gen'rous racer flies,
And all his art each panting rider tries,
While show'rs of gold and praises warm his breast,
And gen'rous emulation fires the beast.

    His trusty club *Pygmalion* dauntless plies:
The ball ambitious climbs the lofty skies;
But soon, ah! soon, descends upon the field,
The adverse winds the lab'ring orb repell'd.
Thus when a fowl, whom wand'ring sportsmen scare,
Leaves the sown land, and mounts the fields of air,
Short is his flight; the fiery *Furies* wound,
And bring him tumbling headlong to the ground.

    Not so *Castalio* lifts th' unerring club,
But with superior art attacks the globe;
The well-struck ball the stormy wind beguil'd,
And like a swallow skimm'd along the field.

    An harmless sheep, by Fate decreed to fall,
Feels the dire fury of the rapid ball;
Full on her front the raging bullet flew,
And sudden anguish seiz'd the silent ewe;
Stagg'ring, she falls upon the verdant plain,
Convulsive pangs distract her wounded brain.
Great PAN beheld her stretch'd upon the grass,
Nor unreveng'd permits the crime to pass:
Th' *Arcadian* God, with grief and fury stung,
Snatch'd his stout crook, and fierce to vengeance sprung;

The Goff

His faithful dogs their master's steps pursue;
The fleecy flocks before their father bow,—
With bleatings hoarse salute him as he strode,
And frisking lambkins dance around the God.
The sire of sheep then lifted from the ground
The panting dam, and piss'd upon the wound:
The stream divine soon eas'd the mother's pain;
The wise immortals never piss in vain:
Then to the ball his horny foot applies;
Before his foot the kick'd offender flies;
The hapless orb a gaping face detain'd,
Deep sunk in sand the hapless orb remain'd.

    As VERDURILLA mark'd the ball's arrest,
She with resentment fired *Castalio's* breast:
The nymph assum'd *Patrico's* shape and mien,
Like great *Patrico* stalk'd along the green;
So well his manner and his accent feign'd,
Castalio deem'd *Patrico's* self complain'd.
Ah, sad disgrace! see rustic herds invade
GOLFINIAN plains, the angry Fairy said.
Your ball abus'd, your hopes and projects crost,
The game endanger'd, and the hole nigh lost:
Thus brutal PAN resents his wounded ewe,
Tho' Chance, not you, did guide the fatal blow.

    Incens'd *Castalio* makes her no replies,
T' attack the God, the furious mortal flies;
His iron-headed club around he swings,
And fierce at PAN the pond'rous weapon flings.
Affrighted PAN the dreadful missive shunn'd;
But blameless *Tray* receiv'd a deadly wound:

The Goff

Ill-fated *Tray* no more the flocks shall tend,
In anguish doom'd his shorten'd life to end.
Nor could great PAN afford a timely aid;
Great PAN himself before the hero fled:
Even he, a God, a mortal's fury dreads,
And far and fast from bold *Castalio* speeds.

 To free the ball the Chief now turns his mind,
Flies to the bank where lay the orb confin'd;
The pond'rous club upon the ball descends,
Involv'd in dust th' exulting orb ascends;
Their loud applause the pleas'd spectators raise;
The hollow bank resounds *Castalio's* praise.

 A mighty blow *Pygmalion* then lets fall;
Straight from th' impulsive engine starts the ball,
Answ'ring its master's just design, it hastes,
And from the hole scarce twice two clubs' length rests.

 Ah! what avails thy skill, since Fate decrees
Thy conqu'ring foe to bear away the prize?

 Full fifteen clubs' length from the hole he lay,
A wide cart-road before him cross'd his way;
The deep-cut tracks th' intrepid Chief defies;
High o'er the road the ball triumphing flies,
Lights on the green, and scours into the hole:
Down with it sinks depress'd *Pygmalion's* soul.
Seiz'd with surprise, th' affrighted hero stands,
And feebly tips the ball with trembling hands;
The creeping ball its want of force complains,
A grassy tuft the loit'ring orb detains.
Surrounding crowds the victor's praise proclaim,
The echoing shore resounds *Castalio's* name.

The Goff

For him *Pygmalion* must the bowl prepare,
To him must yield the honours of the war,
On Fame's triumphant wings his name shall soar
Till time shall end, or GOFFING be no more.

THE HONOURABLE THE EDINBURGH COMPANY OF GOLFERS

THE date of the institution of THE HONOURABLE THE EDINBURGH COMPANY OF GOLFERS (incorporated by a Charter from the Magistrates of Edinburgh in 1800) is lost in antiquity, but the first of a regular series of Minutes, signed by President Forbes of Culloden, bears date 1744. In March of the same year, the Magistrates of Edinburgh, having been "from time to time applied to," authorised their "Treasurer to cause make a SILVER CLUB, not exceeding the value of Fifteen pounds sterling, to be played for annually"; and with the exception of the years 1746-47 and 1832-35, the SILVER CLUB has been regularly played for down to the present time. On referring to the immediately pre-

Honourable Company of Golfers

ceding poem of *The Goff*, it will be found that the heroes of the poem,—Forbes (Lord President of the Court of Session), Macdonald, Dalrymple, Rattray, etc., were all Members of the Club.

Until the year 1768, when the Golf House at the southwest corner of the Links at Leith was built, the Club used to meet in a tavern called Luckie Clephan's; but from 1768 downwards the business and social meetings were held in the Golf House. In 1831, some alterations having been made on the Links, and the green ceasing to be attractive, it was deemed advisable to dispose of the Club House and furniture; and it is much to be regretted that various pictures of old Members, painted expressly for the Club, and forming part of its history, were not reserved. The pictures were sold for trifling sums to parties unconnected with the Club; but there is a probability that some of them may again become the Club's property. After an interregnum of five years, the Club was revived at Musselburgh in 1836, and continued to increase to such an extent as to render quite inadequate the accommodation provided at the Grand Stand. In 1865 the Club House at Musselburgh was built.

But by and bye the game became so popular, and the players so numerous, as to force the Club to again look out for "fresh fields and pastures new"; and in 1891 suitable ground was found at Muirfield (a lease of nineteen years having been acquired from Mrs. Hamilton-Ogilvy), whereon a handsome Club House was erected. Muirfield is the private green of the Club, and all the Medals are now competed for over it.

The following Extracts, which give a glimpse into the social life of those who reigned before us, will no doubt prove interesting to all Golfers.

The Hon. Duncan Forbes of Culloden
Lord President of the Court of Session.
First Captain of the Gentlemen Golfers 1744

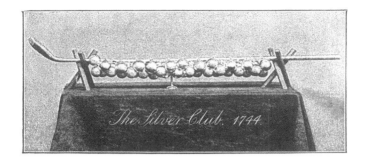

EXTRACTS FROM THE RECORD BOOK OF THE GENTLEMEN GOLFERS

ACT of COUNCIL and REGULATIONS to be observed by those who play for THE CITY OF EDINBURGH'S SILVER CLUB.

AT EDINBURGH, the 7th day of March 1744 years, The Lord Provost, Magistrates, and Council, with the Deacons of Crafts Ordinary and Extraordinary of the City of Edinburgh, being in Council assembled — And it being represented to them That several Gentlemen of Honour, skilfull in the ancient and healthfull exercise of the GOLF, had from time to time applied to several members of Council for a SILVER CLUB to be annually plaid for on the Links of Leith, at such time and upon such conditions as the Magistrates and Council should think proper: And it being reported that the GENTLEMEN GOLFERS had drawn up a Scroll, at the desire of the Magistrates, of such Articles and Conditions as to them seemed most expedient, as proper Regulations to be observed by the Gentlemen who should yearly offer to play for the said SILVER CLUB, which were produced and read in Council, the tenor whereof follows :—

I. As many Noblemen or Gentlemen, or other Golfers, from any part of Great Britain or Ireland, as shall book themselves eight days before, or upon any of the lawfull days of the week immediately preceding the day appointed by the Magistrates and Council for the Annual Match, shall have the privilege of playing for the said CLUB, each signer paying Five shillings sterling at signing, in a Book to be provided for that purpose, which is to lye in Mrs. Clephan's house in Leith, or such other house as afterwards the Subscribers shall appoint ; and the Regulations approved of by the Magistrates and Council shall be recorded at the beginning of said Book.

Extracts from the Record Book

IV. The Crowns given in at signing are solely to be at the disposal of the Victor.

V. Every Victor is to append a Gold or Silver piece, as he pleases, to the CLUB, for the year he wins.

VI. That every Victor shall, at the receiving of the CLUB, give sufficient caution to the Magistrates and Council of Edinburgh for Fifty pounds sterling for delivering back the Club to their hands ONE MONTH before it is to be played for again.

VII. That the CLUB is declared to be always the property of the Good Town.

IX. That the Victor shall be called CAPTAIN OF THE GOLF, and all disputes touching the Golf amongst Golfers, shall be determined by the Captain, and any two or three of the Subscribers.

Lastly, It is Declared, that upon no pretence whatsoever, The City of Edinburgh shall be put to any sort of expense upon account of playing for the said CLUB annually, except to intimate by TUCK OF DRUM, through the City, the day upon which it shall be annually played for, and to send the SILVER CLUB to Leith upon the morning appointed for the Match.

WHICH REGULATIONS having been considered by the Magistrates and Council, they, with the Extraordinary Deacons, approved thereof; And they hereby authorize the Treasurer to cause make a SILVER CLUB, not exceeding the value of Fifteen pounds sterling, to be played for annually upon the above conditions, ... And do hereby appoint the first Monday of April yearly as the day for playing the Annual Match for the SILVER CLUB.

Extracted furth of the Council Records of the City of Edinburgh upon this and the three preceding pages by me,

JOS. WILLIAMSON.

LIST of THOSE who are to play for the SILVER CLUB upon Monday the 2d of April 1744.

DUN. FORBES.[1]	DAV. DALRYMPLE.
HEW DALRYMPLE.	JA. CARMICHAELL.
GEO. SUTTIE.	WILLIAM CROSSE.
JOHN RATTRAY.	JA. LESLIE.
ROBERT BIGGAR.	RICHD. COCKBURN.
JAMES GORDON.	JA. VEITCH.

---

[1] Forbes, Dalrymple, Rattray, Biggar, etc., are all mentioned in Mathison's Poem of *The Goff*, published in 1743.

THE PROCESSION OF THE SILVER CLUB

From an Original Drawing by David Allan in 1787, in the Possession of the late David Laing, Esq., LL.D.

Extracts from the Record Book

Leith, April 2, 1744.

THE SILVER CLUB having been played for, Mr. John Rattray, Surgeon in Edinburgh, is declared to have won the same.—In witness whereof the whole players are hereunto subscribing.

      HEW DALRYMPLE.   ROBERT BIGGAR.
      GEO. SUTTIE.   DAV. DALRYMPLE.
      JA. LESLIE.   WILLIAM CROSSE.
      JA. CARMICHAELL.   JAMES GORDON.
      RICHD. COCKBURN.

Leith, April 1, 1745.[1]

THE SILVER CLUB having then been played for, Mr. John Rattray, Surgeon in Edinburgh, is again declared to have won the same.—In testimony whereof all those who played for the Club do hereto subscribe.   DUN. FORBES,
And eleven others.

Leith, August 4, 1753.

The Captain and his Councill, considering that Mr. David Lyon, ane eminent Golfer, after subscribing and engaging himself to play for the SILVER CLUB this day, has not only not started for the Club, but has, contrary to the duty of his allegiance, withdrawn himself from the Captain and his Company, and has dined in another house after having bespoke a particular dish for himself in Luckie Clephan's, The Captain therefore, with advice of his Councill, appoints the Procurator-Fiscall to indyte the said David Lyon for his above offence, and ordain William M'Ewen and William Alston to assist the Procurator-Fiscall to prepare and prosecute the same, and hereby orders the culprit to be cited to answer here on Saturday next.   HENRY SETON.

Leith, August 11, 1753.

In consequence of the above order of the Captain and his Company, Mr. Lyon was this day tryed for the above offence of breach of allegiance, and punished according to his deserts.

Leith, March 9, 1754.

Robert Douglas, writer in Edinburgh, having represented to the Captain and Gentlemen Golfers present, that several gentle-

---

[1] The next Meeting of the Club took place on 18th March 1748, the "troublous times" no doubt accounting for the interregnum.

Honourable Company of Golfers

men of the county of Fife had contributed for a SILVER CLUB[1] to be played for annually upon the Links of St. Andrews, and he in their name desired to know what day would be most convenient for the Gentlemen Golfers here to honour the Gentlemen of Fife with their presence on that occasion,—It was the opinion of the Captain and Gentlemen Golfers present, that Tuesday the 30th of April next would be the most convenient time for them, and they appointed Sir Henry Seton, Bart., Col. Robert Horn, Mr. David Dalrymple, with the said Robert Douglas one of their number, as a Committee to correspond with the Gentlemen of Fife, and to know of them if the said 30th of April next was a convenient and agreeable time for them, and if so the Gentlemen Golfers here would do themselves the honour to attend accordingly. WILLIAM CROSSE.

Leith, March 7, 1761.

The Captain and his Councill Do appoint that Mr. Patrick Robertson, Jeweller and Goldsmith in Edinburgh, one of their number, shall in all time coming be Ball-maker to the Honourable Society of Golfers. WM. ST. CLAIR, *Captain*.

EXCERPT from ACT of COUNCIL of the Lord Provost and Magistrates, of date 11th January 1764, altering the Condition on which the SILVER CLUB is to be played for.

"That your Petitioners and the other Captains of the Golf should be authorized to admit such Noblemen or Gentlemen as they approve of to be Members of the Company of Golfers.

"*Secondly*. That no person whatever, other than the Members of the Golf Company, shall be entitled to play for the Silver Club given by the Good Town."

Which being read in presence of and considered by the Magistrates and Council, They Did, and hereby Do, authorize the Petitioner and the other Captains of the Golf, To Admit such Noblemen or Gentlemen as they approve of to be Members of the Company of Golfers, And ENACT and ORDAIN That no

---

[1] The St. Andrews Silver Club was first played for on 14th May 1754 (the date of the first Minute and institution of the Club), and gained by Bailie William Landale, merchant in St. Andrews.

Extracts from the Record Book

person whatever other than Members of the Golf Company shall be entitled to play for the SILVER CLUB given by the good Town.
JOS. WILLIAMSON.

Leith, March 15, 1764.

The Captain and Council taking into their serious consideration the deplorable situation of the Company in wanting a godly and pious Chaplain, They did intreat the Reverend Doctor John Dun, Chaplain to the Right Honourable the Earl of Galloway, to accept the office of being Chaplain to the Golfers; which desire the said Doctor, out of his great regard to the Glory of God and the good of the Souls of the said Company, was Religiously pleased to comply with. Therefore the Company and Council Did and Do hereby nominate, present, and appoint the said Rev. Doctor John Dun to be their Chaplain accordingly. The said Reverend Doctor did accept of the Chaplaincy, and in token thereof said Grace after dinner.

From the BETT BOOK.   *Leith, January* 4, 1766.

It is understood that no match shall be plaed for more than one hundred merks on the day's play, or one guinea the round.

Each person who lays a Bett in company of the Golfers, and shall fail to play it on the day appointed, shall forfeit to the Company a pint of wine for each guinea, unless he give a sufficient excuse to their satisfaction.

Leith, March 3, 1766.[1]

WILLIAM ST. CLAIR of Roslin, Esq., *Captain.*

The SILVER CLUB given by the Good Town of Edinburgh to the Company of Gentlemen Golfers having been this day played for, the same was won by William St. Clair of Roslin, Esq., and delivered over to him as Captain.
ROB. HORN ELPHINSTONE.

---

[1] SMOLLETT, writing of this date, thus notices the Game :—Hard by, in the fields called the Links, the citizens of Edinburgh divert themselves at a game called Golf, in which they use a curious kind of bats tipped with horn, and small elastic balls of leather, stuffed with feathers, rather less than tennis-balls, but of a much harder consistence. These they strike with such force

Honourable Company of Golfers

Golf House, Leith, March 11, 1769.

The late Captain, Mr Alexander Keith, moved, That in honour of the memory of the late Lord Drummore, that his Picture should be put up in the Large Room of the New Golf House, which motion the gentlemen present unanimously agreed to, and ordered the best Half-Length copy of his Lordship's picture to be got and put up at their expense.

THOS. STODDART, *C.*

Leith, July 2, 1768.

This day William St. Clair of Roslin, Esq., the undoubted representative of the Honourable and Heretable G.M.M. of Scotland,[1] In presence of Alexander Keith, Esq., Captain of the Honourable Company of Goffers, and other worthy Members of the Goffing Company, all Masons, The G.M., now in his GRAND CLIMAX of GOFFING, laid the Foundation of the GOFFING HOUSE in the S.E. corner thereof, by THREE STROKES with the Mallet.

ALEXR. KEITH, *C.*
WM. ST. CLAIR, *G.M.M.*

---

and dexterity from one hole to another, that they will fly to an incredible distance. Of this diversion the Scots are so fond, that, when the weather will permit, you may see a multitude of all ranks, from the senator of justice to the lowest tradesman, mingled together, in their shirts, and following the balls with the utmost eagerness. Among others, I was shown one particular set of golfers, the youngest of whom was turned of four-score. They were all gentlemen of independent fortunes, who had amused themselves with this pastime for the best part of a century, without having ever felt the least alarm from sickness or disgust; and they never went to bed without having each the best part of a gallon of claret in his belly. Such uninterrupted exercise, co-operating with the keen air from the sea, must, without all doubt, keep the appetite always on edge, and steel the constitution against all the common attacks of distemper.

[1] William St. Clair (the first Grand Master of the Grand Lodge of Scotland) was the last who bore the office of Hereditary Grand Master of the Freemasons of Scotland—a dignity vested in his family by one of our ancient Kings, which he voluntarily resigned to the community. On his death he was much regretted by "the brethren of the mystic tie," to whom he had ever been a warm friend and a liberal benefactor. At a meeting held by them in consequence of his decease, Sir William Forbes delivered a speech, in which his numerous virtues and merits were properly eulogised; and which, for animation and beauty of language, would have done honour to *any* orator.

Golf House, Leith, March 11, 1771.

The Company of Gentlemen Golfers having resolved to have their present Captain's (Wm. St. Clair) picture [1] in full length in his Golfing Dress in their Large Room, requested him to sit for the same, which he having agreed to, Sir George Chalmers is appointed to paint the same, which is to be done at the Golfers' expense as soon as conveniently the same can be done.

ROB. HORN ELPHINSTONE.

---

[1] This fine picture was disposed of at the sale of the Club's effects in 1831. It is now in the Hall of the Royal Company of Archers. Mr. St. Clair is in the costume of a Golfer, with a round blue Scotch bonnet, and stands in the attitude of driving a ball from the *tee*. Sir Walter Scott describes St. Clair

Honourable Company of Golfers

Leith, Nov. 16, 1776.

This day Lieutenant James Dalrymple, of the 43rd Regiment, being convicted of playing five different times at Golf without his uniform, was fined only in Six Pints, having confessed the heinousness of his crime.   JA. CHEAP.

At his own request he was fined of Three Pints more.

---

as being "a man considerably above six feet, with dark-grey locks, a form upright, but gracefully so, thin-flanked and broad-shouldered, built it would seem for the business of war or the chase, a noble eye of chastened pride and undoubted authority, and features handsome and striking in their general effect, though somewhat harsh and exaggerated when considered in detail. His complexion was dark and grizzled, and we as schoolboys, who crowded to see him perform feats of strength and skill in the old Scottish games of Golf and Archery, used to think and say amongst ourselves the whole figure resembled the famous founder of the Douglas race pointed out, it is pretended, to the Scottish monarch on the conquered field of battle as the man whose arm had achieved the victory, by the expressive words, *Shoito Dhuglas,*— 'behold the dark-grey man.'" He died in 1778, æt. 78, and was buried among his mail-shrouded ancestors in Roslin Chapel.

There are twenty of Roslin's barons bold
Lie buried within that proud chapelle.

Extracts from the Record Book

Golf House, Dec. 11, 1779.

The Meeting resolve to adhere strictly to that ancient and proper regulation by which the Preses is bound to call a Bill after a Chopin bottle of Claret has been called in for each person in the company, and that in case the Preses shall neglect to call the Bill within the proper time, and allow the reckoning to exceed that quantum, the surplus shall be paid by himself.

WILLIAM HAGART.

Golf House, Jan. 19, 1782.

That Port and Punch shall be the ordinary Drink of the Society unless upon these days when the SILVER CLUB and CUPS are played for. At those Meetings Claret or any other Liquor more agreeable will be permitted.

ALEX. DUNCAN, *Captain.*

Golf House, May 3, 1783.

Same day Mr. John Gray was with one voice appointed Clerk to the Betts, and that no Golfer should presume to write in the Bett Book when he is present. WILL. INGLIS.

Golf House, Oct. 18, 1783.

This being a General Meeting, it was proposed, and unanimously agreed to, that in all time coming every person who may be assumed a Member shall have a Diploma[1] or Certificate of his admission, for which there shall be paid Half-a-Guinea, and it was remitted to the Captain and Council to consider of and adjust the form of such Diploma, and of the proper Seal to be thereto affixed. WILL. INGLIS.

Golf House, Nov. 22, 1783.

The Company having collected a small sum for David Lindsay, an old ball-maker and caddie, now very old and infirm, being above 80 years of age, It was agreed that he should have one half-crown weekly during pleasure out of the Funds—to commence next Saturday. WILL. INGLIS.

---

[1] The illustration by David Allan, on p. 39, is from the heading of the Diploma.

Honourable Company of Golfers

Golf House, May 14, 1785.

Mr. DAVID ALLAN, Painter in Edinburgh, was this day unanimously chosen an Honorary Member for his good services done the Society. WILL. INGLIS.

Golf House, Nov. 17, 1787.

An Uniform for the Golfers was presented by the Captain and his Council, which was unanimously approved of. John Paterson, Tailor in Edinburgh, was appointed Tailor for the Society, and the Members were requested to appear in the Uniform as soon as conveniently they can. ELCHO, *C.*

Golf House, Jan. 12, 1788.

The Hon. Henry Erskine, Dean of the Faculty of Advocates, was unanimously admitted a Member by ballot.

THOS. STODDART, *C.*

Golf House, March 22, 1788.

Upon motion from the Captain, It was agreed that Robert the waiter, for his faithful services, shall have out of the Funds One Guinea per quarter. ELCHO, *C.*

Golf House, May 31, 1788.

It was unanimously agreed to that every Member of the Society shall dine in his uniform at every public meeting of the Club, and that the Members of the Club shall appear in the uniform when they play upon the Links. ELCHO.

Golf House, Oct. 16, 1790.

As a spur to Golfing, it was proposed that a GOLD MEDAL, value about Five Guineas, should be played for and worn by the winner for the year, and the winner not to be excluded from playing for it again. The Gainer's name and year to be engraved on it. WM. SIMPSON.

Golf House, Nov. 13, 1790.

The GOLD MEDAL was played for this day, and won by Mr. Robert Allan, and delivered to him by the Captain in proper form. WM. SIMPSON.

Extracts from the Record Book

Golf House, Jan. 28, 1792.

Mr. HENRY RAEBURN, formerly proposed by Mr. William Grant, and seconded by the Captain, was this day ballotted for and admitted. JAMES DALRYMPLE, *Captain*.

Golf House, May 4, 1793.

It is the unanimous opinion of this Company that no Member shall play on the Links with Irons all, without the consent of the Captain and Council, and it is recommended by the Meeting that they will not grant the desire of such application.

JAMES DALRYMPLE.

Golf House, June 7, 1794.

Remit to Mr. Gilbert Innes, the Secretary, and Recorder, to make Regulations to enforce the good behaviour of the caddies.

ROBERT ALLAN.

Golf House, Aug. 1, 1795.

Messrs. David Ramsay, printer, and Peter Hill,[1] bookseller, were this day ballotted for and duly admitted Members.

ROBERT ALLAN.

November 14, 1795.

Mr. James Balfour, Secretary and Treasurer to the Society, having died on Tuesday 20th October last, no Meeting has been held until the present that has conveened in consequence of the following Advertisement which was repeated in all the Edinburgh Newspapers :—

Edinburgh Golf Club.

A General Meeting of the Club is to be held, in Memory of their late worthy Secretary, in the Golf House, Leith, upon Saturday the 14th inst. The Members who mean to attend are requested to send their names to the Golf House on the Wednesday preceding. And it is expected they will appear in Mourning.

---

[1] Mr. Hill published the Third Edition of Mathison's poem of *The Goff* in 1793.

Engraved by William Walker from a Picture by Sir Henry Raeburn, R.A.

Henry Raeburn

Walker & Boutall Ph Sc

Honourable Company of Golfers

Accordingly appeared,—

Robert Allan, Esq., present Captain, in the Chair.

The Right Hon. Sir James Stirling, Bart., Lord Provost of the City of Edinburgh.

And 27 others. All dressed in mourning, agreeable to the Advertisement.

Immediately after Dinner the Captain gave the following Toasts :—

I. The Health of the Company.

> Then rising up slowly, which the Company also did, said—I well know you all feel with me on the melancholy cause of this meeting, and will join in dedicating this glass

II. To the Memory of our Worthy and late departed Friend, Mr. James Balfour, whose benevolent and cheerful dispositions, and happy social powers, while they captivated all, particularly endeared him to his numerous friends.

> Being again seated, after a pause—

III. Comfort and Consolation to the Friends and Relatives of Mr. Balfour.

IV. May the Offices in this Society held by Mr. Balfour be agreeably supplied and attended to with that accuracy and precision for which he was peculiarly distinguished.

> During this solemnity, which was truly affecting, a profound silence was observed.

The Captain then proceeded to general Toasts.

In the course of conversation it was early proposed by the Captain, and unanimously agreed to by the company, to have an Engraving of Mr. Balfour taken from the striking portrait or painting of him, the property of the Company, done by Mr. Raeburn,[1] to be executed by a first-rate artist; and for that purpose a Subscription Paper was opened under the following title :—

---

[1] *Edinr.*, 6*th May* 1793.—Received from James Balfour, Esq., the sum of Thirty Guineas for his own portrait, done for the Society of Golfers.

HENRY RAEBURN.

Extracts from the Record Book

"Subscribers for a print of Mr. James Balfour. The money paid to be accounted for by Mr. Robert Allan, present Captain of the Golf, agreeable to his initials."
Proof, £1 : 1s.   Other Copy, 10s. 6d.

The whole Company having subscribed, some for more copies than one, and for friends, the total was forty-five proof copies at one guinea each, and four other copies at 10s. 6d. each.

And for obtaining the work done in such way and manner as might be judged most eligible, the fullest powers were given to the following, named a Committee, viz.—

Capt. ROBERT ALLAN.   Mr. HENRY RAEBURN.
Sir JAMES STIRLING, Bart.   *And six others.*

The following notice of Balfour is extracted from Chambers's *Traditions of Edinburgh* :—

One of the most notable jolly fellows of the last age was James Balfour, an accountant, usually called *Singing Jamie Balfour*, on account of his fascinating qualities as a vocalist. There used to be a portrait of him in the Leith Golf-House, representing him in the act of commencing the favourite song of *When I ha'e a Saxpence under my thoom*, with the suitable attitude, and a merriness of countenance justifying the traditional account of the man. Of Jacobite leanings, he is said to have sung *The wee German lairdie ; Awa, Whigs, awa ;* and *The sow's tail to Geordie*, with a degree of zest there was no resisting.

Report speaks of this person as an amiable, upright, and able man ; so clever in business matters that he could do as much in one hour as another man in three ; always eager to quench and arrest litigation rather than to promote it ; and consequently so much esteemed, professionally, that he could get business whenever he chose to undertake it, which, however, he only did when he felt himself in need of money. Nature had given him a robust constitution, which enabled him to see out three sets of boon-companions, but, after all, gave way before he reached sixty. His custom, when anxious to repair the effects of intemperance, was to wash his head and hands in cold water ; this, it is said, made him quite cool and collected almost immediately. Pleasure being so predominant an object in his life, it was thought surprising that at his death he was found in possession of some little money.

The powers of Balfour as a singer of Scotch songs of all kinds, tender and humorous, are declared to have been marvellous, and he had a happy gift of suiting them to occasions. Being a great peacemaker he would often

Honourable Company of Golfers

accomplish his purpose by introducing some ditty pat to the purpose, and thus dissolving all rancour in a hearty laugh. Like too many of our countrymen he had a contempt for foreign music. One evening, in a company where an Italian vocalist of eminence was present, he professed to give a song in the manner of that country. Forth came a ridiculous cantata to the tune of *Aiken Drum*, beginning, "There was a wife in Peebles," which the wag executed with all the proper graces, shakes, and appogiaturas, making his friends almost expire with suppressed laughter at the contrast between the style of singing and the ideas conveyed in the song. At the conclusion their mirth was doubled by the foreigner saying very simply, "De music be very fine, but I no understand de words."

A lady, who lived in the Parliament Close, told a friend of mine that she was wakened from her sleep one summer morning by a noise as of singing, when, going to the window to learn what was the matter, guess her surprise at seeing Jamie Balfour and some of his boon-companions (evidently fresh from their wonted orgies) singing *The King shall enjoy his own again*, on their knees, around King Charles's statue. One of Balfour's favourite haunts was a humble kind of tavern called *Jenny Ha's*, opposite to Queensberry House, where, it is said, Gay had boosed during his short stay in Edinburgh, and to which it was customary for gentlemen to adjourn from dinner-parties in order to indulge in claret from the butt, free from the usual domestic restraints. Jamie's potations here were principally of what was called *cappie ale*, that is, ale in little wooden bowls, with wee thochts of brandy in it. But indeed no one could be less exclusive than he as to liquors. When he heard a bottle drawn in any house he happened to be in, and observed the cork to give an unusually smart report, he would call out, "Lassie, gi'e me a glass o' *that*," as knowing that, whatever it was, it must be good of its kind.

Sir Walter Scott says, in one of his droll little missives to his printer Ballantyne, "When the press does not follow me I get on slowly and ill, and put myself in mind of Jamie Balfour, who could run when he could not stand still." He here alludes to a matter of fact, which the following anecdote will illustrate: Jamie, in going home late from a debauch, happened to tumble into the pit formed for the foundation of a house in James's Square. A gentleman passing heard his complaint, and going up to the spot was entreated by our hero to help him out. "What would be the use of helping you out," said the by-passer, "when you could not stand though you *were* out?" "Very true, perhaps, yet if you help me up I'll *run* you to the Tron Kirk for a bottle of claret." Pleased with his humour the gentleman placed him upon his feet, when instantly he set off for the Tron Church at a pace distancing all ordinary competition, and accordingly he won the race, though at the conclusion he had to sit down on the steps

Extracts from the Record Book

of the church, being quite unable to stand. After taking a minute or two to recover his breath—"Well, another race to Fortune's for another bottle of claret!" Off he went to the tavern in question, in the Stamp-office Close, and this bet he gained also. The claret, probably with continuations, was discussed in Fortune's, and the end of the story is that Balfour sent his new friend home in a chair, utterly done up, at an early hour in the morning.

June 11, 1796.

The SILVER CLUB was this day played for, and won by Mr. John Gray, and delivered to him in the usual form.

ROBERT ALLAN.

EXCERPT FROM MINUTE OF COUNCIL
26TH MARCH 1800

Read Report from the Magistrates, old Magistrates, and Convener, in consequence of the Remit on the Petition presented by John Gray, Writer to the Signet, *Captain*, Alexander Osborn, Solicitor of the Customs, *Secretary*, and David Murray, Deputy-Clerk of Session, *Treasurer*, of the Honourable the Edinburgh Company of Golfers, for themselves and in name and behalf of the other Members of the said Company, and which petition is of the following tenor :—"Unto the Right Honourable the Lord Provost, Magistrates, and Council of the City of Edinburgh, The Petition of John Gray, Writer to the Signet, *Captain*, Alexander Osborn, Solicitor of the Customs, *Secretary*, and David Murray, Deputy-Clerk of Session, *Treasurer*, of the Honourable the Edinburgh Company of Golfers, for themselves, and in name and behalf of the other Members of the said Company,—Humbly Sheweth, That the Edinburgh Company of Golfers has existed as a Club or Society for these great number of years, and they have occasionally got the aid of Acts of Council for preserving of the Links of Leith in a proper state for their favorite amusement of Golf, They are also Lessees of the Links, and in 1767 obtained a Feu of a piece of Ground adjacent thereto for payment of an Annual Feu-duty, upon which they, at a considerable expence, erected a House and Offices for the accommodation of themselves and workmen connected with the exercise ; But not being a legal society or Body Corporate they were under the necessity of holding the Property in name of a trustee—To remedy which,

Walker & Boutall, Ph. Sc

James Balfour Esq.
Secretary & Treasurer of the Edinburgh Company of Golfers 1793.
By Desire of The Company.

Honourable Company of Golfers

and in order to enable them to manage their Funds and regulate their affairs with proper effect, the present Application is presented. May it therefore please the Right Honourable the Lord Provost, Magistrates, and Council, to grant a Seal of Cause Constituting and Erecting the said Company, and all others who shall hereafter be entered with them, into one Body politic and corporate, or legal Corporation or Society, under the Title and Name of 'THE HONOURABLE THE EDINBURGH COMPANY OF GOLFERS,' And as such and by that name to have a perpetual endurance and succession, so as to entitle your Petitioners and their Successors in office, for the use and behoof of the said Company, to hold Property, real or personal, and with power, with consent of the said Company, at a Meeting upon the first Saturday of any Month, to make Bye-Laws and Regulations for the Management of their Society and Funds; And to be able, in name of their said Captain, Secretary, and Treasurer, for the time being, to sue, plead, and defend, and to be sued and defended in all or any Courts of Justice.—In respect whereof, (Signed) JOHN GRAY, for himself and the other Petitioners." Which Petition and Report thereon having been considered by the Lord Provost, Magistrates, and Council, they agreed that the Prayer thereof shall be granted, And ordered a Seal of Cause to be made out and granted to the Petitioners, Constituting, Erecting, and Incorporating the said Company, and all others who shall hereafter be entered with them, into one Body politic and Corporate, or legal Incorporation or Society, under the Title and Name of "THE HONOURABLE THE EDINBURGH COMPANY OF GOLFERS," and as such, and by that name, to have a perpetual endurance and succession, and to be able and capable of acquiring, holding, and conveying Property, real or personal; And in name of their said Captain, Secretary, and Treasurer for the time being, of suing, pleading, defending, and answering, and of being sued, impleaded, defended, and answered in all or any Courts of Judicature; And with power to the said Captain, Secretary, and Treasurer, with the Consent of the said Company, at a Meeting upon the first Saturday of any Month, to make Bye-Laws and Regulations for the Management of their Society and Funds, and other necessary ends and purposes, with this restriction, that any Bye-Laws or Regulations to be adopted by the said Society shall only be effectual upon receiving the Sanction of the Lord Provost, Magistrates, and Council for the time being.

Extracts from the Record Book

Golf House, Dec. 3, 1808.

The married gentlemen of the party are to play a match at Golf with the Batchelors on the 18th day of January next for a Claret Dinner on that day.

The Batchelors won the match by six holes.

Golf House, 15*th May* 1819.

Mr. Menzies bets with Mr. Guthrie that Baron Norton shall succeed the present Lord Chief Baron.

A Magnum advanced by Mr. Guthrie.

Mr. Menzies bets Mr. Guthrie that a Member of the Club shall be the first Judge named in the Court of Session.

Another Magnum advanced by Mr. Guthrie.

Golf House, Leith, 26*th May* 1827.

The SILVER CLUB to be played for on Saturday, the 30th June, and the Magistrates to be asked in the usual manner.

HENRY M. LOW.

Golf House, Leith, 8*th March* 1828.

It was agreed that the Club should dine at Musselburgh on the 24th current, and that the Magistrates and Council of the " Honest Town" should be invited. HENRY M. LOW.

Golf House, Leith, 5*th June* 1830.

The GOLD MEDAL was played for this day, and gained by Mr. John H. Wood.

Barry's Hotel, 26*th July* 1836.

The Members present unanimously elected Mr. William Wood to be Captain for the year, and resolved in the meantime to meet at Musselburgh, within M'Kendrick's Inn, on the first Saturday of each of the three ensuing months.

The meeting unanimously resolve that the entry money shall in future be Two Guineas.

Musselburgh, 3*rd June* 1837.

The MEDAL was played for, and after a keen contest by 22 players, was gained by William Wood, Esq., at 87 strokes.

Mr. John Wood was fined two tappit hens for appearing on the Links without a red coat. JOHN MANSFIELD.

Honourable Company of Golfers

Musselburgh, 12th July 1856.

The GOLD MEDAL was this day gained by W. M. Goddard holing 2 rounds of the Links in 76 strokes.

ALEX. MACKENZIE, C.

Edinburgh, 17th December 1859.

The Treasurer brought before the meeting the circumstance of Dr. Sanderson having carried on the litigation at his own expense in defence of the rights of Golfers on Musselburgh Links, in which he had been successful in obtaining Interdict against the Magistrates of Musselburgh, and thus preventing them from encroaching on the Links by feuing thereon. The Secretary was directed to summon a meeting of Council to consider and determine in what manner the Honourable Company should mark their approbation of Dr. Sanderson's conduct.

ROBERT COWAN, C.

Edinburgh, 13th Jan. 1860.

The meeting unanimously elected Dr. Henry Sanderson of Musselburgh an Honorary Member of the Honourable Company, as a mark of their appreciation of his services in conducting at his own expense the litigation in defence of the rights of Golfers; and the Secretary was directed to write Dr. Sanderson, inviting him to dine with the Honourable Company on a day to be named by himself.

DINNER given to HENRY SANDERSON, Esq., Surgeon, R.N., on 4th of Feb. 1860—the CAPTAIN in the Chair.

After dinner a silver centre-piece was placed on the table; and, after the usual loyal toasts, the Captain addressed Dr. Sanderson, and, referring to the obligations the Honourable Company are under to him for having defeated the attempt to feu the Musselburgh Links, informed him that he had been elected an Honorary Member, and requested, in name of the Honourable Company and of the subscribers, his acceptance of the piece of silver plate, which bore the following inscription:—
"Presented to Henry Sanderson, Surgeon, R.N., by the Honourable Company of Edinburgh Golfers, as a mark of their sense of the public spirit and energy with which, at his own risk, he successfully resisted the attempt to feu the Links of Musselburgh,

Extracts from the Record Book

by which the enjoyment of the present and future generations of Golfers would have been seriously interfered with."

Dr. Sanderson, in replying to the speech of the Captain, expressed his gratitude for the present, and his satisfaction that his services had met with the approbation of the Honourable Company of Edinburgh Golfers.   ROBERT COWAN, *C.*

Musselburgh, 13*th April* 1865.

The SILVER CLUB given by the City of Edinburgh was this day gained by the Right Hon. John Earl of Stair.[1]

The GOLD MEDAL was afterwards competed for over the Golfing course, when it was found that G. M. Innes, Robert Clark, and H. J. Wylie had tied at 83 strokes each on the two rounds of 16 holes. Those gentlemen played eight holes to decide the winner, which resulted in Mr. G. M. Innes gaining the medal in 37 strokes on the eight holes.

From the BETT BOOK.

13*th February* 1868.

Captain (Captain Kinloch) v. Clark with one Club. Won by Clark.

Musselburgh, 15*th Nov.* 1877.

Thirty-eight members started for the WINTER MEDAL, which was gained by Mr. Robert Clark with a score of 86 strokes.
JOHN WHARTON TOD, *C.*

Musselburgh, 5*th April* 1878.

Twenty-nine couples started for the GOLD MEDAL, which was won by Captain A. M. Brown, R.A., with a score of 82 strokes.
JOHN WHARTON TOD, *C.*

Musselburgh, 14*th Nov.* 1878.

Twenty-four couples competed for the WINTER MEDAL, which was won by Mr. John Wharton Tod with a score of 83 strokes.
WILLIAM J. MURE, *C.*

Musselburgh, 3*rd April* 1879.

Twenty-two couples competed for the GOLD MEDAL, which was won by Mr. W. J. Mure with a score of 82 strokes.
WILLIAM J. MURE, *C.*

---

[1] With the exception of the years 1746-47 and 1832-35, the Silver Club has been regularly played for from the year 1744 down to the present time.

Honourable Company of Golfers

NEW SILVER CLUB

At a DINNER given to the LORD PROVOST and MAGISTRATES of the City of Edinburgh on 26th February 1880, on the occasion of the presentation of a SILVER CLUB (*the third*), presented by the Magistrates to the Club,—

The Lord Provost (the Right Hon. T. J. Boyd) proposed the Toast of the Club, and made the presentation.

Musselburgh, 6th April 1882.

Twenty-eight couples competed for the GOLD MEDAL, which was won by Mr. L. M. Balfour with a score of 81 strokes.

B. HALL BLYTH, *C.*

February 7, 1884.

The Recorder was instructed to minute in the Record Book the following motion, which was carried upon a show of hands, viz.,— That in the event of a match being halved, the money in all bets where odds are laid is to be added together and divided.

J. M.

Musselburgh, 12*th April* 1887.

Twenty-one couples competed for the GOLD MEDAL, which was won by Mr. John E. Laidlay with a score of 79 strokes.

W. G. SIMPSON, *C.*

November 8, 1888.

Captain James Syme in the chair. At this dinner the Captain and several ex-captains appeared in Red Coats for the first time, in accordance with the resolution of the Club passed at the General Meeting of the Club in April last.

February 7, 1889.

Captain James Syme in the chair and 21 members present. The following motion was unanimously adopted,—At this the first dinner of the Honourable Company of Edinburgh Golfers which has been held since the death of the Recorder,—James Mansfield,—the members present desire to record their sense of the great loss which they, in common with the other Members of the Club, have sustained through that event, and also their high

Extracts from the Record Book

appreciation of the able manner in which for many years Mr. Mansfield discharged the duties of Recorder; and they instruct this to be engrossed in the Record Book of the Club.

B. H. B.

OPENING OF MUIRFIELD GREEN

On Saturday, 2nd May 1891, the new Green of the Honourable Company of Edinburgh Golfers, at Muirfield, Gullane, was opened for play in very unfavourable weather, rain falling steadily throughout the day.

In the afternoon about 130 Members and Guests sat down to Luncheon in a Marquee erected on the ground, the Captain, Colonel Anderson, presiding.

Musselburgh, 5th Nov. 1891.

Thirty-eight players competed for the Company's WINTER MEDAL, which was won by Mr. Alexander Stuart with a score of 80 strokes.

OPENING OF THE NEW CLUB HOUSE

On Saturday, 5th Dec. 1891, the New Club House at Muirfield was opened for the use of the Members, about forty of whom were present. The weather was most unpropitious.

The Recorder moved,—That after this date Muirfield shall be the Club Green, and that all matches made at the dinners of the Club shall consist of two rounds of that green, unless any other green be specified at the time of making the match.

This motion was also unanimously agreed to.

B. H. B.

Muirfield, 5th April 1892.

Forty-six players competed for the Company's GOLD and SILVER[1] MEDALS, the former of which was won by Mr. Leslie M. Balfour with a score of 79 strokes, and the latter by Mr. John E. Laidlay with a score of 80 strokes.[2]

---

[1] Presented to the Club by Sir Walter G. Simpson, Bart.
[2] The first time the Medals were played for on the Club's Private Green at Muirfield.

Honourable Company of Golfers

Muirfield, 6th April 1893.

Twenty-one couples competed for the Company's GOLD and SILVER MEDALS, the former of which was won by Mr. John E. Laidlay with a score of 78 strokes, and the latter (after a tie with Mr. A. Stuart) by Mr. R. H. Johnston in 85 strokes.

ALEX. STUART, C.

DINNER BILL

Golf House, Leith, August 29, 1801

		£	s.	d.
Dinner	.	2	0	0
Bread and Biscuit	.	0	2	0
Porter, Ale, and Spruce	.	0	8	0
Gin and Brandy	.	0	6	8
Port and Sherry (7 bottles)	.	1	13	6
Claret (16 bottles)	.	5	12	0
Tody, Glasses, Wax Lights, and Servants	.	0	11	2
		£10	13	4

CITY OFFICERS, etc.

		£	s.	d.
Dinner. Porter, Rum, and Tody	.	0	18	8
Club and Ball Maker, and Caddies	.	0	10	0
Waiter	.	0	12	0
		£12	14	0
To be paid by the Club	.	4	6	0
Remainder by 14 at 12s. each	.	£8	8	0

FORE!

THE ROYAL AND ANCIENT GOLF CLUB OF ST. ANDREWS

ST. ANDREWS, the old Ecclesiastical Metropolis of Scotland, though decayed from its ancient grandeur, has still a good many attractions at once for the permanent resident and the temporary sojourner. Persons of an antiquarian turn of mind generally employ a good deal of their time in mooning about the picturesque and historically-interesting ruins; whilst for others, in summer time, the sea, with its splendid sands and fine bathing facilities, is the great attraction. The Golfer, however—if in the least he be worthy of the name—does not greatly concern himself with such things. He eschews the ruins; and his sole concernment with the sea (after his morning plunge in it) is when, by evil hap, his ball takes a dip into that pestilent nook of it which comes across him at the High Hole. For the votaries of the game, nothing at St. Andrews can practically be said

Royal and Ancient Golf Club

to exist save the Club-house and the famous "Green." For not a few of the residents Golf is the main, or even sole, business of life; and the visitors who throughout the summer come to the Ancient City, drawn thither by the charm of the game pure and simple, very much outnumber those who come for all other reasons whatever.

The admitted supremacy of St. Andrews as a golfing centre may in various ways be accounted for. Socially and otherwise, the place has always been a pleasant one; even in its decay some savour of the ancient *prestige* has continued to cling to it; and the Club—one of the oldest in the kingdom—has thus from the first been one of much more than merely local celebrity. For the purposes of the game the Links are, on the whole, unrivalled by any other Links in Scotland; and since the year 1852, when railway communication was opened with St. Andrews, access to them is easy. In consequence, the Club has of late years developed enormously, so that the "Royal and Ancient" may now fairly be called, without dispute, the "National" Golf Club of Scotland. Nearly all Golfers of note are members; and to the Spring and Autumn meetings they flock from all parts of the kingdom. The Autumn meeting is considerably the more important; and its first prize—the KING WILLIAM MEDAL—may be termed the Blue Ribbon of Golf. To carry off this is the ambition of all Golfers; and nowadays, when upwards of sixty couples start for the much-coveted prize, it is easier to name an Epsom or St. Leger winner than to prophesy of the winner of this. The SILVER CROSS of the Spring meeting ranks next in importance; and no honour to be won anywhere at Golf can be held comparable to either.

The Royal and Ancient

Some little jottings of the history of this famous Club may here be not out of place. The St. Andrews Golf Club was instituted in 1754, the Silver Club having been played for in May of that year, and gained by Bailie William Landale, merchant in St. Andrews. The Honourable Company of Golfers, then called the "Gentlemen Golfers" of Leith, joined in the competition. In the year 1766 the Members met once a fortnight at eleven o'clock, played a round of the Links, and afterwards dined in the house of Bailie Glass, each paying a shilling for his dinner—the absent as well as the present. In October 1786 a Ball was given for the first time. In 1827 the funds were at so low an ebb that in that year the Club discontinued the allowance of Two Guineas to the Leith clubmaker for attending the annual general meeting. In 1834, His late Majesty, King William the Fourth, was graciously pleased to become Patron of the Club, and to approve of its being in future styled "The Royal and Ancient Golf Club of St. Andrews"; and in 1837 he presented a magnificent Gold Medal, "which His Majesty wished should be challenged and played for annually." In 1838, Her Majesty the Queen Dowager, Duchess of St. Andrews, became Patroness of the Club, and presented a handsome Gold Medal—"The Royal Adelaide"—as a mark of her approbation; with a request that it should be worn by the Captain, as president, on all public occasions. In 1854 the Union Club and the Royal and Ancient Golf Club of St. Andrews were amalgamated—Members of the latter being declared also Members of the Union; and since that time all entering Members are made free of both Clubs. In June 1863 His Royal Highness the PRINCE OF WALES became

Golf Club of St. Andrews

Patron of the Club, and in the following September was elected Captain by acclamation.

Up to the year 1835 the Club was without any distinct "local habitation." For some time after, it had modest accommodation in a small house at the foot of Golf Place known as the "Union Parlour," consisting of a reading-room, to which latterly a small billiard-room was attached. Shortly after the opening of the railway, the Club took a fresh start; the influx of Golfers speedily became so great that new arrangements were imperative, and the present Union Club House was built. Originally projected on an ample scale, it has since been extended and improved, and may now be held, in the matter of accommodation, to leave little to be desired. The prime mover in all such matters, whilst he lived, was Major (afterwards Sir Hugh) Playfair, an exceedingly striking and characteristic likeness of whom has appropriate place on the wall of the main room,—a specially fine, airy, and spacious apartment. Opposite, with equal appropriateness, has been hung a fine portrait of J. Whyte-Melville, Esq., of Bennochy and Strathkinness, who had through life identified himself with the interests of the Club. This picture is from the brush of the late Sir Francis Grant, President of the Royal Academy, and as a work of art is much admired. It was some years since subscribed for, in recognition of Mr. Melville's services to the Club, and as a token of the general esteem in which he was held by its Members.

Whilst he lived, the famous Allan Robertson, in some unofficial and unremunerated way, exercised a general supervision of the green; organised the meetings, adjusted the

The Royal and Ancient

handicaps, etc.; and was admittedly the fit arbiter in all matters of dispute. After his death in 1859 it speedily became obvious that a void existed which it would be necessary to fill; and a proposal was made to invite Tom Morris, then at Prestwick, to become keeper of the St. Andrews green, at a moderate salary. Though it met with considerable opposition, this proposal was approved by a majority of the Members, and was carried out. The wisdom of the arrangement has probably long since been admitted even by those who at the time could not see its necessity. Tom's services have proved invaluable; and it is hardly too much to say that we owe it to his careful and skilful management that the Links—with the immense amount of play upon them, from year to year on the increase—remain at this day in a playable condition. In particular, a good many of the putting greens had lapsed into a shameful state; but under Tom's steady and continuous doctoring, they have of late years wonderfully improved.

From the great amount of play upon it, the St. Andrews green is now necessarily year after year a good deal cut up, so that bad-lying balls are rather more frequent than of old. It is, however, on the whole much easier than it used to be, from the gradual disappearance of whin and bent, and the consequent great widening of the course. A reference to the Medal scores will of itself sufficiently establish this, every due allowance being made. It may be of interest to note that the crack score of last century was that of James Durham, Esq., of Largo, who won the Silver Club in 94 strokes, for the time an extraordinarily fine performance; and that the score of George Glennie, Esq., for the King William the Fourth Medal

Golf Club of St. Andrews

in 1855, in 88 strokes, remained unbeaten for 29 years, when Horace G. Hutchinson, Esq., broke the record for this Medal.

The ground gone over in a round of these Links used vaguely to be put at about five miles. No doubt it may be so to an erratic driver; but some years ago an accurate measurement was made, and the distance was ascertained as exactly 3 miles 1154 yards as the crow flies.

Of late years the ladies, as an improvement on such drivelling games as croquet and lawn-billiards, have taken vigorously to Golf; and the Ladies' Green at St. Andrews is now a very charming feature of the place. On occasion of playing for prizes, a very large field turns out; and when the day is reasonably propitious, the sun being gallant enough to light up for us the fancy costumes, a prettier and gayer sight is not readily to be found. The skill of the fair competitors is by no means to be despised; and on their own ground the best of them would be backed freely against the "Cracks" of the Royal and Ancient.

The Royal and Ancient

EXTRACTS FROM THE MINUTE BOOKS

> The Right Hon. Earl of Elgin and Kincardine.
> The Right Hon. James Earl of Wemyss.
> The Hon. Thomas Leslie.
> The Hon. James Leslie.
> The Hon. Francis Charteris.
> Sir James Wemyss, Baronet.
> Sir Robert Henderson, Baronet.
> Lieut.-General James St. Clair.
> David Scot of Scotstarvet.
> James Oswald of Dunnikier.
> Mr. David Young, Professor of Philosophy.
> James Lumsdain, Esq., Provost of St. Andrews.
> James Wemyss of Weemysshall.
> Walter Wemyss of Lathockar.
> John Bethune of Blebo.
> Henry Bethune of Clato.
> Thomas Spens the Younger of Lathallan.
> James Cheap of Sauchie.
> Arthur Martin of Milntoun.
> Maurice Trent of Pitcullo.
> Robert Douglas, Esq.
> Mr. John Young, Professor of Philosophy.

The Noblemen and Gentlemen above named being admirers of the antient and healthfull Exercise of the Golf, and at the sametime having the interest and prosperity of the Antient City of St. Andrews at heart, being the ALMA MATER of the GOLF, Did in the year of our Lord 1754 contribute for a SILVER CLUB, weighing   pounds   ounces, and having a St. Andrew engraved on the head thereof, to be played for on the Links of St. Andrews upon the 14th day of May said year, and yearly in time coming, subject to the Conditions and Regulations following, viz.—

> [Here follow the Conditions and Regulations, which are almost identical with those of the Honourable Company. See p. 41.]

Golf Club of St. Andrews

St. Andrews, 14th May 1754.

The Silver Club was this day played for, in terms of the Regulations, and gained by Bailie William Landale, merchant in St. Andrews.   JOHN SMART.

St. Andrews, 4th October 1764.

The Captain and Gentlemen Golfers present are of opinion that it would be for the improvement of the Links that the four first holes should be converted into two,[1]—They therefore have agreed that for the future they shall be played as two holes, in the same way as presently marked out.   WM. ST. CLAIR.

St. Andrews, 4th May 1766.

We, the Noblemen and Gentlemen subscribing, Did this day agree to meet once every fortnight, by Eleven of the Clock, at the Golf House, and to play a round of the Links; to dine together at Bailie Glass', and to pay each a Shilling for his dinner,—the absent as well as the present.

St. Andrews, 3rd September 1767.

This day the Silver Club was played for, and gained by James Durham of Largo, Esq., by holing the Links at 94 strokes.[2]
                                        WM. ST. CLAIR.

St. Andrews, 27th June 1771.

The Captain and Company agree and appoint that in time coming, the caddies who carry the clubs or run before the players, or are otherwise employed by the Gentlemen Golfers, are to get Fourpence sterling for going the length of the hole called the Hole of Cross, and if they go farther than that hole, they are to get Sixpence, and no more. Any of the gentlemen transgressing this rule are to pay two pint bottles of claret at the first meeting they shall attend.   HENRY BETHUNE.

---

[1] Previous to this the round consisted of 22 holes.

[2] Considering what must have been the state of the green more than a century ago, and that it was in the days of "feather and leather," this is a remarkably fine score.

The Royal and Ancient

St. Andrews, 2nd October 1771.

This day a Gold Medal,[1] value Seven Guineas, given by the Society of Golfers, was played for by the gentlemen mentioned in the Book of Record of the Monthly Meetings, and gained by Mr. Beveridge by holing the Links at 101 strokes.

HENRY BETHUNE.

St. Andrews, 28th May 1773.

It is agreed that no person should be allowed to play for the Silver Cup to be given this year except members of either this or the Leith Society. HENRY BETHUNE.

St. Andrews, 6th October 1773.

This day the Silver Cup (of Eight pounds value) was played for, and Mr. Arnot holed the Links at 105 strokes, but upon an objection made that he had transgressed the Rules by pulling back his ball, the Captain and Society appoint the Cup to be again played for on Friday next.

St. Andrews, 8th October 1773.

The Silver Cup[2] was this day played for and gained by Mr. Halket, by holing the Links at 114 strokes. PAT. RIGG.

St. Andrews, 4th September 1779.

It is enacted that whoever shall be Captain of the Golf, and does not attend all the meetings to be appointed throughout the year, shall pay Two Pints of Claret for each meeting he shall be absent at,—to be drunk at such meeting; but this regulation is not to take place if the Captain be not in Fife at the time.

WALTER BOSWELL.

St. Andrews, 4th August 1780.

The Society took into their consideration that their Golfing Jackets are in bad condition,—Have agreed that they shall have new ones—viz. Red with yellow buttons. The undermentioned

---

[1] This Medal was open to be played for, according to advertisement, by any Gentleman Golfer.

[2] This cup became the property of the winner.

Golf Club of St. Andrews

gentlemen have likewise agreed to have an Uniform Frock—viz. a Buff colour with a Red Cap. The Coat to be half lapelled, the Button white.
BALCARRES,
and Ten others.

St. Andrews, 22nd October 1783.

Lord Balcarres, Mr. Durham, Mr. Anstruther, Mr. Sandilands, Mr. Cheape, and Captain Cheape, having engaged to dine here this day, and having neither come, nor sent, this meeting has decerned them to pay One Scotch Pint of Claret each at the first meeting they shall be present, under pains and penalties.
WM. MORISON, *Captain.*

St. Andrews, 15*th September* 1786.

The Captain appoints the Silver Club to be played for on the 4th of October next. A Ball on Friday the 6th of October as usual.[1]
JOHN CHEAPE.

St. Andrews, 3rd August 1792.

It is proposed that a Fête Champêtre for the Ladies shall take place in the week of the October meeting. The Captain is instructed to give orders for the Room at Robertson's to be fitted up.
ALEX. DUNCAN, *Captain.*

St. Andrews, 3rd September 1796.

The Captain appoints the Silver Club to be played for on Wednesday the 5th day of October next. A Ball upon Friday as usual—the Secretary to obtain the Gows for the music if possible.
ALEX. ANDERSON.

St. Andrews, 3rd October 1806.

This day the Gold Medal was played for and gained by Walter Cook, Esq., Writer to the Signet, by holing the Links at 100 strokes.

St. Andrews, 7th September 1810.

The Meeting authorise the Secretary to employ a tradesman to repair the Golfers' Bridge at the Links, which is at present almost impassable, and to pay the expense thereof.

---

[1] First notice of a Ball.

The Royal and Ancient

St. Andrews, 2nd October 1816.

Which day John Whyte-Melville, Esq., of Bennochy, was admitted a member.

St. Andrews, 6th March 1818.

The Secretary stated to the Club that from the subscriptions obtained from the Members he had paid the Club's subscription of One hundred Guineas for the privilege of the Town Hall and Supper Rooms above the same.

Eo. Die.

The Club, taking into consideration that the Meetings have of late been thinly attended by the Members residing in town, in consequence of several Members giving parties on the ordinary days of meeting, and thereby preventing those who would otherwise give their presence at the Club from attending them,—Do Resolve that in future such Members as shall invite any of their friends, Members of this Club, to dinner on the days of meeting, shall forfeit to the Club a Magnum of Claret for himself, and one bottle for each Member so detained by them, for each offence, and the Captain and Council appoint this Resolution to be immediately communicated to General Campbell.

St. Andrews, 16th Sept. 1825.

Which day the present Captain, having imposed on himself a fine of a Magnum of Claret for failure in public duty, imposed a similar fine on the old Captains present.

RALPH A. ANSTRUTHER.

St. Andrews, 17th Oct. 1827.

The Captain proposed that as the funds of the Club were at present inadequate to payment of their debt, the salary or allowance of Two Guineas now payable annually to the Leith Clubmaker for attending at the General Meeting should be discontinued.   J. CHEAPE, *C.*

St. Andrews, 25th Sept. 1833.

Previous to Captain Halkett Craigie resigning the chair, Captain Melville rose and stated, that on 3rd Nov. 1820, a Bet having been made by the late Sir David Moncrieffe, Bart., and himself, by which it was stipulated that the survivor should purchase and present to the Club A NEW SILVER PUTTER, with

Golf Club of St. Andrews

the arms of the parties engraved on it; Captain Melville, in the most feeling and appropriate terms, expressed his deep regret that the Club had been deprived of one of its most zealous and distinguished supporters, and although he had great pleasure in fulfilling the duty that Bet imposed on him, he could not but regret the event which had led to it; he therefore begged to present to the Club a New Silver Putter, and to suggest that the Gold Medals should be attached to it, so that as the Silver Club handed down to posterity the names of those who presided over its meetings, the Putter might transmit, in a similar manner, the names of those who had signalised themselves by the superiority of their play.

St. Andrews, 26th Sept. 1834.

Which day the Gold Medal was played for over the Links of St. Andrews, and gained by Robert Oliphant, Esq., younger of Rossie, by holing the course at 97 strokes.

ROBERT ANSTRUTHER, C.

St. Andrews, 4th May 1836.

It having been the anxious wish of a very great number of Members of the Royal and Ancient Golf Club of St. Andrews to convey to Charles Grace, Esq., their Secretary, some particular mark of the high and grateful sense they entertain of the very kind and handsome manner in which he has for a period of twenty-four years gratuitously devoted his time and attention to the management of their affairs, and at the same time bearing in mind that his late respected father contributed his valuable services in a similar manner for thirty years,—The Club, at a meeting held here this day, unanimously Resolve, That, in testimony of the regard and esteem in which Charles Grace, Esq., is held by the Members, and as a mark of the heartfelt gratitude they entertain towards him for the zealous and conscientious manner in which he has gratuitously discharged the duties of Secretary for twenty-four years,—PLATE, amounting in value to a sum of not less than One hundred Guineas, be presented to him by the Club; and that a Subscription, limited to One Sovereign each, be immediately entered into.

St. Andrews, 4th May 1836.

Which day the Captain proposed His Grace the Duke of Buccleuch as a member; seconded by the Master of Gray.

The Royal and Ancient

Major Belshes then stated that as the Gold Medal was the only prize now given by the Club, and as there were numerous first-rate players who competed for it, he conceived that it would tend to increase the interest in that game among these competitors were an additional prize competed for yearly; and entertaining this opinion, he had great pleasure in now presenting to the Club a "Silver Cross of St. Andrew." The Club unanimously accepted of the very handsome gift, and begged to record their sense of the deep interest which the Major has on all occasions manifested for the prosperity of the Club.   J. MURRAY BELSHES, C.

St. Andrews, 3rd May 1837.

Which day Captain Belshes stated to the Club that he had the great pleasure of communicating to them a Letter which Major-General Sir Henry Wheatley had, by command of His Majesty, the Patron of the Club,[1] done him the honour of addressing to him as its Captain, and which accompanied a magnificent Gold Medal which His Majesty had most graciously directed to be presented as a gift from him to the Royal and Ancient Golf Club of St. Andrews:—

St. James' Palace, 6th Jan. 1837.

SIR—I have the honour to transmit, by the King's command, a Gold Medal, with Green Ribband, which His Majesty desires you will present in His name to "The Royal and Ancient Golf Club of St. Andrews," and which His Majesty wishes should be challenged and played for annually by that Society. The King orders me to add, that His Majesty has great satisfaction in availing himself of this opportunity to evince his approbation of that ancient Institution.—I have the honour to be, Sir, your most obedient servant,   H. WHEATLEY.

To Major Murray Belshes.

St. Andrews, 4th May 1837.

Which day the Club had the honour of entertaining at a Public Dinner Lieut.-Col. M. Belshes, their present Captain, in testimony of their high respect and esteem for him, and to mark their sense of the deep interest he has uniformly taken not only in the prosperity of the Club, but also in, first, obtaining for it His Majesty's permission to assume the high and distinguished

---

[1] His Majesty was graciously pleased to become Patron of the Club, and to approve of it being in future styled "The Royal and Ancient Golf Club of St. Andrews," in January 1834.

Golf Club of St. Andrews

title of "The Royal and Ancient Golf Club of St. Andrews"; but, secondly, in successfully using his influence to procure for it from His Gracious Majesty the King the splendid Royal Medal presented to the Club yesterday. Lieut.-Gen. Sir John Oswald of Dunnikier, G.C.B., presided, and discharged the duties of the Chair in the most able, dignified, and efficient manner.

St. Andrews, 20th June 1838.

Colonel M. Belshes presented to the Club a splendid Case for containing the Royal Medal, and having therein finely-burnished plates for engraving the names of the winners of that Medal. The Club accepted with great satisfaction this very handsome gift, and a vote of thanks for the same to Colonel Belshes was unanimously carried.

St. Andrews, 3rd Oct. 1838.

On the Chair being vacated by Colonel Belshes and taken by Captain Bruce, the Colonel rose and expressed the high satisfaction he felt in making known to the meeting that Her Majesty the Queen Dowager, Duchess of St. Andrews,[1] had been graciously pleased to present this Royal and Ancient Club with a handsome Medal, as a mark of her approbation, with a request that it should be worn by the Captain, as President, on all public occasions, and with which accordingly Colonel B. proceeded to invest the present Captain. To mark their high sense of the honour which had thus been conferred on the Club by the Queen Dowager, it was proposed by Colonel Belshes that the Medal should be called the "Royal Adelaide Medal," and be worn by the Captain of the Club at all their meetings.

J. MURRAY BELSHES.

St. Andrews, 15th June 1842.

The Captain stated to the meeting that, in consequence of the death of Mr. Henry Berwick, it had become necessary to elect a person to the office of Secretary, and he accordingly proposed that Mr. Stuart Grace be appointed Honorary Secretary to the Club, which motion was unanimously agreed to.

---

[1] Her Majesty had been graciously pleased to become Patroness of the Club in the previous March.

The Royal and Ancient

St. Andrews, 16th Oct. 1850.

The Club Gold Medal having to-day been gained by Mr. George Condie, who holds the Silver Cross, and as, in conformity with the Rules of the Club, the Silver Cross falls to be surrendered to the Club and competed for to-morrow, the meeting accordingly directed that the Cross should be played for to-morrow morning at half-past nine o'clock.　　J. O. FAIRLIE.

St. Andrews, 12th Oct. 1853.

Which day the Gold Medal of the Club was played for over the Links of St. Andrews, and gained by James Balfour, Esq., Edinburgh, by holing the course at 93 strokes.

EGLINTON AND WINTON.

St. Andrews, 21st Sept. 1855.

As David Anderson, the present keeper of the Golf course, has resigned his office, the meeting resolve to appoint Walter Alexander and Alexander Herd, caddies, in his place, at a salary of Six pounds betwixt them.

St. Andrews, 17th Oct. 1855.

Which day the Royal Medal, the gift of His late Majesty King William the Fourth, was played for over the Links of St. Andrews, and gained by GEORGE GLENNIE, Esq., by holing the course at **88** strokes.　　LOUGHBOROUGH.

St. Andrews, 22nd Oct. 1856.

The Club had under their consideration the proposal to erect a New Town Hall in St. Andrews, which is to contain a spacious Ball-room, with Supper-room and Dressing-rooms; and it was resolved to agree to contribute the sum of £50 from the funds of the Club towards aiding in the erection of the building,—on condition that the Club be secured by the Town Council of St. Andrews of the right to use the building for their Meetings and Balls, as fully in all respects as the Club are at present entitled to make use of the rooms in the present Town Hall.

St. Andrews, 2nd May 1860.

Mr. Whyte-Melville moved the following resolution, which was seconded by Sir Thomas Moncrieffe, and agreed to unanimously:—That this Club consider some acknowledgment to be due to the eminent services of the late Allan Robertson in improving the game of Golf and extending its practice through-

Golf Club of St. Andrews

out the kingdom, and are of opinion that for this purpose a moderate annuity should be purchased for his widow.

St. Andrews, 6th May 1863.

Which day the Silver Cross of St. Andrew was played for over the Links of St. Andrews, and gained by Gilbert Mitchell Innes, Esq., by holing the course at 97 strokes. Same day, the Bombay Silver Medal was played for, when Sir Thomas Moncrieffe, Bart., Thomas Hodge, Esq., St. Andrews, Andrew Nicoll, Esq., of Bonnytown, and Robert Clark, Esq., Edinburgh, came in equal, each having holed the course at 100 strokes; and the parties having played a second round, the said Medal was gained by Mr. Clark, he having gone the round in 92 strokes.

J. WHYTE-MELVILLE, *Actg. C.*

Copy of the REPLY to the ADDRESS to His Royal Highness the PRINCE of WALES on his Marriage.

Marlborough House, 25th June 1863.

Lieut.-General Knollys has had the honour of laying before the Prince of Wales the Address of the Captain and Members of the Royal Golf Club of St. Andrews on the occasion of his marriage, and praying His Royal Highness to be Patron of their Club; and General Knollys is directed to convey His Royal Highness' thanks for their congratulations, and to signify the pleasure it will give him to become their Patron.

To the Earl of Dalhousie, Captain.

The Chairman further stated that he had heard from Lord Dalhousie intimating that His Royal Highness the Prince of Wales had signified his intention of becoming Captain of the Club for the ensuing year. The Chairman therefore moved that His Royal Highness be elected a member of the Club by acclamation, which having been done, the Chairman nominated His Royal Highness as Captain for the ensuing year in the usual manner. J. WHYTE-MELVILLE, *C.*

St. Andrews, 30th Sept. 1863.

His Royal Highness the PRINCE OF WALES having this day gained the SILVER CLUB (being represented by John Whyte-Melville, Esq., of Strathkinness), Mr. Whyte-Melville, in the name and at the special request of His Royal Highness, took the Chair as Captain of the Club.

The Royal and Ancient

Same day the Royal Medal, the gift of His late Majesty King William the Fourth, was played for over the Links of St. Andrews, and gained by Lieut.-Col. William Heriot Maitland Dougall of Scotscraig, by holing the course at 95 strokes.
J. WHYTE-MELVILLE, *Actg. C.*

St. Andrews, 4th May 1864.

Major Boothby moved, That Tom Morris of Prestwick, formerly of St. Andrews, be brought here as a professional Golfer, at a salary of Fifty pounds a year, on the understanding that he shall have the entire charge of the Golf Course under the Green Committee.

St. Andrews, 28th Sept. 1870.

Which day the Royal Medal, the gift of His late Majesty King William the Fourth, and the Gold Medal of the Club, were played for over the Links of St. Andrews, when Gilbert Mitchell Innes, Esq., and Dr. D. Argyll Robertson came in equal, each having holed the course at 89 strokes; and they having played a second round, the Royal Medal was gained by Mr. Innes, he having holed the round at 86 strokes, and the Gold Medal was gained by Dr. Robertson. ROBERT HAY, *C.*

St. Andrews, 30th Sept. 1874.

Which day the Royal Medal, the gift of His late Majesty King William the Fourth, was played for over the Links of St. Andrews, and gained by Samuel Mure Fergusson, Esq., by holing the course at 91 strokes.

Same day the Gold Medal of the Club was played for over the Links of St. Andrews, and gained by Leslie Melville Balfour, Esq., by holing the course at 97 strokes. W. P. ADAM, *C.*

St. Andrews, 27th Sept. 1876.

His Royal Highness PRINCE LEOPOLD having this day gained the SILVER CLUB, he was duly installed as Captain of the Club and took the Chair accordingly.

St. Andrews, 26th Sept. 1877.

Which day the Silver Club given by the Royal and Ancient Golf Club of St. Andrews, and the Royal Adelaide Medal, were played for over the Links of St. Andrews, and gained by the Right Hon. John Inglis of Glencorse.

Golf Club of St. Andrews

The Late J. Whyte-Melville, Esq.

St. Andrews, 25th Sept. 1883.

At this the first meeting of the Royal and Ancient Golf Club since the death of John Whyte-Melville, Esq., Chairman of the Committee of Management, it was agreed unanimously to record in the Minutes an expression of regret at Mr. Melville's death, and of the deep sense entertained by all the Members of the Club of the services rendered by Mr. Melville during his long connection with it of upwards of sixty years, and particularly of the uniform urbanity and courtesy with which he had discharged the duties of Chairman of Committee of Management for a period of over thirty years.

St. Andrews, 24th Sept. 1884.

Which day the Silver Club given by the Royal and Ancient Golf Club of St. Andrews, and the Royal Adelaide Medal, were played for over the Links of St. Andrews, and gained by George Glennie, Esq.

St. Andrews, 3rd March 1886.

The Committee of the Royal and Ancient Golf Club of St. Andrews cannot allow their first business meeting after the lamented death of the Very Reverend Principal Tulloch to pass without placing on record their deep regret at the loss of their associate and colleague in the management of the Club, of which for about 30 years he has been an honoured Member—in which he took so much pleasure, and where he was wont to unbend from the cares and anxieties of his busy life, and where his dignified presence and genial manner endeared him to all who had the pleasure either of his friendship or acquaintance.

Retirement of Mr. Stuart Grace.

St. Andrews, 4th May 1886.

The following Minute, which had been prepared by the late Principal Tulloch and Major Bethune, as requested at the last General Meeting of the Club, was read and approved of, viz.—"The Royal and Ancient Golf Club cannot part with Mr. Stuart Grace, who has so long and with so much acceptance filled the office of Honorary Secretary to the Club, without recording their most cordial thanks to him for his long-continued and faithful services.

The Royal and Ancient

A comparatively small institution in 1842 when Mr. Grace entered upon his office, it has grown to its present large and prosperous position under his fostering management and that of the successive committees with which he has acted. Without any remuneration or formal acknowledgment of his services—which he has consistently refused—Mr. Grace has spared no pains to advance the interests of the Club, and to conduct its business—frequently involving a large expenditure of time and trouble—with courtesy and kindness to all. The Members of the Club desire to express their indebtedness for so many years of his gratuitous services and their best wishes for him now that he has retired from official connection with the Club."

St. Andrews, 4th May 1892.
Which day the Silver Cross of St. Andrew was played for over the Links of St. Andrews, and gained by Francis A. Fairlie, Esq., by holing the course at 86 strokes.
RALPH ANSTRUTHER, *C.*

St. Andrews, 28th September 1892.
Which day the Silver Club given by the Royal and Ancient Golf Club of St. Andrews, and the Royal Adelaide Medal, were played for over the Links of St. Andrews, and gained by Andrew Graham Murray, Esq., M.P.   RALPH ANSTRUTHER, *C.*

Same day the Royal Medal, the gift of His late Majesty King William the Fourth, was played for over the Links of St. Andrews, and gained by Edward B. H. Blackwell, Esq., by holing the course at 82 strokes.   A. GRAHAM MURRAY, *C.*

St. Andrews, 3rd May 1893.
Which day the Silver Cross of St. Andrew was played for over the Links of St. Andrews, and gained by Allan Fullarton Macfie, Esq., by holing the course at 82 strokes.
A. GRAHAM MURRAY, *C.*

Golf Club of St. Andrews

WINNERS OF THE GOLD MEDAL

Given by the Club, from 1806 to 1836

During which period this Medal was the only one competed for

		Strokes
1806	Walter Cook, Esq., W.S.	100
1807	Do.	101
1808	William Oliphant, Esq.	102
1809	Do.	103
1810	Dr. James Hunter, United College, St. Andrews	111
1811	Do. do.	116
1812	Robert Pattullo, Esq., of Balhouffie	109
1813	Do.	114
1814	Do.	118
1815	Dr. James Hunter, United College, St. Andrews	101
1816	David Moncrieffe, Esq., yr. of Moncrieffe	111
1817	Walter Cook, Esq., W.S.	113
1818	Captain H. L. Playfair	111
1819	Sir David Moncrieffe, Bart., of Moncrieffe	102
1820	Edward D'Oyley, Esq.	108
1821	Henry M. Low, Esq., W.S.	108
1822	Charles Shaw, Esq., Leith	109
1823	Henry M. Low, Esq., W.S.	120
1824	Do.	110
1825	Samuel Messieux, Esq.	105
1826	Robert Pattullo, Esq., junior	104
1827	Samuel Messieux, Esq.	111
1828	Robert Pattullo, Esq., junior	105
1829	Major Holcroft, R.A.	109
1830	Do.	111
1831	David Duncan, Esq., Rosemount	111
1832	John H. Wood, Esq., Leith	104
1833	Major Holcroft, R.A.	103
1834	Robert Oliphant, Esq., yr. of Rossie	97
1835	Do.	105
1836	Major William Wemyss	104

The Royal and Ancient

WINNERS OF THE GOLD MEDAL
Presented by His late Majesty King William the Fourth

		Strokes
1837	J. Stuart Oliphant, Esq.	104
1838	Captain J. Hope Grant	100
1839	J. H. Wood, Esq., Leith	99
1840	Major H. L. Playfair	105
1841	Sir David Baird, Bart.	100
1842	James Condie, Esq., Perth	103
1843	W. M. Goddard, Esq., Leith	103
1844	J. Hamilton Dundas, Esq.	111
1845	James Calvert, Esq., Montrose	100
1846	Do.	111
1847	N. J. Ferguson Blair, Esq.	105
1848	George Condie, Esq., Perth	104
1849	W. M. Goddard, Esq., Leith	105
1850	Sir David Baird, Bart.	100
1851	O'Brian B. Peter, Esq., Kirkland	105
1852	Robert Hay, Esq.	99
1853	John C. Stewart, Esq., 72nd Highlanders	90
1854	William Archibald Hamilton, Esq.	97
1855	**GEORGE GLENNIE, ESQ.**	**88**
1856	Captain W. H. Maitland Dougall	92
1857	James Ogilvie Fairlie, Esq., of Coodham	101
1858	Patrick Alexander, Esq.	96
1859	Thomas D. M'Whannell, Esq.	96
1860	William C. Thomson, Esq., Dundee	104
1861	Thomas D. M'Whannell, Esq.	98
1862	James Ogilvie Fairlie, Esq., of Coodham	99
1863	Captain W. H. Maitland Dougall	95
1864	Robert Clark, Esq., Edinburgh	94
1865	Lieut.-Colonel W. H. Maitland Dougall	92
1866	Thomas Hodge, Esq.	97
1867	Do.	96
1868	Charles Anderson, Esq., Fettykill, Leslie	95
1869	Thomas Hodge, Esq.	89
1870	Gilbert Mitchell Innes, Esq.	89
1871	Thomas Mackay, Esq.	91
1872	Sir Robert Hay, Bart.	94
1873	Henry A. Lamb, Esq.	92
1874	Samuel Mure Fergusson, Esq.	91

Golf Club of St. Andrews

		Strokes
1875	Leslie M. Balfour, Esq.	93
1876	Do.	91
1877	Do.	89
1878	Henry A. Lamb, Esq.	90
1879	Charles Anderson, Esq.	88
1880	Alexander Stuart, Esq.	89
1881	S. Mure Fergusson, Esq.	90
1882	Alexander Stuart, Esq.	88
1883	Leslie M. Balfour, Esq.	88
1884	Horace G. Hutchinson, Esq.	87
1885	John Ernest Laidlay, Esq.	87
1886	S. Mure Fergusson, Esq.	84
1887	John Ernest Laidlay, Esq.	83
1888	S. Mure Fergusson, Esq.	85
1889	Leslie M. Balfour, Esq.	87
1890	Horace G. Hutchinson, Esq.	85
1891	Alexander Stuart, Esq.	85
1892	E. B. H. Blackwell, Esq.	82
1893	S. Mure Fergusson, Esq.	79

The Royal and Ancient

WINNERS OF THE SILVER CROSS
Presented by Colonel J. Murray Belshes of Buttergask

		Strokes
1836	James Condie, Esq., Perth	110
1837	John H. Wood, Esq., Leith	100
1838	C. Robertson, Esq.	108
1839	Do.	104
1840	Samuel Messieux, Esq.	109
1841	Robert Haig, Esq.	104
1842	Do.	104
1843	Captain David Campbell	103
1844	Robert Haig, Esq.	111
1845	Captain A. O. Dalgleish	99
1846	Robert Lindsay, Esq.	110
1847	Captain David Campbell	104
1848	Robert Hay, Esq.	101
1849	J. O. Fairlie, Esq., of Coodham	100
1850	George Condie, Esq., Perth	96
1851	George Glennie, Esq.	99
1852	Captain W. H. Maitland Dougall, Scotscraig	96
1853	Henry Jelf Sharpe, Esq.	96
1854	J. O. Fairlie, Esq., of Coodham	95
1855	Captain W. H. Maitland Dougall	98
1856	William Playfair, Esq.	102
1857	W. C. Thomson, Esq., Dundee	96
1858	Sir Thomas Moncrieffe of Moncrieffe, Bart.	95
1859	James C. Lindsay, Esq., Broughty Ferry	101
1860	James Ogilvie Fairlie, Esq., of Coodham	99
1861	Thomas Hodge, Esq.	92
1862	Henry Mackechnie, Esq.	94
1863	Gilbert Mitchell Innes, Esq.	97
1864	William C. Thomson, Esq., Dundee	95
1865	Gilbert Mitchell Innes, Esq.	98
1866	William C. Thomson, Esq., Dundee	92
1867	Robert Clark, Esq., Edinburgh	92
1868	Major Robert T. Boothby	92
1869	Robert Clark, Esq., Edinburgh	92
1870	Do.	92
1871	Henry A. Lamb, Esq.	93
1872	Ross W. Ochterlony, Esq.	98
1873	Henry A. Lamb, Esq.	99

Golf Club of St. Andrews

		Strokes
1874	W. J. Mure, Esq., Edinburgh.	90
1875	Captain Alexander Dingwall Fordyce	92
1876	Major Robert T. Boothby	92
1877	William J. Mure, Esq.	97
1878	A. Frank Simson, Esq.	89
1879	William J. Mure, Esq.	86
1880	Charles Anderson, Esq.	87
1881	Elliot S. Balfour, Esq.	88
1882	Alexander Stuart, Esq.	88
1883	Do.	83
1884	William S. Wilson, Esq.	91
1885	S. Mure Fergusson, Esq.	89
1886	Bruce E. Goff, Esq.	90
1887	Horace G. Hutchinson, Esq.	84
1888	Do.	87
1889	Allan Fullarton Macfie, Esq.	90
1890	Leslie M. Balfour, Esq.	83
1891	H. S. C. Everard, Esq.	88
1892	F. A. Fairlie, Esq.	86
1893	Allan Fullarton Macfie, Esq.	82

THE MUSSELBURGH GOLF CLUB was instituted in 1774. The Minutes for the first ten years of its existence are unfortunately amissing, but the Medals attached to the quaint old Cup, and which severally bear the name of the winner for the year, satisfactorily carry back its existence as a Club to that year. This now venerable Cup was presented to the Club by Thomas M'Millan, Esq., of Shorthope, in 1774, who gained it that year and became Captain of the Club. The Rev. Dr. Carlyle of Inveresk was the victor of 1775. With one or two interregnums, the Cup has been regularly played for at the autumn meeting. A new Club House at the west end of the Links was opened to the Members in April 1873; and in it the Centenary Festival was held—Sir Archibald Hope, Bart., President, in the Chair.

The Musselburgh Golf Club

EXTRACTS FROM THE MINUTE BOOKS

Mrs. Sheriff's, Dec. 10, 1784.

The Company of Golfers met this day, according to adjournment, when they proceeded, agreeably to fifth rule, to a re-election of Members for the ensuing year, when the following were re-elected, viz.—

Rev. Dr. CARLYLE, Bailie COCHRAN, *and* 23 *others*.

The meeting chose Mr. Davidson as Secretary for the ensuing year, and then fined Mr. Gillies in Three shillings for having forbidden Mrs. Sheriff to prepare a dinner for the Club upon Friday, 8th Oct. last.

Mr. Ward's, April 8, 1785.

The Company of Golfers met here this day, when the SILVER CUP was played for, and won by Bailie George Young.

Sheriff's, Dec. 9, 1785.

In order to remedy the inconvenience that has been found in collecting the eightpences for the dinners of absent members, according to Rule 8, the Company do this day unanimously resolve that each member shall pay into the Treasurer's hand Six shillings sterling to pay for the dinners of the Nine meetings of the ensuing year; that the Treasurer always pay the dinner to the house, and collect the money from the several members. The overplus to remain in Treasurer's hands, and to be disposed of by order of the Company.

Paid for thirteen dinners of this day, 8s. 8d., and to Officer for to-day, and for collecting the Six shillings from the Members, 3s.—In all, 11s. 8d.

Ward's, Jan. 13, 1786.

This day the Company of Golfers met according to adjournment. Captain Young took the Chair.

They then took under consideration Dr. Carlyle's card intimating his desire to demit, and also Mr. George Baillie's to same purport, and accepted of both their demissions.

The Musselburgh Golf Club

Sheriff's, April 21, 1786.

The Silver Cup was this day played for, and won by the Rev. Mr. Smith.

Order Seven shillings and sixpence to be given to Mr. Murray for balls to his scholars.

Captain Fairfax was fined One shilling for playing upon the Links and not dining.

Paid house for 17 dinners 11s. 4d.

Thom's, Jan. 11, 1788.

The Preses must call for a bill before it shall exceed Two shillings and sixpence each, else he shall be liable to pay the overplus.

The Preses shall allow only Port Wine and Sherry, Rum, Brandy, Gin, and Small Beer, and these in any manner any member shall think fit, to be put into the bill. What is drunk before dinner must be paid by those who call for it.

Two shillings per bottle is to be paid in future for the wine. Neither more nor less than Sixpence each hole shall be played for on a Club day.

Kedzlie's, Feb. 11, 1791.

The Club met according to adjournment, Captain Smart in the chair.

The Club, taking Mr. Macmillan's card of resignation into consideration, resolve that, *since he has put himself to death*, they don't chuse to try their hands for his resurrection.

Musselburgh, Jan. 11, 1793.

The Club met according to adjournment. The meeting was so merry that it was agreed that matching and every other business should be delayed till next month.

Musselburgh, 11*th May* 1798.

This day the Club met at Moir's, Lieut.-Col. Stuart in the chair. The question was put whether the funds should be disposed of by the members present or delayed till December meeting, when it was resolved by a majority that the company *present* should determine it. And it being put to the vote whether the funds should be drunk or part of them taken to give their Myte to the Voluntary Subscription in aid of the Government,

The Musselburgh Golf Club

—It was carried unanimously that Five Guineas of the funds should be presented to the Voluntary Subscription in name of the Club, and that the remainder of the funds should be disposed of at the December meeting.

Moir's, Dec. 12, 1800.

This day the Club met, when Governor Bruce was unanimously admitted.

Resolved, That as the price of provisions is very high, Mr. Moir should be allowed 1s. 6d. each for dinner.

Moir's, 26th June 1807.

The members of the Club met this day at Moir's, and thereafter went to the Links, when the Cup was played for by Sir John Hope, Bart., of Craighall, and Colonel Charles Stuart, and won by Sir John.

Musselburgh, 26th July 1808.

Sir James Baird, Bart., was proposed as a member, and admitted with the greatest approbation.

The Secretary was authorised to give the boys at Mr. Taylor's two dozen of golf-balls, and to those at Mr. Grierson's school one dozen. JOHN HOPE, *C.*

Moir's, 16th February 1810.

Resolve, That an annual subscription of One Guinea be paid by each member, from which fund the expense of the dinners is to be in future defrayed, but all the expenses of liquors to be defrayed by the company present. And any overplus at the end of each season to be sunk in a General *Gaudeamus*.

JOHN HOPE, *Preses.*

Musselburgh, 14th Dec. 1810.

The Club resolve to present by subscription a new Creel and Shawl to the best female golfer who plays on the annual occasion on 1st Jan. next, old style (12th Jan. new), to be intimated to the Fish Ladies by the Officer of the Club.

Two of the best Barcelona silk handkerchiefs to be added to the above premium of the Creel. ALEX. G. HUNTER, *C.*

The Musselburgh Golf Club

Musselburgh, 4th June 1819.
This being the King's Birthday, the members present did everything loyal in honour of the day by drinking the health of the Royal Family with every demonstration of loyalty.

J. STIRLING, *C.*

Musselburgh, 31st Oct. 1828.
Captain Hope challenges Mr. Sanderson for a match to be played on Saturday, 1st Nov., at 2 o'clock,—the Captain to shoot with a bow and arrow, and Mr. Sanderson to use a Club and ball, he being allowed to tee the ball at every stroke.[1]

Mr. Jameson and Mr. Sanderson presented, for the acceptance of the Club, a Snuff-box made from a shell picked up by Mr. Jameson on the coast of Africa, and which Mr. Sanderson got mounted in silver and suitably inscribed. The President returned the best thanks of the Club for this handsome donation.

JOHN HOPE, *C.*

Musselburgh, 8th Oct. 1830.
The Captain of the Club reported that some members of the Bruntsfield Links Golfing Society had proposed to match themselves against a certain number of the Members of this Club upon Musselburgh Links. Friday, the 15th current, was fixed for the match, and the Secretary was instructed to write to the Society that six members of this Club would be ready to meet an equal number from that Society on the above day.

Musselburgh, 5th Nov. 1830.
It was reported that on the day fixed the Bruntsfield Links Society had won the match by three holes, but that the same match had been played again this day, when the Musselburgh Club won by one hole.

Musselburgh, 14th Sept. 1833.
Mr. Robert Chambers, author of the *Traditions of Edinburgh*, etc., being present at the meeting, was, on the motion of Mr. Moir, seconded by Mr. Wells, unanimously admitted an Honorary Member.

---

[1] Captain Hope gained this match "with great ease."

The Musselburgh Golf Club

Musselburgh, 23rd Sept. 1834.

It is resolved that the boys employed as caddies shall be paid, For one round, Threepence; and for two or more Twopence each round. An engagement for the day not to exceed One shilling. Golfers from other places will see the propriety of giving effect to this resolution.

Musselburgh, 12th Oct. 1838.

The meeting agree to allow W. Doleman £3 for taking charge of the boxes of members, and Tom Alexander £2 for taking charge of the holes and green.

Musselburgh, 25th July 1857.

Mr. J. Cundell proposed that Mr. W. Marjoribanks and Mr. Robert Chambers jr. should represent the Club at the National Golf Tournament at St. Andrews, which was carried unanimously.

Their score was 92 for the eighteen holes.

Musselburgh, 2nd April 1870.

Sir Archibald Hope, Bart., who was President of the Club in 1857, and was present at the meeting to-day, was unanimously re-elected President of the Club.

OPENING OF NEW CLUB HOUSE

Club House, 16th Oct. 1873.

The Members and their Friends, to the number of forty-four, dined in the Club House, under the presidency of Mr. A. D. M. BLACK, *Captain.*

Club House, 9th July 1874.

The Secretary read a letter received from Mr. Inches, in which he expressed the desire to present, through the Council, a GOLD MEDAL. The meeting desired the Secretary to accept Mr. Inches' proposal, and to convey their best thanks for his handsome offer. A. D. M. BLACK, *C.*

Club House, 16th July 1874.

Mr. Thomson moved, — "That the present year being the Centenary of the Club, a GOLD MEDAL should be subscribed for

The Musselburgh Golf Club

amongst the Members, to be played for in October, and the winner of the Medal to retain same."

Club House, 15*th Oct.* 1874.
The Members with their Friends dined together in the Club House. The Chair was taken by Sir Archibald Hope, and Mr. A. D. M. Black acted as Croupier.

Club House, 21*st Oct.* 1875.
This day the SILVER CUP was won by Mr. Marcus J. Brown in 84 strokes. JAMES MELLIS, *C.*

Club House, 5*th Sep.* 1876.
The Secretary read a letter received from Major Pickard giving HIS ROYAL HIGHNESS THE DUKE OF CONNAUGHT'S consent to become Honorary President of the Club.
JAMES MELLIS, *C.*

Club House, 19*th Dec.* 1876.
The Secretary read a letter from Sir Howard Elphinstone intimating that H.R.H. the DUKE OF CONNAUGHT, President of the Club, had no objections to the title of "ROYAL" being appended to the name of the Club.

Club House, 16*th Oct.* 1884.
This day the SILVER CUP was won by Mr. Marcus J. Brown in 79 strokes. DAVID WHITELAW, *C.*

Club House, 9*th Oct.* 1890.
This day the SILVER CUP was won by Mr. A. W. Millar in 87 strokes. Thirty-nine Members and Friends afterwards dined in the Club House. THOS. CARMICHAEL, *C.*

THE names of the Founders of the BRUNTSFIELD LINKS GOLF CLUB have not been handed down to us, and there is reason to fear that they are irrecoverably lost: nor is there any positive evidence when the Club was established. No records of its earlier years can be found. The first Minute-Book in the possession of the Club dates from 1787, in which year the Club underwent conversion from a Society into a Club, whatever that may mean. In a Minute, dated 1790, it is stated that the Club had then existed for thirty years, which points to the year 1760 as the date of its foundation. The Centenary of the Club was celebrated in 1861 in the Freemasons' Hall, Edinburgh, the Lord Provost, Francis Brown Douglas, Esq., and several leading citizens being present.

The Club House is at Musselburgh. The Membership has gradually been increased from time to time, there being

Bruntsfield Links Golf Club

now considerably over 100 Members. Two stated half-yearly competitions for prizes are held at Musselburgh, after each of which the Members dine in the Club-room. There is also a special competition in the spring of each year at North Berwick or Gullane, for prizes presented by the Members. Besides these gatherings, there are several other competitions during the season for Club and other prizes.

EXTRACTS FROM THE MINUTE BOOKS

Bruntsfield Links, 10*th June* 1787.
MINUTE OF SEDERUNT in Thos. Comb's.
Present—Messrs. Alexander Brown, and Nine others.

This Society having been formerly, by general consent, instituted into a Club for the healthful exercise of Golf, of this date agreed to continue the same monthly, on a Saturday which shall be judged most convenient for the Members, and to assume six additional gentlemen, each of whom to be proposed by a present Member, and to lye on the table till the following monthly meeting before admission.   ALEX. THOMSON, *Preses*.

Bruntsfield Links, Thos. Comb's, 31*st May* 1788.

The meeting of the Society being very full, it was agreed that the last Saturday of June be appointed as the anniversary day of the Club.

Every Preses is hereby directed to call the dinner bill in due time; for when any dinner bill shall exceed the quota of Two shillings to each Member, the Preses for the day shall be liable for the overplus, except on the quarter days, when a little more latitude is allowable.

Bruntsfield Links, 29*th Nov.* 1788.

At this Meeting Mr. Brown presented the Arms of the Society blazoned thus :—Vert two Golf Clubs in Saltyr, their Heads in chief proper between four Golf Balls Argent. Motto in an escroll above the shield, *Inde Salus.*

Bruntsfield Links Golf Club

Bruntsfield Links, 30th July 1790.

As this Golfing Society had subsisted above thirty years, a proposal had been some time ago made for having an Uniform. Mr. A. Brown produced a design, viz. two clubs crossed with four balls, with the opposite motto below—*Inde Salus*. This was considered and approved by the Meeting.

Bruntsfield Links, 30th June 1792.

Mr. Longlands produced a subscription for making a road on the west side of the Wrights Houses, for the purpose of preserving the Links entire. The whole Members paid in a subscription of 10s. 6d. each, which Mr. Longlands had advanced to the Lord Provost and Magistrates of Edinburgh, and the Society voted their thanks to the said Lord Provost and Magistrates, and also to Mr. Longlands, for their great attention in this business.

Bruntsfield Links, 27th April 1793.

It was proposed, for the good regulation of the Society, that a Captain should be chosen annually, and Mr. Hepburn was proposed and elected Captain without a dissenting voice. It was also proposed that the Captain should have a caddie to attend him, clothed at the expense of the Society.

Bruntsfield Links, 29th August 1801.

There being fourteen Members present, Mr. Maugham, agreeably to last minute, was admitted. No other business. The meeting as usual cracked their jocks over a glass, and enjoyed the evening harmoniously with a song.   JAMES TOD, *C.*

Bruntsfield Links, 31st Oct. 1801.

It was recommended to the Treasurer to purchase a dozen caps and aprons, or to get Mrs. Henderson to buy the same, the expense to be paid out of the admission fund.   JAMES TOD.

Bruntsfield Links, 27th March 1802.

The Preses requested that a new pack of cards be procured for the use of the Club.   JAMES TOD.

Bruntsfield Links Golf Club

Bruntsfield Links, 30th Oct. 1802.

Captain Tod intimated to the Preses and company that the Gentlemen Burgess Club of Golfers had a wish that their Club and ours should have a friendly meeting once or twice a year, which was cordially agreed to.   ALEX. THOMSON, *C.*

Bruntsfield Links, 21st May 1803.

The two Clubs met and dined—Captain Bruce in the chair; Provost M'Vicar on his right, and Captain Scott of the Burgess Society on his left. The company consisted of thirty-eight, sixteen of which belonged to the Bruntsfield Links Club. The evening spent with great harmony, and some fine songs.

ADAM BRUCE.

Bruntsfield Links, 27th July 1805.

Captain Walker renewed the motion he made 29th June last, that no more wine be used in the Club room; it was agreed unanimously that the Captain (for the time being) had it in his power to call for wine, but no other Member to do so.

JAMES WALKER.

Bruntsfield Links, 29th Oct. 1814.

The Captain and Secretary having received a special invitation to dine with the Burgess Golfing Society at their last quarterly meeting, they accepted of it, and were received with very marked attention by Captain Scott and the other Members of that Club. It was therefore judged proper, in order to show the sense this Club entertained of the reception of their two Members, to invite Captain Scott and Treasurer Reid of the Burgess Club to dine with them, who accordingly this day honoured the meeting with their company. It was stated from the chair that nothing would be so gratifying as to keep up that cordiality and good understanding which subsisted betwixt the two Clubs.

ROBT. STODART.

Bruntsfield Links, 24th June 1815.

No particular business occurred at this meeting, but as the news had that morning arrived of the entry of the Allies into Paris, it put the whole Members into such spirits that the glass

Bruntsfield Links Golf Club

circulated pretty freely, and the usual hour of departure was protracted to the detriment of the stock. Bill, £4 : 8 : 6 ; whereof from stock, £2 : 0 : 6.   ROBT. STODART.

Bruntsfield Links, 28th Oct. 1815.

It was resolved that in future the Captain should have a person in some sort of uniform to carry his clubs as officer to the Society, and it was recommended to the Captain to select one at his conveniency.   ROBT. STODART.

Bruntsfield Links, 31st Jan. 1818.

Mr. Gray informed the meeting that he had received a letter from Mr. M'Candlish enclosing a biographical sketch of the late John Graham, historical painter in Edinburgh, taken from *Blackwood's Magazine* of December last, and requested the same might be preserved in the Society's box.

CAMP. GARDNER.

Bruntsfield Links, 25th April 1818.

The following Report was read and approved of :—

REPORT OF THE COMMITTEE OF THE BURGESS AND
BRUNTSFIELD LINKS GOLFING SOCIETIES.

It being the unanimous wish of the Members of the above Societies to have a joint meeting annually, for the better establishing the game of Golf, and for cementing more firmly that friendship which ought ever to subsist among Golfers,—It has been resolved that the first Annual Meeting shall take place on the fourth day of June next, when it is proposed the new ground shall be opened, and such regulations adopted as will best tend to promote that healthful exercise.

It is proposed that in the arrangements for dinner the most strict economy should be observed, and little if any wine introduced. The dinner hour to be exactly at 4, and the bill to be called precisely at 8.

Captain Duncan is to take the Chair at this meeting, he being Captain of the senior Club, and Captain Gardner to act as Croupier.

The two Clubs shall meet at one o'clock, and the two Captains shall make the matches.   CAMP. GARDNER, *C.*

Bruntsfield Links, 4th June 1818.

The new ground at the south end of the Links was opened this day for the first time, and the hole played for by Captain

Bruntsfield Links Golf Club

Gardner and Mr. Graham of our Society against Captain Duncan and Mr. Edington of the Burgess Club, when it was gained by the former, and at the suggestion of Captain Gardner was to be from that time called the " Union " hole.

The Members of both Societies dined together—thirty-eight in number—Captain Duncan in the chair.

CAMP. GARDNER, *C.*

Bruntsfield Links, 30th Jan. 1819.

The appointment of an officer to the Society having again been brought forward, agreeably to the minute of 31st October last,—after some consideration Peter M'Ewan, clubmaker, was considered as a very fit person to fill that office, when a committee was appointed to see him provided with a proper coat and uniform suitable to the Society, and to which there would be attached the very handsome present of a badge voluntarily offered by Bailie Tullis. NATH. GRANT, *C.*

Bruntsfield Links, 27th March 1819.

The Gold Medal of the Club was this day played for, and won by Mr. James Smith in 68 strokes for the two rounds.

NATH. GRANT, *C.*

Bruntsfield Links, 29th Jan. 1820.

Captain Gray having presented the Club with a handsome silver-mounted snuff-horn, it was proposed by Mr. Struthers, and unanimously agreed to, that Mr. Gray's name should be inscribed on the same as having been presented by him.

JOHN GRAY, *C.*

Bruntsfield Links, 29th July 1820.

Mr. Douglas proposed that the Prize Balls in future should be " Gourlay " balls instead of those given at present.

JOHN GRAY, *C.*

Bruntsfield Links, 27th April 1822.

Captain Kilgour informed the meeting that Mr. Williamson had sent a small cask of spirits of his own manufacture as a present to the Club. The Secretary was ordered to transmit the

Bruntsfield Links Golf Club

thanks of the Society to Mr. Williamson, and to inform him that he was unanimously elected an Honorary Member.

The Gold Medal was then played for and gained by Mr. Edward Henderson in 62 strokes. JA. KILGOUR, C.

Bruntsfield Links, 27th March 1824.

Peter M'Ewan, the officer to the Club, intimated his wish that the Society would accept of his son Douglas to carry the Captain's clubs on the Saturdays, and that he would attend the dinners as usual, it being very inconvenient for him to be absent from his business between the hours of one and three.

Bruntsfield Links, 24th April 1830.

The Society dined in the University Tavern. The evening was spent in the most convivial manner, and the hilarity of the company was increased by some excellent Champagne [1] presented to them by Mr. Brown. SAM. AITKEN.

Bruntsfield Links, 29th March 1834.

The Secretary was then directed to record the match betwixt the Musselburgh Club and this Club, which came off on Musselburgh Green on the first of last month, showing that the Musselburgh Club was beaten on the day's play by five holes. The match was for one dozen of wine—ten players on each side.
GEORGE BROWN, C.

Bruntsfield Links, 28th Sep. 1839.

Captain Cairns stated that as the period of his Captaincy was drawing to an end, he intended presenting the Club with a Medal before resigning office, to be played for on Musselburgh Links.

The Medal was won by Mr. Aitken in 90 strokes.

During the evening the Secretary sang the following impromptu :—

>   Come, all you Golfers stout and strong,
>   Who putt so sure and drive so long,
>   And I will sing you a good song,
>   About old Captain Aitken.

---

[1] First notice of Champagne.

Bruntsfield Links Golf Club

> There is no Golfer in our view
> Who drives so far, and putts so true,
> With left hand down, his Club does wield,
> 'Tis ten to one against the field,
> And soon he'll be our Dean of Guild.
>   The glorious Captain Aitken.

Bruntsfield Links, 29th Jan. 1842.

A very large party dined at Cork's, and the evening was spent with more than stereotyped happiness, harmony, and hilarity. A number of matches were made. Mr. S. Aitken (not of course when "madness ruled the hour") pledged himself if, and when, Deacon Scott married, to present to the Club half a dozen of wine, and the like quantity to the object (lovely of course) of his choice! This happy meeting, though "through many a bout of linked sweetness long drawn out," partook of the transitory nature of all earthly things, and as one of our poets says—broke up!

                                      JAS. MITCHELL, C.

Bruntsfield Links, 17th Dec. 1842.

Matches were then arranged (handicap [1]) to compete for the Prize Clubs presented by Mr. Stewart, and after a keen and spirited contest Captain Mitchell was found to be the gainer, having holed the two rounds in 57 strokes.

A large party afterwards dined at Goodsman's, and spent a very happy evening, not the less so that some Member, to the company unknown, made the handsome present of half-a-dozen of Champagne. Mr. Brown, after some very apposite remarks, read an interesting paragraph from the *Bombay Times* of the 19th October last, noticing certain proceedings of a Golf Club formed in the East Indies, which gave rise to much felicitous discussion, and the appointment of a deputation, consisting of the Captain and Mr. Paterson, to meet and compete with the like, or any number, of the Indian Club,—the deputation to travel at the Club's expense and by the new Aerial Transit, which is expected to start early in February next.

In the course of the evening the Secretary, Mr. Donaldson, intimated that he intended presenting the Club with a Silver Quaigh to be competed for annually by handicap.

---

[1] First notice of a Handicap prize.

Bruntsfield Links Golf Club

The meeting, which had been kept up with great spirit, then separated. J. D., *Sec.*

Musselburgh, 18th Oct. 1845.

The object of the Meeting being to compete for the Cairns Medal, the Members proceeded to the Green, and though the wind blew a perfect hurricane, accompanied by showers, the competition was animated. It terminated in the success of the Secretary, Mr. Cameron.

The Club dined in the Musselburgh Arms Inn, and spent a very happy evening; but the meeting having been prolonged beyond the period at which the omnibus (in which seats had been taken) started, the Members found it necessary to walk the greater part of the way to town! W. H. C., *Sec.*

Bruntsfield Links, 22nd Jan. 1852.

MEETING OF COUNCIL.

Before proceeding to the business of the meeting, the Captain retired, and communicated with Mrs. Gilchrist and Mary as to their intention in regard to the occupation of the house; and after a lengthened and confidential interview, he found that they were not disposed to remain unless at a reduced rent. The meeting were of opinion, in the interest of the Club, that they should remain—particularly Mary—so that the comfort and pleasure of the Members might, as hitherto, be secured. The meeting

Bruntsfield Links Golf Club

agreed, on the part of the Club, to pay £9 : 14s. of yearly rent —Mrs. Gilchrist paying the remaining £5 ; and finding this arrangement satisfactory to Mrs. Gilchrist and Mary, the meeting spontaneously joined in a song—" Mary the Maid of the Inn for me." J. M., *Sec.*

Bruntsfield Links, 24th July 1852.

On the motion of Mr. Miller, it was agreed that on 25th September there should be second, third, and fourth prizes, to consist of six, four, and two Gutta Percha[1] balls respectively.

J. R., *Sec.*

Bruntsfield Links, 29th Jan. 1853.

Captain Cameron, as intimated at last meeting, then moved " That the Annual Subscription be raised to One pound," which was carried unanimously.

Matches were then arranged for Prize Balls.

The Members thereafter dined in the Club-room, and spent a most harmonious evening, the conviviality being increased by a presentation of Champagne by Mr. Greenhill on the occasion of a very interesting " Match " which he had just made.

J. B. S., *Sec.*

JOINT COUNCIL MEETING of the BRUNTSFIELD LINKS GOLF CLUB and the EDINBURGH BURGESS GOLFING SOCIETY

Bruntsfield Links, 9th February 1854.

The Meeting having been called to take steps for procuring the Joint Medal to be competed for annually by the two Societies, and to make the necessary arrangements for the first Competition, after some discussion the following design was unanimously approved of :—A circular pedestal of ebony with three Golf Clubs rising from it in triangle, which support a Silver Golf Ball as a Snuff-Box. A Silver Medal to be inserted in the base, with the following inscription :—

---

[1] First notice of Gutta Percha balls ; "Gourlays" had been given previously.

Bruntsfield Links Golf Club

FOR ANNUAL COMPETITION
BETWEEN
The Edinburgh Burgess Golfing Society
AND
The Bruntsfield Links Golf Club

1854

The first competition took place on Saturday, 11th March— 10 players a side; when it was found that the total score of the "Burgess" was 675 and the "Bruntsfield" 688—the Burgess Golfing Society thus winning the Joint Medal for the first time by 13 strokes.[1]

Bruntsfield Links, 19th May 1854.

Treasurer Stewart, in name of the Club, presented "Mary" with the sum of £3, which had been raised for her by subscription among the Members,—Mary replying in a neat and appropriate speech. Dr. Mackay then sung with his usual taste, "*Thou art gane awa' frae me, Mary.*"[2] A. B. TAWSE, *Sec.*

Bruntsfield Links, 29th March 1856.

The Members then proceeded to play for the Gold Medal, which was gained by Mr. John Dun in 53 strokes, being the fewest number the Medal had ever been gained in,—Mr. Sibbald being second with 55 strokes. J. R., *Sec.*

Bruntsfield Links, 28th March 1857.

The Members then proceeded to play for the Gold Medal, when Messrs. Clark and Dun having holed the two rounds in 55 strokes each, they played another round, and Mr. Clark having holed the third round in 26 and Mr. Dun in 28 strokes, Mr. Clark was declared the winner. ALEX. JAMES, *Sec.*

Bruntsfield Links, 9th Oct. 1858.

It was suggested by Captain Greenhill that it would be very desirable that the Club should have a special meeting to rejoice

---

[1] The second competition took place on 10th March 1855, when the "Bruntsfield" beat their opponents by 14 strokes.

[2] "Mary" was going to Australia.

Bruntsfield Links Golf Club

with our Member, Mr. Robert Chambers, as the Champion Golfer of Great Britain; and it was unanimously carried that Mr. Chambers should be invited to a dinner for that purpose, and that the Council be entrusted with the arrangements.

W. COTTON, *Sec.*

Musselburgh, 26th May 1860.

The members present played for the Cairns Medal, which was found to have been gained by Mr. Greenhill, who holed the two rounds in 87 strokes.   A. M'KINLAY, *Sec.*

Edinburgh, 28th March 1861.

This day being the Centenary of the Club, the Members celebrated the occasion by dining together with their friends in the Masonic Hall, George Street. Invitations were issued to the Lord Provost, Sheriff Gordon, Dr. Sanderson, Musselburgh, etc. Ninety-eight sat down to dinner.

The chair was ably filled by Josiah Livingston, Esq., Captain of the Club, supported on the right by Francis Brown

Bruntsfield Links Golf Club

Douglas, Esq., Lord Provost of Edinburgh. The duties of croupier were discharged by Messrs. Cameron and Greenhill.

The "Glee Union," whose services were engaged for the occasion, proved a great acquisition, and the whole proceedings were a complete success.

In replying to the toast of the evening, which was proposed by the Lord Provost, the Chairman gave a sketch of the rise and progress of the Club. THOS. USHER, *Sec.*

Musselburgh, 7th June 1870.

The Cairns Medal was competed for here this afternoon, and gained by Mr. David Croall in 90 strokes.

ALEX. WHYTE, *Sec.*

Musselburgh, 5th May 1874.

The first competition for the Ladies' Prize and the Russell Challenge Cup came off to-day at Musselburgh. Forty players started. Dr. W. Bryce proved himself the winner by doing the two rounds of the green (18 holes) in the score of 79 after deducting his handicap of 7. THOS. USHER, *C.*

Musselburgh, 18th May 1875.

The Annual Competition with the BURGESS came off to-day, BRUNTSFIELD winning by 29 holes. THOS. USHER, *C.*

Musselburgh, 1st May 1877.

After two rounds of the green, it was found that the GOLD MEDAL had been won by Mr. Andrew Usher with the very excellent score of 84. JOSIAH LIVINGSTON, *C.*

Musselburgh, 7th May 1878.

The GOLD MEDAL was won by Mr. A. S. Douglas with a score of 85. J. CLAPPERTON, *C.*

Musselburgh, 3rd July 1879.

The Competition between the BRUNTSFIELD and BURGESS Clubs took place to-day, and resulted in a victory for the BURGESS by 43 holes. CHAS. N. COWPER, *C.*

Bruntsfield Links Golf Club

NEW CLUB HOUSE

Musselburgh, 27th May 1886.

The NEW CLUB HOUSE being now completed, was opened to-day, when the Members played for the following Prizes :—

The GOLD MEDAL, the LADIES' CUP, and the MORRISON-TURNBULL CUP, with the following results,—the Gold Medal won by Captain Bloxsom with the net score of 90,—the Ladies' Cup and Morrison-Turnbull Cup by Mr. George Morison with a score of 106, less 18, 88.[1]

Thereafter the Members and Guests, to the number of 90, dined together and spent a most enjoyable and pleasant evening. The Captain, Mr. Kirkhope, and Mr. A. W. Usher entertained the company with song, — the Glee Club also sustaining their well-earned reputation.   W. GIBSON BLOXSOM, *C.*

North Berwick, 3rd July 1886.

The Competition between the BURGESS and BRUNTSFIELD Clubs took place to-day at North Berwick, and resulted in a victory for the BRUNTSFIELD by 19 holes.

At the termination of the play the Members of the two teams dined together in the Royal Hotel.

W. GIBSON BLOXSOM, *C.*

Gullane, 4th June 1887.

The Competition between the BURGESS and BRUNTSFIELD Clubs took place to-day at Gullane, and resulted in a victory for the BURGESS by a majority of 57 holes.

Musselburgh, 6th May 1890.

The GOLD MEDAL of the Club was this day played for and won by Mr. Duncan Maclaren in 83 strokes.

Musselburgh, 18th Oct. 1892.

The CAIRNS MEDAL was competed for this day and won by Mr. John Taylor with a score of 82 strokes.

WILLIAM B. GLEN, *C.*

---

[1] The scores were high, a downpour of rain lasting the whole day.

EDINBURGH BURGESS GOLFING SOCIETY

THIS SOCIETY claims to have been instituted in 1735. The Members of it were constituted a "body politic and corporate, or legal incorporation or society, under the name and title of the EDINBURGH BURGESS GOLFING SOCIETY," by a Charter or "Seal of cause" granted by the Lord Provost, Magistrates, and Council of the city of Edinburgh, dated 2nd July 1800. This charter bears that "the Edinburgh Burgess Golfing Society has existed as a club or society for upwards of twenty years, and had occasionally got the aid of the Town-Council of Edinburgh for preserving of Bruntsfield Links in a proper state for their favourite amusement of golf." The minute-books of the Society are in existence continuously since 1773, and the following Extracts may prove interesting to Golfers generally. The Society, which formerly held its meetings at Bruntsfield Links, has now erected a spacious and commodious golf-house at Musselburgh.

Edinburgh Burgess Golfing Society

EXTRACTS FROM THE MINUTE BOOKS

*At Bruntsfield Links, near Edinburgh,
the 8th day of April* 1773.

We, Daniel Ker, Alexander Milne, and Charles Rhind, three of the members of the Society of Golfers in and about Edinburgh, taking into our consideration the present state of the said Society, and that most of the old members are either dead or have neglected to attend the meetings of the same, and we being inclined that the said Society should be continued,—Have therefore resolved to admit and receive the persons after named to be members, and who are to be subject and liable to the rules and regulations hereafter insert, in place of the old rules of the said Society, and to such other rules as may be regularly enacted in time coming.

In consequence of the above resolution, the following gentlemen appeared and were admitted, viz.—

ORLANDO HART and 14 others,

who all agreed to and subscribed the rules hereto annexed.

Bruntsfield Links, 30*th April* 1773.

Resolved, That all the members shall pay in Two shillings and sixpence sterling to the Treasurer as a fund for the Society.

ORLANDO HART, *P.*

Bruntsfield Links, 1*st July* 1774.

The meeting was of opinion that a Boy should be made choice of and engaged to call on each member every Saturday morning, and take the names of those who propose dining on that day, and that he shall serve as waiter in time of dinner, and also attend the Preses on the Saturdays, as a caddie for carrying his clubs. They also agreed that a suit of cloaths be immediately furnished, to be worn by him on Saturdays and Sundays only. In consideration of his trouble he is to be paid Six shillings per quarter from the funds of the Society.

Edinburgh Burgess Golfing Society

Bruntsfield Links, 11*th April* 1783.
The Preses moved, That the roll, how soon it comes to three score of members, shall be closed, and the Society unanimously approved thereof.

Bruntsfield Links, 9*th April* 1784.
The Society authorise the Treasurer to pay the officer the price of a pair of shoes on account of the late increase of members, which occasioned a great deal of additional walking to him.

Bruntsfield Links, 12*th June* 1790.
That in future the members of this Society shall wear an uniform, as is universally done by other Societies of Golfers, and that the uniform be a scarlet jacket, black neck, and badge, as presently worn by some of the members.

Bruntsfield Links, 16*th June* 1792.
The petitions of Mr. Andrew Milligan, watch-case maker, and Mr. Alexander Nasmyth, landscape-painter in Edinburgh, came this day to be considered, and a ballot having taken place separately for each candidate, they were both duly admitted.

Bruntsfield Links, 12*th April* 1794.
Some bottles of port wine introduced to drink to the memory of Lord Rodney and the glorious 12th of April.

Bruntsfield Links, 5*th July* 1800.
Convener Rankine presented a Seal of Cause granted by the city of Edinburgh to the Society, " constituting and erecting the said Club or Society into one body politic and corporate, or legal incorporation, under the name and title of THE EDINBURGH BURGESS GOLFING SOCIETY, and as such, and by that name and title, to have a perpetual endurance and succession," etc.
JAMES STIRLING, *Provost.*

Bruntsfield Links, 21*st December* 1811.
The Captain and Council were appointed a Committee to look after the interest of the Club in the making of the new race-course on the Links.

Edinburgh Burgess Golfing Society

Bruntsfield Links, 2nd July 1814.

Various applications having been made to the Captain requesting that a backgammon box should be purchased for the use of the members, the Treasurer was directed to procure one.

JOHN SCOTT, C.

Bruntsfield Links, 13*th May* 1815.

Mr. Scott betted One Guinea with Mr. M'Dowall that he would drive a ball from the Golf House, Bruntsfield Links, over Arthur Seat, at 45 strokes.

Mr. Scott lost.

Mr. Brown betted with Mr. Spalding one gallon of whisky that he would drive a ball over Arthur Seat on the same terms and at the same number of strokes as the above bet.

Mr. Spalding lost, as Mr. Brown drove his ball in 44 strokes.

Bruntsfield Links, 13*th January* 1816.

The Silver Club and Box were presented to the Society at this meeting, and gave universal satisfaction.

Bruntsfield Links, 1*st June* 1816.

The Gold Medal was played for this day, and was gained by Mr. Andrew Spalding.

Bruntsfield Links, 30*th July* 1816.

Mr. Reid stated that a quantity of rum had been received from the island of St. Vincent, as a present to the Society, from Mr. Charles M'Dowall, one of its members, and that, owing to the amount of the funds being insufficient to defray the government duties, which would amount to upwards of £43, he had called the present meeting to consider what measures should be adopted.

The Council therefore unanimously assessed themselves in £2 each to make up the deficiency.

Young's Tavern, High Street, 2*nd Oct.* 1817.

The Captain stated that as the stock of rum belonging to the Society was nearly done, he had ordered a stock of whisky to be laid in.

Edinburgh Burgess Golfing Society

Bruntsfield Links, 25th April 1818.

In the course of the evening the Society were honoured with a deputation from the Bruntsfield Links Golfing Society, who were received with every mark of respect and attention.

Bruntsfield Links, 16th April 1825.

The Gold Medal was played for this day, and after a keen contest, was gained by Mr. James Reid at 58 strokes.

Bruntsfield Links, 4th December 1830.

On the motion of Captain Birrell, James Sheridan Knowles, Esq., author of *Virginius*, etc., was unanimously admitted an Honorary Member of the Society.

Bruntsfield Links, 7th November 1835.

The Silver Medal was played for and keenly contested; and Messrs. J. Martin and A. Wilson having holed the two rounds at 62 strokes each, they played again two rounds more, and having severally holed the first round at 31, and the second at 32 strokes, were still equal. Darkness, however, having put an end to the play, the decision was postponed to a future day.

Bruntsfield Links, 4th April 1840.

Thereafter the members proceeded to the green to compete for the Gold Medal, which was gained by Mr. Martin at the unprecedented number of 52 strokes.

Bruntsfield Links, 4th September 1841.

At this meeting the usual fine of Champagne, on the occasion of his marriage, was presented to the Society by old Captain Alexander M'Millan, and the meeting did not fail to drink in a flowing bumper prosperity to the happy couple.

Bruntsfield Links, 8th January 1848.

Treasurer Scott reported that he had collected from the members of the Society the sum of Ten guineas, which he had paid over to the Treasurer of the Royal Infirmary.

Bruntsfield Links, 14th January 1854.

The Society had the pleasure of receiving at their table to-day Mr. Macdougall, the Treasurer of the Royal Infirmary, to whom,

Edinburgh Burgess Golfing Society

before dinner, there had been handed the sum of Fifteen pounds for the funds of the Infirmary from the Members of the Society. After dinner Mr. Macdougall, in name of the managers, thanked the Society for their very handsome donation, and for the excellent example they had set to similar institutions.

Bruntsfield Links, 4th November 1854.

Mr. Scott proposed that the Society should vote a subscription of Ten pounds from its funds towards the "Patriotic Fund." The motion was seconded by Mr. Bishop, and unanimously agreed to.

Bruntsfield Links, 5th April 1862.

The business before the meeting being concluded, the Gold Medal was then competed for, and gained by Dr. Argyll Robertson at 52 strokes.

Bruntsfield Links, 1st April 1868.

The Committee appointed to report on the Braid Hills as a Golfing green, played there to-day, and enjoyed the game amazingly. The green is splendid.

Bruntsfield Links, 3rd April 1869.

It was moved by Mr. Stevenson, and unanimously agreed to, that there be recorded in the Minute Book of the Society an expression of sincere regret at the death of John Gourlay of Musselburgh, who for many years had held the office of Ball-maker to this Society.

Bruntsfield Links, 22nd May 1874.

Plans for a Club House at Musselburgh having been laid before the meeting, Mr. Tod moved that the plans be approved of. Seconded by Mr. Cunningham, and agreed to.

OPENING OF NEW CLUB HOUSE

Musselburgh, 24th June 1875.

The New Club House at Musselburgh was opened this day. The weather was extremely favourable, and the turnout of players was very strong, 24 couples starting for two rounds of the green,

Edinburgh Burgess Golfing Society

Mr. Murray Thomson winning the SILVER CUP presented by Captain Mann in 84 strokes.

In the evening a large company of Members and their friends (82) sat down to dinner, Captain Mann in the chair. Lord Provost Falshaw proposed "The Edinburgh Burgess Golfing Society," which was responded to by the Captain.

Musselburgh, 7th April 1876.

The Gold Medal was this day, for the first time, competed for over Musselburgh, and won by Mr. H. B. Ferrier in 85 strokes.

Musselburgh, 10th October 1878.

The Gold Medal was this day competed for, and won by Mr. Alex. Ross in 84 strokes.

Musselburgh, 3rd July 1879.

The Annual Match with the Bruntsfield Links Golf Club took place to-day, the "Burgess" winning by 43 holes.

Musselburgh, 13th October 1881.

The Gold Medal was this day competed for, and won for the fifth time in succession by Mr. A. M. Ross with the remarkably fine score of 76—38 to each round.

Musselburgh, 13th October 1882.

The Gold Medal was this day competed for, and on this occasion taken from the custody of Mr. Ross by Mr. T. R. Pinkerton, who did the two rounds in 81 against Mr. Ross's 86.

Musselburgh, 6th April 1893.

Twenty-one couples this day competed for the Gold Medal, which was won by Mr. A. M. Ross in 78 strokes.[1]

---

[1] Same day at Muirfield twenty-one couples competed for the Gold Medal of the Honourable Company, which was won by Mr. J. E. Laidlay in 78 strokes.

THE XIV. PARLIAMENT of KING JAMES the Second, halden at *Edinburgh*, the sext daie of the Moneth of March, the zeir of God, ane thousand, foure hundreth, fiftie seven zeires.

Weapon-schawinges, Fute-ball, Golfe, and Archers.

ITEM, It is decreeted & ordained, that the Weapon-schawinges be halden be the Lordes and Barronnes Spiritual and Temporal, foure times in the zeir. And that the *Fute-ball and Golfe be utterly cryed downe, and not to be used.* And that the bow-markes be maid at ilk Parish Kirk a pair of Buttes, & schutting be used. And that ilk man schutte sex schottes at the least, under the paine to be raised upon them, that cummis not at the least, twa pennyes to be given to them, that cummis to the bowe-markes to drinke. And this to be used fra *Pasche* till *Alhallow-mes* after. And be the nixt Midsommer to be reddy with all their graith without failzie. And that there be a bower and a fledgear in ilk head town of the Schire. And that the town furnish him of stuffe and graith, after as needs him thereto, that they may serve the countrie with. And as tuitching the *Fute-ball and the Golfe*, to be punished be the Barronnis un-law, and gif he takis not the un-law, that it be taken be the Kingis Officiares. And that all men, that is within fiftie, and past twelve zeires, sall use schutting.

THE VI. PARLIAMENT of KING JAMES the Third, halden at *Edinburgh*, the sext daie of the Moneth of Maij, the zeire of God, ane thousand, foure hundreth, seventie ane zeires.

The length of speares, and that Zeamen have targes.

ITEM, It is thought expedient, that na Merchandes bring speares in this Realme out of ony uther cuntry, bot gif they conteine sex elne of length, and of a clyft: nor that na bower within this cuntrie make na speares, bot gif they conteine the samin length. And quha that dois the contrair, that the speares be escheited, and the persones punished at the Kingis will. Also, that ilk zeaman that cannot deale with the bow, that he have ane gude axe, and ane targe of ledder, to resist the schot of *England*, quhilk is na coist bot the value of a hide. And that ilk Schireffe, Stewart, Baillie, and uthers Officiares, mak weapon-schawinges within the boundes of their office, after the tenour of the acte of Parliament, sa that in default of the said weapon-schawinge our Soveraine Lords Lieges be not destitute of harnes, quhen they have need. And that the *Fute-ball and Golfe be abused in time cumming*, and that the buttes be maid up, and schuting used, after the tenour of the acte of Parliamente maid thereupon.

Acts of the Scots Parliament

THE III. PARLIAMENT of KING JAMES the Fourth, halden the auchtenth day of the Moneth of Maij, the zeir of God, ane thousand, foure hundreth, ninetie ane zeires.

Fute-ball and Golfe forbidden.

ITEM, It is statute and ordained that in na place of the Realme there be used *Fute-ball*, *Golfe*, or uther sik unproffitable sportes, but for commoun gude of the Realme & defense thereof. And that bowes and schutting be hanted, and bow-markes maid therefore ordained in ilk parochin, under the paine of fourtie shillinges to be raised be the Schireffe and Baillies foresaid. And of ilk Parochin ilk zeir, quhair it beis found in, that bow-markes beis not maid, nor schutting hanted, as is before said.

THE KINGS MAJESTIES DECLARATION TO HIS SUBJECTS CONCERNING LAWFULL SPORTS TO BE USED. 1618.

By the King (James VI.)

WHEREAS upon our returne the last yeere out of Scotland, wee did publish our pleasure touching the recreations of our people in those parts under our hand: For some causes us thereunto mooving, we have thought good to command these our directions then given in Lancashire with a few words thereunto added, and most appliable to these parts of our Realmes, to be published to all our subjects.

Whereas we did justly in our progresse through Lancashire rebuke some Puritanes and precise people, and tooke order that

Declaration concerning Sports

the like unlawfull cariage should not bee used by any of them hereafter in the prohibiting and unlawfull punishing of our good people for using their lawfull recreations, and honest exercises upon Sundayes and other holy dayes, *after the afternoone sermon or service:* Wee now find that two sorts of people wherewith that countrey is much infested (wee meane Papists and Puritanes), have maliciously traduced and calumniated those our just and honourable proceedings. And therefore lest our reputation might upon the one side (though innocently) have some aspersion layd upon it, and that upon the other part our good people in that countrey bee misled by the mistaking and misinterpretation of our meaning: We have therefore thought good hereby to cleare and make our pleasure to bee manifested to all our good people in those parts.

It is true that at our first entry to this Crowne and Kingdome, wee were informed, and that too truely, that our county of Lancashire abounded more in Popish Recusants then any countie of England, and thus hath stil continued since to our great regret, with little amendment, save that now of late, in our last riding through our said county, wee find both by the report of the judges, and of the bishop of that diocesse that there is some amendment now daily beginning, which is no small contentment to us.

The report of this growing amendment amongst them, made us the more sory, when with our owne eares wee heard the generall complaint of our people, that they were barred from all lawfull recreation, and exercise upon the Sundayes afternoone, *after the ending of all Divine service*, which cannot but produce two evils: the one, the hindering of the conversion of many, whom their Priests will take occasion hereby to vexe, perswading them that no honest mirth or recreation is lawfull or tollerable in our religion, which cannot but breed a great discontentment in our peoples hearts, especially of such as are peradventure upon the point of turning; the other inconvenience is, that this prohibition barreth the common and meaner sort of people from using such exercises as may make their bodies more able for warre, when wee or our successors shall have occasion to use them. And in place thereof sets up filthy tiplings and drunkennesse, and breeds a number of idle and discontented speaches in their alehouses. *For when shal the common people have leave to exercise, if not upon the Sundayes and holydayes, seeing they must apply their labour, and winne their living in all working dayes?*

Declaration concerning Sports

Our expresse pleasure therefore is, that the lawes of our kingdome, and canons of our church bee as well observed in that county, as in all other places of this our kingdome. And on the other part, that no lawfull recreation shall bee barred to our good people, which shall not tend to the breach of our aforesaid lawes and canons of our church: which to expresse more particularly, our pleasure is, that the bishop, and all other inferiour churchmen, and churchwardens, shall for their parts bee carefull and diligent, both to instruct the ignorant, and convince and reforme them that are misled in religion, presenting them that will not conforme themselves, but obstinately stand out to our judges and justices: whom we likewise command to put the law in due execution against them.

Our pleasure likewise is, that the bishop of that diocesse take the like straight order with all the Puritans and Precisians within the same, either constraining them to conforme themselves, or to leave the countrey according to the lawes of our kingdome, and canons of our church, and so to strike equally on both hands, against the contemners of our authoritie, and adversaries of our church. And as for our good peoples lawfull recreation, our pleasure likewise is, *that after the end of divine service*, our good people be not disturbed, letted, or discouraged from any lawfull recreation; such as dauncing, either men or women, archerie for men, leaping, vaulting, or any other such harmlesse recreation . . . . so as the same be had in due and convenient time, without impediment or neglect of divine service . . .

And likewise we barre from this benefite and libertie, all such knowne as Recusants, either men or women, as will abstaine from comming to church or divine service, being therefore unworthy of any lawfull recreation after the said service, that will not first come to the church and serve God: prohibiting in like sort the said recreations to any that, though conforme in religion, are not present in the church at the service of God, before their going to the said recreations. Our pleasure likewise is, that they to whom it belongeth in office shall present and sharply punish all such as, in abuse of this our libertie, will use these exercises before the ends of all divine services for that day. And we likewise straightly command, that every person shall resort to his owne parish church to heare divine service, and each parish by it selfe to use the said recreation after divine service. Prohibiting likewise any offensive weapons to be caried or used in the said times of recreations.

Declaration concerning Sports

And our pleasure is, that this our declaration shal be published by order from the bishop of the diocesse, through all the parish churches, and that both our judges of our circuit, and our justices of our peace be informed thereof.

> Given at our mannour of Greenwich the foure and twentieth day of May, in the sixteenth yeere of our raigne of England, France and Ireland, and of Scotland the one and fiftieth.
>
> GOD SAVE THE KING.

DECLARATION CONCERNING LAWFULL SPORTS. 1633.

By the King (Charles I.)

OUR deare father of blessed memory, in his returne from Scotland, comming through Lancashire, found that his subjects were debarred from lawful recreations upon Sundayes after evening prayers ended, and upon holy dayes: And hee prudently considered, that if these times were taken from them, the meaner sort who labour hard all the weeke, should have no recreations at all to refresh their spirits. And after his returne, hee farther saw that his loyall subjects in all other parts of his kingdome did suffer in the same kinde, though perhaps not in the same degree: and did therefore in his princely wisedome publish a declaration to all his loving subjects concerning lawfull sports to be used at such times, which was printed and published by his royall commandement in the yeere 1618. In the tenor which hereafter followeth.

[Here follows Declaration by James VI.]

NOW out of a like pious care for the service of God, and for suppressing of any humors that oppose trueth, and for the ease, comfort, and recreation of our well deserving people, wee doe ratifie and publish this our blessed father's declaration: the rather because of late in some counties of our kingdome, wee finde that under pretence of taking away abuses, there hath been a generall forbidding, not onely of ordinary meetings, but of the feasts of the dedication of the churches, commonly called wakes. Now our expresse will and pleasure is, that these feasts with others shall be observed, and that our justices of the peace in their

Declaration concerning Sports

severall divisions shall looke to it, both that all disorders there may be prevented or punished, and that all neighbourhood and freedome, with manlike and lawfull exercises be used. And we farther command our justices of assize in their severall circuits, to see that no man doe trouble or molest any of our loyall and duetifull people, in or for their lawfull recreations, having first done their duetie to God, and continuing in obedience to us and our lawes. And of this wee command all our judges, justices of the peace, as well within liberties as without, maiors, bayliffes, constables, and other officers, to take notice of, and to see observed, as they tender our displeasure.

Given at our palace of Westminster the eighteenth day of October, in the ninth yeere of our reigne.

GOD SAVE THE KING.

"Prophaning the Lord's Sabbath."

EARLY NOTICES OF GOLF FROM BURGH AND PARISH RECORDS, Etc.

Archbishop Hamilton's acknowledgment of License granted to him by the City of St. Andrews to plant cuniggis in the Links, and Ratification by him of the City's rights in the Links, dated 25th Jan. 1552.

WE JOHNE be the mercie of God archebischop of Sanctandros primat et legat natie of the haill realme of Scotland grantis us to have obtenit licience and tollerance be the free consent of our lovittis provest bailleis conseill and communitie off our cittie of Sanctandros to plant and planis[1] cuniggis[2] within the northe pairt of thair commond linkis nixt adjacent to the Wattir of Eddin and that it salbe lesum to uss to tak the profitt of the saidis cuniggis and to uss thame to our

---

[1] Plenish. [2] Rabbits.

Early Notices of Golf

utilitie and plesour Reserveing alwais to our saidis provest balleis consell and communitie all maner of rycht and possessioun proprietie and communitie of the saidis linkis baith in pastoring of thair gudis casting and lading of divattis and scherettis [1] to thair uis and profitt playing at golf futball schuting at all gamis with all uther maner of pastyme as ever thai pleis als weill quhair the saidis cuniggis salbe plantit and planisit as utheris pairtis of the saidis linkis withottin ony closing or dyking to be maid be us of ony pairt off the saidis linkis or ony propirtie to be hed be us and our successouris of ony pairt thairof bot alanerlie we to tak the profitt of the saidis cuniggis for our tyme alanerlie sua that nay persone sall tak distroy holl or delf furth ony of the saidis cuniggis bot the linkis and cuniggis to be usit in maner foirsaid AND WE thairfoir be thir presentis for us and our successouris and withe consent of our chaptour confermis ratifeis and apprevis the rycht and possessioun propirtie and communite of the saidis linkis in pastoring of gudis casting and leding of dovettis and scherettis playing at golff futball schuteing at all gamis with all uther maner of pastyme als weill quhair the saidis cuniggis salbe plenisit as utheris pairtis of the saidis linkis as said is to pertene and remane pecebill and perpetuall withe the saidis provest balleis consell communitie and inhabitaris of our said cittie without ony dykin or closing of ony pairt thairof fra thame or impediment to be maid to thame thairintill in ony tyme cuming IN WITNESING heirof to thir presentis subscrivit withe our hand our rond seill togidder withe the commone seill [2] of our chaptour ar appendit at our said cittie of Sanctandros the tuenty fyve day of the monethe of Januar in the yeir of God ane thousand fyve hundrethe fyftie tua yeris befoir thir witnes Maister Alexander Forest

---

[1] Green turf. *Jamieson*. The burgesses of St. Andrews still claim the right of "casting feal and divots" on the Links.

[2] Both seals are still attached, and are in a very fair state of preservation.

Early Notices of Golf

provest of Logy-montrois Robert Hammylton chammillane Robert Forseyth withe utheris diverss.

JHONE ARCHEBISCHOP OF SANCTANDROS.
From the Original in St. Andrews University Library.

Dec. 18, 1583. The quhilk day, it is delatit that Alexander Milleris tua sonis ar inobedient to him, and that thai, with Nicholl Mane, William Bruce and utheris, thair complices, playit in the golf feildis Sonday last wes, tyme of fast and precheing, aganis the ordinances of the kirk. The sessioun ordanis thame to be warnit and accusit thairfor.

Register of St. Andrews Kirk Session, Scot. Hist. Soc., ii. 515.

Upon Tuisday, the 13th of Februar [1592-3], Mr Johne Graham of Halyairds went out of Edinburgh toward Leith, being charged to depart off the toun. The duke and Sir James Sandilands following as it were, with clubs in their hands,[1] and comming doun Leith Wynde, one of Mr Johne's companie looking backe, and seing them, they turned to make resistance. The duke [Lennox] sent, and willed them to goe fordward, promising no man sould invade them, yitt Mr Johne Graham's companie shott; wherupon the duke suffered Sir James and his companie to doe for themselves. Mr Johne was shott; his companie fled before ever he was caried to a hous. Sir Alexander Stewart's page, a Frenche boy, seing his maister slaine, followed Mr Johne Graham in to the hous, dowped a whinger into him, and so dispatched him. Before their encounter, Mr Johne was accompanied with three or foure score.

Calderwood's History, Wodrow Society, vol. v. pp. 223, 224.

Feb. 21, 1592. This day compeared John Pitscottie, heir-apparent of Loncarty, Finlay Errol, servitor to the Laird of

---

[1] "Making towards their sport in the sands." (Spottiswoode's *History*, Spot. Soc., vol. ii. p. 428.)

Early Notices of Golf

Balhousie (with several other persons named in the Register), and confessed that on the Sunday of the fast, in the time of preaching in the afternoon, they were playing at the foot-ball in the meadow inch of the Muirtown, and that the same was an offence. Therefore, they were ordained on Sunday next to make their repentance for breach of the Sabbath.

Records of the Kirk Session of Perth.

April 19, 1592. The sam day ordanis proclamatioun to be maid threw this burgh, that seeing the Sabboth day being the Lord's day it becumis everie christiane to dedicat himselff, his houshald, and familie, to the service and worship of God, in hearing the word, meditating thairupoun, and reading the sam, instructing thair fameleis and otherwayis in the exercise of prayer, thairfore commanding and chairgeing in our Soverane lord's name, and in name and behalf of the provest, baillies, and counsall of this burgh, that na inhabitants of the samyn, be thameselffis, thair children, servands, or fameleis, be sene at ony pastymes or gammis within or without the toun upoun the Sabboth day, *sic as Golf*, aircherie, rowbowllis, penny stayne, kactch pullis, or sic other pastymes, and that thai nor thair said servands occupy ony kynd of handie lawbour or wark upoun the said day, and also that thair dochteris and wemen servands be nocht fund playing at the ball, nor singing of profayne sangs, upoun the sam day, under sic paynis as the magestrates sall lay to thair chairge. *Records of the City of Edinburgh.*

April 20, 1593. The quhilk day, Nicol Uddert, provest, the baillies, Den of Gild, Thesaurer, and ane greitt [part] of the counsall and deykins of crafts being convenit, for swomekill as it is regraitit be the Sessioun of the kirk, that dyvers inhabitants of this burgh repaires upoun the Sabboth day to the toun of Leyth, and in tyme of sermonis are sene vagant athort the streits, drynking in tavernis, or otherwayes at *Golf*, aircherie, or

Early Notices of Golf

other pastymes upoun the Lynks, thairby profaning the Sabboth day, and gevand evill exampill to others to do the lyke, thairfoir ordans proclamatioun to be maid, dischairgeing all maner of persouns, indwellers of this burgh, to be fund upoun the Sabboth day in the toun of Leyth vagand threw the streits, or drinkand in howsses the tyme of sermones, or yitt at thair pastymes in the Lynks or other places, quhairby the Sabboth day may be profanet, under the payne of wairding thair persounis quhill thai pay ane unlaw of fourty shillings, and otherwayes be punist in thair persouns at the discretioun of the Magestrates. *Records of the City of Edinburgh.*

March 29, 1598. The quhilk day, Dauid Gray pewderar and Thomas Saith tailyour being callit comperit, and, being accusit for prophaning of the Saboth day in playing at the gouf eftir nune, confest the samin; and becaus thai war nocht apprehendit with the lyik fault of befoir, thai war admonished nocht to do the samin heireftir; and cravit the session forgivenes, and ar with thair awin consentis actit to pay fourtie s. ilk ane of thame, if evir thai be fund violating the Saboth day.
Register of St. Andrews Kirk Session, Scot. Hist. Soc., ii. 846.

Nov. 19, 1599. John Gardiner, James Bowman, Laurence Chalmers, and Laurence Cuthbert, confess that they were playing at the golf on the North Inch in time of the preaching after noon on the Sabbath. The Session rebuked them, and admonished them to resort to the hearing of the Word diligently on the Sabbath in time coming, which they promised to do. *Records of the Kirk Session of Perth.*

Wedinsday, the xix *of December,* 1599.—The quhilk day, the bretheren undirstanding perfytlie that divers personis of thair number the tyme of sessioun passis to the feildis, to the goufe

Early Notices of Golf

and uthir exercise, and hes no regard for keiping of the sessioun conform to the actis maid thairanent, for remeid quhairof it is ordinit that quhatsumevir person or personis of the session that heireftir beis fund playand, or passis to play at the goufe or uthir pastymes the tyme of sessioun, sall pay ten s. for the first fault, for the secund fault xx. s., for the thrid fault publik repentance, and the fourt fault deprivation fra thair offices; and this to be payit to the clerk, without prejudice of the formar actis maid for keiping of the sessioun.

Register of St. Andrews Kirk Session, Scot. Hist. Soc., ii. 913.

Jan. 2, 1604. The visitors report that good order was keeped the last Sabbath, except that they found some young boys playing at the gowf in the North Inch, in the time of preaching afternoon, who were warned then by the officiars, to compear before the Session this day.

Compears Robert Robertson, William Stenis, Andrew Donaldson, Alexander Niving, Adam Paul, Robert Meling: all warned to this day, who were convicted of profaning the Lord's Sabbath, by absenting themselves from hearing of the Word, and playing at the gowf, in time of preaching; and therefore the Session ordained, first, Robert Robertson, who was ringleader to the rest, to pay an merk to the poor; and secondly, ordains him and the rest to compear the next Sabbath into the place of public repentance, in presence of the whole congregation. *Records of the Kirk Session of Perth.*

Feb. 11, 1608. The which day compeirit John Henrie, Pat. Bogie, James Kid, George Robertsoune, and James Watsoune, and being accusit for playing of the gowff everie Sabboth the tyme of the sermonnes, notwithstanding oft admonitioun past befoir, were convict of xx. lib. ilk ane of them, and ordainit to be wardet [put in prison] until the same

Early Notices of Golf

wer payit, and to find cautioun not to do the lyke again at na tyme heirefter, under the paine of c. lib.

Register of the Kirk Session of North Leith.

June 5, 1619. For as meikle as delation being made that John Brown, gardner, permits men to play at the alye bowlls in my Lord Sanquhar's yard the time of the sermons on the Sabbath days, therefore he is warned to compear the morrow, for taking convenient order thereanent.

Records of the Kirk Session of Perth.

Jan. 30, 1621. *David Hairt.* The quhilk day David Hairt, prenteis to Gilbert Bauhop, wrycht, confest prophanatione of the Sabboth in playing at the Goff in the park on the Sabboth aftirnone in tyme of preaching; and therfor is ordenit to pay *ad pios usus* vj s̃ viij d etc.

Register of the Kirk Session of Stirling.

Jan. 31, 1641. The said day James and George Duffus and Charles Stevinson were convict in break of the Sabboth, for playing at the golff, efternoone, in time of sermone, and therfor are ordayned, evrie ane of them, to pay halff a merk, and mak ther repentance the next Sabboth.

Records of the Kirk Session of Cullen.

April 27, 1651. The which day James Rodger, Johne Rodger, Johne Howdan, Andrew Howdan, and George Patersone, were complained upon for playing at the Golf upon ane Lord's day; were ordained to be cited the next day.

May 4. The which day compeired the aforementioned persons, and confessed thair prophaning of the Lord's day by playing at the Golf; were ordained to mak their publick repentance the next day.

The which day Johne Howdan was deposed from his office, being ane deacon.

Register of the Kirk Session of Humbie.

Early Notices of Golf

I. Extract of Letter from Wm. Cramond, LL.D., Cullen, to Editor of *Banffshire Journal*.

Playaris at the Goffe were given to the Session, playing in tyme of sermon.   *Minutes of Kirk Session of Culross*, 1633.

II. Letter from Wm. Cramond, LL.D., Cullen, to Editor of *Banffshire Journal*.

Cullen, 25th Jan. 1892.

Sir,—Will you allow me to supplement my notes in your former issue on the early history of Golf by two quotations from the *Diary of Alexander Brodie of Brodie?*—

"*August* 12, 1672. I did this day begin to drink at the well of Rinns [Rives]; some effect it had as to appearance. I passed this day ther, and made use of golfing for exerceis of the body. Whil I drink let this be noe snar to me.

"*August* 19, 1672. I was this night at Burgi. Mr. Colin Falconer drank with me, and we recreated the bodi by pastim at golf. Lord, let this be noe snar to me!"

The interest of this quotation consists in the fact that it disproves the assertion, not unfrequently made of late, that golf in early times represented shinty, and not golf as understood by us; for let us look at the pleasant picture these extracts present. Who were the players? One was the Laird of Brodie, a staid worthy of the old school, of the age of fifty-five, who had come to the well to obtain relief from an excruciating disease; the other the minister of Forres, a man of forty-nine, who had been previously minister of Essil, and when promoted to Forres "turned Episcopal," and was afterwards appointed Bishop of Moray, and died, its last Bishop, in the Palace of Spynie. These two agree of an afternoon to have a round. To imagine the Laird of Brodie, a rigid Covenanter, with a text in his mouth and stone in the bladder, going away with the minister of Forres to play a game so rough as shinty, were a sight to make the angels weep; but substitute golf as now understood, and all is natural; in fact, is it too much to expect that the angels, at least some of them, for they cannot be all alike, would follow the game of the two pious worthies with a kindly and intelligent interest? Another proof that ancient golf was modern golf, and not shinty, is

Early Notices of Golf

found in the fact that the players who conclude their games in old Kirk Session and other records correspond in number with those of modern golf, but not with those of shinty.—I am, etc. WM. CRAMOND.

III. EXTRACT of LETTER from WM. CRAMOND, LL.D., Cullen, to Editor of *Banffshire Journal.*

Gordon, the famous parson of Rothiemay, states that the inhabitants of Aberdeen used to "recreat" themselves on the links with "several kynds of exercises, such as foot-ball, goffe, bowling, and archerie." In 1642 the Town Council of Aberdeen granted "licence and tolerance to John Dickson to use and exercise his trade of making gowff ballis within this burgh in respect ther is not sich ane tradisman in this burgh."

Sept. 9, 1637. The Borrow or Justice Court of the Burgh off Banf haldin within the tolbuithe of the samen be hono[ll]. men George Baird of Auchmedden, provest of the said burghe etc presentit Franceis Broune, sone to John Broune wabster in Banff with the dittay and fang wnderwreittin tackin and apprehendit as ane theiff upon the sext day of September instant and than put in firmance in the stocks q[r]in he hes remanit quhill this present tyme.

Followes the poyntis of the said dittay aganis the said Franceis : . . . Fourthlie, Thow art indytet for cumyng about midnicht on Saterday the secound day of September instant to the said burghe to the marcat place theroff accompanied with Jo[n.] Cryistie, vagabound, banischit abefoir furthe of this burghe. . . . Thow past to Patrik Schand his buithe and therefter thow haid brokin wp the window of the said Patrik his buithe w[t.] ane aix thow past in therat and thair thifteouslie stole out of the said buithe and cariet away with the gudis and geir following viz some dolors worthe of turnoris or therby . . . sume golff ballis . . . Confessit the steilling of Patrik Schand his geir and that he sauld twa of the golf ballis to

Early Notices of Golf

Thomas Urquhart servand. The judges remit the case to an assize of fifteen persons who convict him *inter alia* of stealing the golf balls and "convictis the said Francis as ane leud liver and boy of ane evill lyiff and conversatioun and as ane daylie remainer fra the kirk in tyme of dyvyne worschip." The judges "ordanit the said Francis to be presentlie tackin and cariet to the Gallowehill of this burghe and hangit on the gallows therof to the death wherof William Wat dempster of the said assyis gawe doome." *Annals of Banff*, i. 77.

The numerous references to club-makers in the records of that burgh leave little if any doubt that golf has, at least since the above date, been played continuously on the links of Banff. In Banff Museum is a skull, labelled that of Macpherson, the noted freebooter. The skull was found prior to a recent complete examination of the burgh records, and when the belief was entertained that Macpherson alone suffered death on the Gallows Hill. The evidence points, however, more strongly towards the skull being that of this infamous golf-ball stealer, and I would respectfully suggest to the Museum Committee that the skull be re-labelled as that of the aforesaid Francis Brown in order to point a moral and serve as a warning to all future generations of the danger and disgrace of stealing golf balls. W. C.

May 23, 1658. James Winchester delaitted to have clume nests upon the Lord's day, and James Waldie to have plaid att the golfe with the herds of Mulben; being present they are called into the Session and being both found guiltie they were rebuked for making so little conscience of the Lord's day, and ordained to make their publick repentance three Lord's days. *Kirk Session Records of Boharm, Banffshire.*

EXTRACTS FROM THE NOTE-BOOKS OF SIR JOHN FOULIS, BART., OF RAVELSTOUN [1]

[The sums are in Scots money.]

1672.

Jan. 6.	For a dozen and a half Golfe balls	4	7	0
13.	Lost at Golfe with Pittarro and Comissar Munro	0	13	0
	Lost at Golfe with Lyon and Harry Hay	1	4	0
Feb. 14.	Spent at Leith at Golfe	2	0	0
26.	Spent at Leith at Golfe	1	9	0
Mar. 2.	For three Golfe balls	0	15	0
	Lost at Golfe at Mussleboorgh with Gosfoord, Lyon, etc.	3	5	0
Apr. 13.	To the boy who carried my Clubs, when my Lord Register and Newbyth was at the Links	0	4	0
Nov. 19.	Lost at Golfe with the Chancellour, Lyon, Master of Saltoune, etc.	5	10	0
	For Golfe balls	0	12	0
30.	Lost at Golfe with the Chancellour, Duke Hamilton, etc.	4	15	0
Dec. 7.	For a Golfe Club to Archie	0	6	0

[1] From *Nugæ Scoticæ. Miscellaneous Papers, illustrative of Scotish affairs*, (1535-1781) MDXXXV.-MDCCLXXXI. Edited by Mr. James Maidment. Edinburgh, 1829, 8vo. (No. 18). Privately printed.

Extracts from Note-Books

THESE Extracts show that in 1672 Golf was the fashionable amusement of the Scottish Edinburgh aristocracy, and that, as now, Leith and Musselburgh were the ordinary places for enjoying the game. Sir John Foulis was a baronet of an ancient family, and his curious books of expenditure are still, it is presumed, in possession of his representative. Being on intimate terms with the late Sir James Foulis, Bart., of Woodhall, he kindly gave me access to them, and various extracts were taken and printed in the collection previously noticed, of which not more than six copies are now presumed to be in existence.

Sir John's associates were of the highest quality at the time. The Lord Chancellor was Duke of Rothes; the Lord Register was Sir Archibald Primrose; Newbyth was Sir John Baird, made a Lord of Session 4th November 1664, whose descendant, the late Sir David, was one of the best and most popular of gentlemen players in Scotland; Gosfoord was Sir Peter Wedderburn, also a Lord of Session, 17th July 1668; the Duke of Hamilton was William Douglas, who by marriage with Anne, Duchess of Hamilton, was created a Duke for life. He died in 1694.

J. M.

Extracts from Accounts

EXTRACTS from the ACCOUNTS of the Lords High Treasurers of Scotland

1503-4, Feb. 3. Item to the King *to play at the Golf* with the Erle of Bothuile . . . . xlij s̃

Item *to Golf Clubbis and Ballis* to the King that he playit with . . . ix s̃

1505-6, Feb. 22. Item for xij Golf Ballis to the King . iiij s̃

1506, July 18. Item the xviij day of Julij for ij Golf Clubbes to the King . . . ij s̃

THE following SCRAP relative to GOLF, by THOMAS SHADWELL, occurs in a very rare work entitled *Westminster Drollery*, 12mo, London 1671, p. 28.

A Song called—

"*And to each pretty Lass
We will give a green Gown.*"

THUS all our life long we are frolick and gay,
And instead of Court revels, we merrily play
At Trap, at Rules, and at Barly-break run:
At GOFF, and at Foot-ball, and when we have done
These innocent sports, we'll laugh and lie down,
    *And to each pretty Lass
    We will give a green Gown.*

COCK OF THE GREEN.

THE COCK O' THE GREEN [1]

ALEXANDER M'KELLAR, the "Cock o' the Green," was probably one of the most enthusiastic golf-players that ever handled a club. When the weather would at all permit, he generally spent the whole day on Bruntsfield Links; and he was frequently to be found engaged at the "short holes" by lamp-light. Even in winter, if the snow was sufficiently frozen, he might be seen enjoying his favourite exercise alone, or with any one he could persuade to join him in the pastime. M'Kellar thus became well known in the neighbourhood of the green; and his almost insane devotion to golf was a matter of much amusement to his acquaintances. So thoroughly did he enter into the spirit of the game that every other consideration seemed obliterated for the time. "By the la' Harry," or "By gracious, this won't go for nothing!" he would exclaim involuntarily, as he endeavoured to ply his club with scientific skill; and when victory chanced to crown his exertions, he used to give way to his joy for a second or two by dancing round the golf-hole. M'Kellar, however, was not a member of any of the clubs; and, notwithstanding his

---

[1] From Kay's *Portraits*. Edinburgh: Hugh Paton, 1838, 4to.

The Cock o' the Green

incessant practice, he was by no means considered a dexterous player. This is accounted for by the circumstance of his having been far advanced in years before he had an opportunity of gaining a knowledge of the game. The greater part of his life had been passed as a butler, but in what family is unknown, nor indeed does it matter much. He had contrived to save a little money, and his wife, on their coming to Edinburgh, opened a small tavern in the New Town. M'Kellar had thus ample leisure for the indulgence of his fancy, without greatly abridging his income; and golf may be said to have virtually become his *occupation;* yet no perseverance could entirely compensate for the want of practice in his younger years.

His all-absorbing predilection for golf was a source of much vexation to his managing partner in life, on whom devolved the whole duty of attending to the affairs of the tavern. It was not because she regretted his want of attention to business,—for probably he would have been allowed to appropriate a very small portion of authority in matters which she could attend to much better herself,—but she felt scandalised at the notoriety he had acquired, and was not altogether satisfied with the occasional outlay to which he was subjected, though he never speculated to any great amount.

No sooner was breakfast over than M'Kellar daily set off to the green; and ten to one he did not find his way home till dusk; and not even then, if the sport chanced to be good. As a practical jest on the folly of his procedure, it occurred to his "better half" that she would one day put him to the blush, by carrying his dinner, along with his nightcap, to the

The Cock o' the Green

Links. At the moment of her arrival M'Kellar happened to be hotly engaged; and apparently without feeling the weight of the satire, he good-naturedly observed that she might *wait*, if she chose, till the game was decided, for at present he had no time for dinner!

So provoked at length was the good dame that she abhorred the very name of golf, as well as all who practised it; and to her customers, if they were her husband's associates on the green, even a regard for her own interest could scarcely induce her to extend the common civilities of the tavern.

What betwixt respect for his wife and his fondness of golf M'Kellar must have been placed in rather a delicate situation; but, great as the struggle might be, all opposition was eventually overcome, and he determined to enjoy his game, and be happy in spite of frowns, lectures, or entreaties. One thing alone annoyed him, and that was the little countenance he was enabled to give his friends when they happened to visit him. At length an opportunity occurred, apparently highly favourable for an honourable *amende* to his long-neglected acquaintances. Having resolved on a trip to the kingdom of Fife, where she calculated on remaining for at least *one* night, his "worthy rib" took her departure, leaving him for once, after many cautions, with the management of affairs in her absence. Now was the time, thought M'Kellar. A select party of friends were invited to his house in the evening: the hour had arrived, and the company were assembled in the best parlour—golf the theme, and deep the libations—when (alas! what short-sighted mortals are we) who should appear to mar the mirth of the revellers but the

The Cock o' the Green

golf-hating Mrs. M'Kellar herself! Both winds and waves had conspired to interrupt the festivity: the ferry had been found impassable, and the hostess was compelled to return. What ensued may be imagined. The contemplated journey was postponed *sine die ;* and M'Kellar internally resolved to make sure, before giving a second invitation, that his spouse had actually *crossed the ferry !*

Happening to be at Leith one day, where his fame as a golfer was not unknown, M'Kellar got into conversation, in the club-maker's shop, with a number of glass-blowers, who were *blowing* very much about their science in the game of golf. After bantering him for some time to engage in a trial of skill, a young man from Bruntsfield Links opportunely made his appearance. "By gracious, gentlemen!" exclaimed M'Kellar, whose spirit was roused,—"here's a boy and I will play you for a guinea!" No sooner said than a match of three games was begun, in all of which the glass-blowers were defeated. The "Cock o' the Green" was triumphant; and, not waiting till the bet had been forthcoming, he ran to the shop of the club-maker, announcing the joyful intelligence,—"By gracious, gentlemen, the old man and the boy have beat them off the green!"

By way of occupying his time profitably on the *seventh* —the only day in the week he could think of employing otherwise than in his favourite amusement—M'Kellar was in the habit of acting as door-keeper to an Episcopalian Chapel. On entering one day, old Mr. Douglas Gourlay, club and ball maker at Bruntsfield, jocularly placed a golf-ball in the plate, in lieu of his usual donation of coppers. As anticipated, the prize was instantaneously secured by M'Kellar, who was

The Cock o' the Green

not more astonished than gratified by the novelty of the deposit.

It was at the suggestion of the late Mr. M'Ewan and Mr. Gourlay that Kay produced the etching of the "Cock o' the Green." Going out purposely to the Links, the artist found him engaged at his usual pastime, and succeeded in taking an accurate and characteristic likeness. When informed what Kay had been doing M'Kellar seemed highly pleased. "What a pity!" said he; "By gracious, had I known, I would have shown him some of my capers!"

The print was executed in 1803. Although then pretty far advanced in life, M'Kellar continued to maintain his title of the "Cock o' the Green" for a considerable time. He died about 1813.

Sanctandrews[1]

St. Andrews! name unmeet for tuneful lay,
And all unapt the Bard for tuneful part—
Be his the task thy features to pourtray,
Thy every charm of nature and of art:
Thy bays, thy rocks, thy ruins that apart
Uplift their towers beneath the pale moon beam,
Thy colleges that form the head and heart,
Professors, which those colleges beseem,
Thy student, golfer-crew—a multifarious theme!

All here are golfers—strangers, natives, all
The sons of science, idleness, and war,
Who can or wield a club, or hit a ball,
Professor, Soldier, Student-lad, and Tar
And country Laird, attracted from afar,
With some mischancy Writer to engage;
Whilst oft the rag, and spirit-chafing *jar*,
Provokes to sudden bet, and smothered rage,
Which twice another round will quietly assuage.

It is indeed a goodly sight to see
These red-coat champions marshalled for the fray,
Driving the ball o'er bunker, rut, and lea,
And clearing, with imperious "fore," the way,
Enlivening still the game with laugh and say,

---

[1] From *Blackwood's Edinburgh Magazine*, September 1819.

Sanctandrews

Whilst trotting club-man follows fast behind,
Prepared with ready hand the "*tees*" to lay,
With nicest eye the devious ball to find,
And of the going game each player to remind.

It is in sooth a goodly sight to see,
By east and west, the Swilcan lasses clean,
Spreading their clothes upon the daisied lea,
And skelping freely barefoot o'er the green,
With petticoats high kilted up I ween,
And note of jocund ribaldry most meet;
From washing-tub their glowing limbs are seen
Veiled in an upward shower of dewy weet!
Oh! 'tis enough to charge an anchorite with heat!

MAIDEN ROCK, ST. ANDREWS BAY

THE LINKS OF ST. RULE [1]

I AM sure that I shall not soon forget the scene which greeted me when I drew aside my bedroom curtain in the morning and looked abroad. It was one of those summer mornings with which we used to be familiar at Interlachen or at Venice, but which have been rarely met with on this side of the Channel until the July of this year of grace 1863. I might write pages about it; but an older pilgrim has described the scene in a few poetic words which cannot be imitated. He, standing on the rocky ledge and looking down—

> Beheld an ocean bay girt by green hills;
> And in a million wavelets tipt with gold
> Leapt the soft pulses of the sunlit sea.

And lo! among the white-edged breakers and upon the yellow sands, the sea-nymphs at their sport, the Sirens with

---

[1] From *Macmillan's Magazine*, September 1863.

The Links of St. Rule

dripping locks, and rosy lips and cheeks, and such soft and musical words and laughter as might wile away the wisest Ulysses of us all. It is impossible to resist the fresh breath of the morning; so—arraying ourselves hastily in dressing-gown and slippers—we hurry to the easternmost headland, to which the sea comes up pure and blue, and where we have a hundred feet of water at our feet. Through the retreating waves we make way swiftly, the sea-mews dipping beside us, an occasional seal dropping from his perch in our wake, the herring-boats, with their wet nets and brown sails, passing us one by one, as they return to the harbour, until we are right below the battlements of a ruined keep—like that which Black Agnes kept so well—

> Great Randolph's fearless daughter,
> Lord March's dame is she;
> Beside the ocean water
> Her towers embattled be.

Then, after brief rest upon a desolate island crag, back once more to the shore from which we started—to the dressing-gown, to the stroll on the beach, to the dish of fresh-gathered strawberries, and the fresh eggs, and the fresh-caught salmon, and the fresh butter and cream, and the fragment of oatcake and fragrant honey or marmalade, which form the outworks of a Scottish breakfast.

But it is time to start, for, ere we reach the Links, haunted by the golfers, we must give you a glimpse of this peerless little city. Not what it once was, indeed, yet still charmingly quaint, old-mannered, and picturesque. Here in "the unhappy, far-off times," not many hundred years after the death of our Lord, came a great Christian missionary,

The Links of St. Rule

bearing with him (reverently, in a silver casket) "three of the fingers and three of the toes" of a yet greater apostle. Here he founded a Christian Church, and converted to the true faith "that bloody, savage, and barbarous people the Pights." Here a long line of saints and bishops, from Adrian to Arthur Ross, lived and died, and were buried in sumptuous tombs which those humble shepherds took care to build for themselves. Here, on a barren promontory, rose an exquisite shrine (300 years they took to raise it), whose burnished copper roof, when struck by the beams of the sun, was seen miles off by the hardy mariners of France and Flanders who ploughed the northern seas. Here grey friars and black friars grew fat and sleek upon the prudent piety of Scottish kings—here high-born and high-bred cardinals and legates kept princely state—here beautiful and subtle French Maries landed and feasted—here martyrs suffered, and their foes followed swiftly.

It could hardly happen that such a history could transact itself, even upon a storm-beaten headland, without leaving some trace behind it. The iconoclasts, indeed, were active and bitter enemies; "the proveist, the magistrates, and the commonalty," as the great reformer has it, "did agree to remove all monuments of idolatry, *quhilk also they did with expeditione*"; but the idolaters had built with such a cunning hand, and with such strength of arm, that even to-day the fragments of their work remain—noble massive towers, windows of exquisite design, sculptured gateways, ivy-grown walls, cloistered walks, a bishop's sepulchre fretted and chased and finished like a Genevese bracelet. The demolition of this noble edifice is graphically described by the late Professor

The Links of St. Rule

Tennent in his *Papistry Storm'd, or the Dingin' Down o' the Cathedral*—

> I sing the steir, strabush, and strife,
> Whan, bickerin' frae the towns o' Fife,
> Great bangs of bodies, thick and rife,
>   Gaed to Sanct Androis town,
> And, wi' John Calvin i' their heads,
> And hammers i' their hands, and spades,
> Enrag'd at idols, mass, and beads,
>   Dang the Cathedral down.

As you walk through the picturesquely irregular streets, you are constantly reminded that a story is attached to each nook and cranny of the place. The life of the castle alone, what a chequered and startling romance it dis-

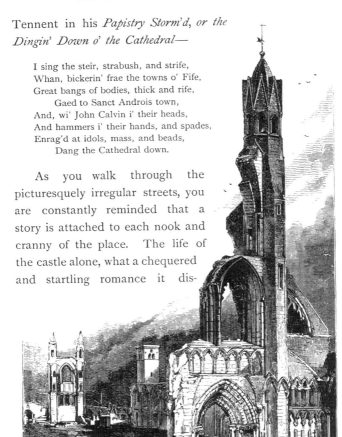

The Links of St. Rule

closes! From its dungeons the son of a king was taken away that he might die in a royal palace a slower and secreter death. In its courtyard the martyrs were condemned—from its battlements they attained,

> Thro' the brief minute's fierce annoy,
> To God's eternity of joy;

while "on rich cushions laid for their ease," high-bred and politic prelates witnessed the translation. There simple and learned men came, "with a glad heart and mind," to give their lives for what they considered the true gospel of Christ. "Some have falsely spoken," said the most gifted of the brethren, as he stood upon the scaffold beside the sea, "'that I should hold the opinion that the souls of men departed sleep after their death until the last day; but I know and believe the contrary, and am assured that my soul shall be this night with my Saviour in heaven.' This said, he bowed his knees, and having conceived a short but most pithy prayer, he was led to the stake, and then cried aloud, 'O Saviour of the world, have mercy upon me! Father in Heaven, I commend my spirit into Thy holy hands!' The executioner having kindled the fire, the powder that was fastened to his body blew up. The captain of the castle, who stood near him, perceiving that he was yet alive, bade him be of good courage, and commend his soul to God. 'This flame,' said he, 'hath scorched my body, yet hath it not daunted my spirit; but he who from yonder high place beholdeth us with such pride shall, within a few days, lie in the same spot as ignominiously as now he is seen proudly to rest himself'"—a prevision which the Cardinal may,

The Links of St. Rule

perhaps, have recalled when, a year afterwards, Norman Leslie dragged him from his bed.

But we must not linger longer among the tombs, for a bright and animated assemblage is gathered along the margin of the links, and the play is about to commence. The stalwart champions of the green have already "played a round." Twenty couples started two hours ago: eighteen of these have died like heroes, and gone to Hades; Drumwhalloch and a single antagonist remain to contest the honours of the day. As they buckle on their armour for the decisive encounter, let us look about at our friends, and try to initiate South-country readers into the mysteries of a noble and ancient pastime.

The "ring" is a gay but somewhat motley one. There are members of "the Royal and Ancient," splendid in martial red: professional players, club-makers, ball-makers, and *caddies;* and on the terrace in front of the club, such a cluster of bright faces and bright dresses, that it is plain the reigning *belles* of St. Rule are not unworthy of the *belles* who welcomed Mary of Guise. "But, when the queen came to her palace," the old chronicler observes, "and met with the king, she confessed unto him that she never saw in France, nor in no other country, so many good faces in so little room as she saw that day in Scotland: for, she said, it was shown to her in France that Scotland was but a barbarous country, destitute and void of all good commodities that used to be in other countries; but now, she confessed, she saw the contrary, for she never saw so many fair personages of men, women, young babes, and children, as she saw that day." It would not be fair to betray the incognito of that throng

The Links of St. Rule

of "sweet girl-graduates"; but you would never forgive me if I neglected to introduce you to this charming old lady—one of the finest specimens of the ancient Scottish gentlewoman. She is as neat, as natty, as daintily dressed (though the dress be made after another fashion), as her granddaughters; and her eyes, which have seen eighty summers, are nearly as bright as theirs, and disclose a fund of shrewd intelligence and sarcastic life. She belongs, in fact, to an earlier matronhood—a matronhood of vigorous actors and vigorous speakers—a matronhood which witnessed a good deal of hard living and hard drinking and hard swearing without being prudishly scandalised. I fear, indeed, that the good old soul is a bit of a heathen at heart. She feels, at least, and sometimes sharply expresses, an immense contempt for sons and grandsons (though she loves "the lads," too, in her way) who want to elevate the lower classes, and to teach them sobriety and continence—who do not swear like troopers, and who cannot take their claret like the men of her rosy youth. A relic of the old times, all the legends of that time cluster around her. She is the centrepiece of a host of stories with which, it may be, she is, as matter of fact, entirely unconnected. Thus her directness of speech and somewhat easy morals are illustrated by her reply to an evangelical matron who, when recommending a cook, assured her that the servant in question was a very decent woman. "Oh, d—n her decency! Can she make good collops?"

It is well-nigh twenty years to-day, my friend, since you and I last stood together on the green; and during the interval time and death have been hard at work. The lads who were our school-fellows are scattered over the face of

The Links of St. Rule

the earth—grave judges in India, wealthy Australian sheep-farmers, naval and military magnates at home and abroad—

> Some lie beneath the churchyard sod,
> And some before the Speaker.

Indian mutinies and Crimean campaigns thinned our ranks sadly—not a few of the brightest and kindliest of the set sleeping now outside the shattered walls of Delhi and Sebastopol. I am sure that not many of the survivors have read a touching passage in Mr. Kinglake's wonderful history unmoved, or without a very tender and wistful glance back into the past: "Then a small childlike youth ran forward before the throng carrying a colour. This was young Anstruther. He carried the Queen's colour of the Royal Welsh. Fresh from the games of English school-life, he ran fast, far heading all who strove to keep up with him; he gained the redoubt, and dug the butt end of the flagstaff into the parapet, and there for a moment he stood, holding it tight, and taking breath. There he was shot dead, but his small hand, still grasping the flagstaff, drew it down along with him, and the crimson silk lay covering the body with its folds: but only for a moment, because William Evans, a swift-footed soldier, ran forward, gathered up the flag, and raising it proudly, made claim to the Great Redoubt on behalf of the Royal Welsh."

Ah! well—*dulce et decorum est*—they sleep well who, with their feet to the foe, die for England; but stalwart men remain, and many of them are present upon the green to-day. But the professionals have suffered a loss that cannot be repaired. One mighty golfer is gathered to his

The Links of St. Rule

fathers. "Allan"—the hero of our boyhood—is dead. "Tom" is a famous player, and he merits his fame; but "Allan" had no peer, and he has no successor. Shall we, or our children, look upon his like again?

That narrow strip of barren sand and *bent* stretching for nearly three miles along the sea-shore (only the other day it was *under* the sea, they say), and lying between the city and the estuary of the Eden, forms the links, or downs, of St. Rule. The *course* on which the game is played, and which runs from end to end of the downs, is covered with a peculiarly soft and scrubby grass, interspersed with whins, sand-holes, etc. These *bunkers*, as they are called, constitute the hazards of the game. The holes are eighteen in number, and are placed at favourable points at unequal distances along the green—the shortest "hole" being about one hundred, and the longest about four hundred yards. The golfing-ground is under the *surveillance* of the Society of Golfers, and is strictly protected. Some years ago the Court of Session granted an interdict, at their instance, to prevent rabbits from burrowing on the green; but the mandate does not appear to have been respected by the parties against whom it was directed, as "rabbit-scrapes" are still the plague of the golfer. The links, in fact, have been frequently in the law-courts—more than once in the House of Lords.

And now Drumwhalloch and "the Captain" are ready to start. The foes are not unequally matched. The chief, indeed—a magnificent specimen of humanity—is double the weight of the other; but every player on the green knows well that this slim and wiry soldier is a tough antagonist, and that, at present, he is in first-rate condition and first-rate play.

The Links of St. Rule

They strike off—Drumwhalloch's ball mounting high into the sky, and descending gracefully on a green bank, within fifty feet of the burn: the Captain's, not so lofty, but quite as far and sure, a low and raking shot, which whistles through the air like the bullet from a Whitworth rifle. I should like much to describe to you, with a little, perhaps, of what Mr. Kinglake calls "the fire of Homer's battles," the varying fortunes of the field: but the patience of the most Job-like editor is not inexhaustible; and therefore I can only allow "Ned"— the *caddie* who accompanies and carries the chief's clubs —to relate briefly, in his own style, the issue of the contest:—

"Weel, you see, sir, they turned a' even—neck and neck. The first hole hame was halved—Drumwhalloch holin' a lang *putt*. The Captain wan the neist and the neist—twa holes to the good, and sax to play—lang odds. But the Laird was cool and keen, and he pit the heather hole in his pooch— the Captain comin' to grief amang the stiff whins on the brae. At the Hole across baith drove weel aff the *tee*, weel on to Elysium; but the Captain's second shot gaed slap into 'Hell'—which settled *him*. A' even again, and four to play —a teuch fecht—the Captain as white as death, and the Laird verra douce, but no canny to come across. Weel, the fourth hole was halved—never seed it played better—but the neist finished the match—the Captain hookit his ba' into the 'Principal's Nose,' and the Laird lay snug on the green at the *like*. After that the Captain never lookit up, and Drumwhalloch wan easy at the burn."

So Drumwhalloch returned radiant and triumphant, to be *fêted* and medalled, and made much of by Isabel and the rest

The Links of St. Rule

of the Naiads. And then, as the sun sank behind the hills, and the shade of the autumnal evening—

> Another kind of shade than when the night
> Shuts the woodside with all its whispers up,

gathered into the sky, and across the sea—we all went home, and—DINED. J. S.

GOLFIANA

OR NICETIES CONNECTED WITH THE GAME OF GOLF

DEDICATED, WITH RESPECT, TO THE

Members of all Golfing Clubs, and to those of St. Andrews and North Berwick in particular.

BY GEORGE FULLERTON CARNEGIE.

Printed privately in 1833.
Edinburgh: William Blackwood and Sons, 1842, small 8vo.

GEORGE FULLERTON CARNEGIE of Pitarrow, author of *Golfiana*, was born at the beginning of this century. His father having died early, he had a long minority, and consequent accumulation of fortune. At the time of his coming of age he was proprietor of Pitarrow, and of Charlton in Forfarshire (within two miles of the links of Montrose), affording, with accumulations, fully £5000 a year.

Carnegie no sooner came into possession than he commenced a gay and extravagant life. There was then living much in Edinburgh a very wild set of young men, who played high, hunted, kept racehorses, and so on. Of this set Carnegie became a well-known member. As an instance of their reckless, mad-like behaviour, is the story of a party of them one day dining, and sitting late at the Royal Hotel, Princes Street—the late Lord Glasgow, then Lord Kelburn, being one of them. They took offence

Golfiana

at one of the waiters, and by way of a gentle punishment pitched him out of the window into the area below. Some one of the house came into the room to tell them that the poor man was seriously injured ; the only answer he got was, " Put him in the Bill."

Carnegie in a very few years had his estates in the hands of his creditors, and was under trust. Before his reverse he married a daughter of Sir John Connell, and a characteristic story is told of his manner of proposing.

Carnegie was a remarkably clever man, and had a wide range of knowledge and exact information. He was of a poetic genius too, though not of the highest. His *Golfiana* made a sensation among golfers of the day, it hit off so humorously the characteristics of the men he introduced in it. He was of a slight make, and short in stature, and, *par excellence*, went by the name of "*Little* Carnegie." Notwithstanding, he was ambitious of the company of tall men, and was generally seen walking with Campbell of Saddell, Major M'Kenzie, Fraser (6 ft. 6 in.), and other comparative giants ; forming an amusing contrast. He was a capital shot, and possessed a gun of extreme length of barrel, which appeared as long as himself. Notwithstanding certain peculiarities, he was a thorough gentleman in manner ; and though small, a manly, hardy man ; he had no spare flesh, and his muscles were whipcord. He had a passion for golf (though never much of a player except as a putter), which continued to the last, playing at St. Andrews, Montrose, and Musselburgh. Though reduced to a comparatively small income, he enjoyed life to near the end, living much with his friends, Ross of Rossie, the late Lord Saltoun, and many others, by whom he was much appreciated. He was born in 1800, and died at Montrose in 1851.

GOLFIANA

ADDRESS TO ST. ANDREWS

St. Andrews! they say that thy glories are gone,
That thy streets are deserted, thy castles o'erthrown:
If thy glories *be* gone, they are only, methinks,
As it were, by enchantment, transferr'd to thy Links.
Though thy streets be not now, as of yore, full of prelates,
Of abbots and monks, and of hot-headed zealots,
Let none judge us rashly, or blame us as scoffers,
When we say that instead there are Links full of Golfers,
With more of good heart and good feeling among them
Than the abbots, the monks, and the zealots who sung them:
We have red coats and bonnets, we've putters and clubs;
The green has its bunkers, its hazards, and *rubs*;
At the long hole across we have biscuits and beer,
And the Hebes who sell it give zest to the cheer:
If this make not up for the pomp and the splendour
Of mitres, and murders, and mass—we'll surrender;
If Golfers and caddies be not better neighbours
Than abbots and soldiers, with crosses and sabres,
Let such fancies remain with the fool who so thinks,
While we toast old St Andrews, its Golfers and Links.

Golfiana

THE GOLFIAD

Arma virumque cano.—VIRGIL, *Æn.* i. l. 1.

BALLS, clubs, and men I sing, who first, methinks,
Made sport and bustle on North Berwick Links,
Brought coin and fashion, betting, and renown,
Champagne and claret, to a country town,
And lords and ladies, knights and squires to ground
Where washerwomen erst and snobs were found!

Had I the pow'rs of him who sung of Troy—
Gem of the learned, bore of every boy—
Or him, the bard of Rome, who, later, told
How great Æneas roam'd and fought of old—
I then might shake the gazing world like them:
For, who denies I have as grand a theme?
Time-honour'd Golf!—I heard it whisper'd once
That he who could not play was held a dunce
On old Olympus, when it teem'd with gods.
O rare!—but it's a lie—I'll bet the odds!
No doubt these Heathen gods, the very minute
They knew the game, would have delighted in it!
Wars, storms, and thunder—all would have been off!
Mars, Jove, and Neptune would have studied Golf,
And swiped—like Oliphant and Wood below—

The Golfiad

Smack over Hell[1] at one immortal go!
Had Mecca's Prophet known the noble game
Before he gave his paradise to fame,
He would have promis'd, in the land of light,
Golf all the day—and Houris all the night!
But this is speculation: we must come,
And work the subject rather nearer home;
Lest in attempting all too high to soar,
We fall, like Icarus, to rise no more.

The game is ancient—manly—and employs,
In its departments, women, men, and boys:
Men play the game, the boys the clubs convey,
And lovely woman gives the prize away,
When August brings the great, the medal day!
Nay, more: tho' some may doubt, and sneer, and scoff,
The female muse has sung the game of Golf,
And trac'd it down, with choicest skill and grace,
Thro' all its bearings, to the human race;
The tee, the start of youth—the game, our life—
The ball when fairly bunkered, man and wife.

Now, Muse, assist me while I strive to name
The varied skill and chances of the game.
Suppose we play a match: if all agree,
Let Clan and Saddell tackle Baird and me.
Reader, attend! and learn to play at Golf;
The lord of Saddell and myself strike off!
He strikes—he's in the ditch—this hole is ours;

---

[1] Hell—a range of broken ground on St. Andrews Links.

Golfiana

Bang goes my ball—it's bunker'd, by the pow'rs.
But better play succeeds, these blunders past,
And in six strokes the hole is halved at last.

O hole! tho' small, and scarcely to be seen,
Till we are close upon thee, on the green;
And tho' when seen, save Golfers, few can prize,
The value, the delight, that in thee lies;
Yet, without thee, our tools were useless all—
The club, the spoon, the putter, and the ball:
For all is done—each ball arranged on tee,
Each stroke directed—but to enter thee!
If—as each tree, and rock, and cave of old,
Had *its* presiding nymph, as we are told—
Thou hast *thy* nymph; I ask for nothing but
Her aid propitious when I come to putt.
Now for the second: And here Baird and Clan
In turn must prove which is the better man:
Sir David swipes sublime!—into the quarry!
Whiz goes the chief—a sneezer, by Old Harry!
"Now, lift the stones, but do not touch the ball,
The hole is lost if it but move at all:
Well play'd, my cock! you could not have done more;
'Tis bad, but still we may get home at four."
Now, near the hole Sir David plays the odds;
Clan plays the like, and wins it, by the gods!
"A most disgusting *steal;* well, come away,
They're one ahead, but we have four to play.
We'll win it yet, if I can cross the ditch:
They're over, smack! come, there's another *sich.*"

The Golfiad

Baird plays a trump—we hole at three—they stare,
And miss their putt—so now the match is square.

    And here, who knows but, as old Homer sung,
The scales of fight on Jove's own finger hung?
Here Clan and Saddell; there swing Baird and I,—
Our merits, that's to say: for half an eye
Could tell, if *bodies* in the scales were laid,
Which must descend, and which must rise ahead.

    If Jove were thus engaged, we did not see him,
But told our boys to clean the balls and tee 'em.
In this next hole the turf is most uneven;
We play like tailors—only in at seven,
And they at six; most miserable play!
But let them laugh who win.   Hear Saddell say,
"Now, by the piper who the pibroch played
Before old Moses, we are one ahead,
And only two to play—a special *coup!*
Three five-pound notes to one!"   "Done, sir, with you."
We start again; and in this dangerous hole
Full many a stroke is played with heart and soul:
"Give me the iron!" either party cries,
As in the quarry, track, or sand he lies.
We reach the green at last, at even strokes;
Some caddie chatters, *that* the chief provokes,
And makes him miss his putt; Baird holes the ball;
Thus, with but one to play, 'tis even all!
'Tis strange, and yet there cannot be a doubt,
That such a snob should put a chieftain out:

Golfiana

The noble lion, thus, in all his pride,
Stung by the gadfly, roars and starts aside;
Clan did *not* roar—*he* never makes a noise—
But said, "They're very troublesome, these boys."
His partner muttered something not so civil,
Particularly, "scoundrels"—"at the devil!"
Now Baird and Clan in turn strike off and play
Two strokes, the best that have been seen to-day.
His spoon next Saddell takes, and plays a trump—
Mine should have been as good but for a bump
That turn'd it off. Baird plays the odds—it's all
But in!—at five yards, good, Clan holes the ball!
My partner, self, and song—all three are done!
We lose the match, and all the bets thereon!
Perhaps you think that, tho' I'm not a winner,
My muse should stay and celebrate the dinner;
The ample joints that travel up the stair,
To grace the table spread by Mrs. Blair;
The wine, the ale, the toasts, the jokes, the songs,
And all that to such revelry belongs:—
It may not be! 'twere fearful falling off
To sing such trifles after singing Golf
In most majestic strain; let others dwell
On such, and rack their carnal brains to tell
A tale of sensuality!—Farewell!

First Hole at St. Andrews

THE FIRST HOLE AT ST. ANDREWS ON A CROWDED DAY

Forsan et hæc olim meminisse juvabit.—ÆN. i. l. 203.

'TIS morn! and man awakes, by sleep refresh'd,
To do whate'er he has to do with zest;
But at St. Andrews, where my scene is laid,
One only thought can enter every head;
The thought of golf, to wit—and that engages
Men of all sizes, tempers, ranks, and ages;
The root—the *primum mobile* of all,
The epidemic of the club and ball;
The work by day, the source of dreams by night,
The never-failing fountain of delight!
Here, Mr. Philp, club-maker, is as great
As Philip—as any minister of state!
And every caddie as profess'd a hero
As Captain Cook, or Wellington, or Nero!
For instance—Davie, oldest of the cads,
Who gives *half-one* to unsuspicious lads,
When he *might* give them *two*, or even *more*,
And win, perhaps, three matches out of four,
Is just as politic in *his* affairs
As Talleyrand or Metternich in *theirs*.
He has the statesman's elements, 'tis plain,
Cheat, flatter, humbug—*anything* for gain;
And, had he trod the world's wide field, methinks,
As long as he has trod St. Andrews Links,

Golfiana

He might have been prime minister, or priest,
My lord, or plain *Sir David* at the least.

   Now to the ground of golf my muse shall fly,
The various men assembled to descry,
Nine-tenths of whom, throughout the rolling year,
At the first hole *unfailingly* appear;
Where "How d'ye do?" "Fine Morning," "Rainy day,"
And "What's the match?" are preludes to the play.
So full the meeting, that I scarcely can,
In such a crowd, distinguish man from man.
We'll take them as they come:—He next the wall,
Outside, upon the right, is Mr. Small;
And well he plays, though, rising on his toes,
Whiz round his head his *supple* club he throws.
There, Doctor Moodie, turtle-like, displays
His well-filled paunch, and swipes beyond all praise,
While Cuttlehill, of slang and chatter chief,
Provokes the bile of Captain George Moncrieffe.
See Colonel Playfair, shaped in form *rotund*,
Parade the unrivall'd Falstaff of the ground;
He laughs and jokes, plays "what you like," and yet
You'll rarely find him make a foolish bet.
Against the sky, displayed in high relief,
I see the figure of Clanranald's Chief,
Dress'd most correctly in the *fancy* style,
Well-whisker'd face, and radiant with a smile;
He bows, shakes hands, and has a word for all—
So did Beau Nash, as master of the ball!
Near him is Saddell, dress'd in blue coat plain,

First Hole at St. Andrews

With lots of Gourlays, free from spot or stain;
He whirls his club to catch the proper *swing*,
And freely bets round all the scarlet ring;
And swears by *Ammon*, he'll engage to drive
As long a ball as any man alive!
That's Major Playfair, man of nerve unshaken,
He knows a thing or two, or I'm mistaken;
And, when he's press'd, can play a tearing game,
He works for *certainty* and not for *Fame!*
There's none—I'll back the assertion with a wager—
Can play the *heavy iron* like the Major.
Next him is Craigie Halkett, one who can
Swipe out, for distance, against any man;
But in what *course* the ball so struck may go,
No looker on—not he himself—can know.
See Major Holcroft, he's a steady hand,
Among the best of all the golfing band;
He plays a winning game in every part,
But near the hole displays the greatest art.
There young Patullo stands, and he, methinks,
Can drive the longest ball upon the Links;
And well he plays the spoon and iron, but
He fails a *little* when he comes to *putt*.
Near Captain Cheape, a sailor by profession
(But not so good at golf as navigation),
Is Mr. Peter Glass, who once could play
A better game than he can do to-day.
We cannot last for ever! and the *gout*,
Confirmed, is wondrous apt to put us out.
There, to the left, I see Mount-Melville stand

Golfiana

Erect, his *driving putter* in his hand;
It is a club he cannot leave behind,
It works the balls so well against the wind.
Sir David Erskine has come into play,
He has not won the medal *yet*, but *may*.
Dost love the greatest laugher of the lot?
Then play a round with little Mr. Scott;
He is a merry cock, and seems to me
To win or lose with equal ecstasy.
Here's Mr. Messieux, he's a noble player,
But something *nervous*—that's a bad affair;
It sadly spoils his putting, when he's *press'd*—
But let him *win*, and he will beat the *best*.
That little man that's seated on the ground
In red, must be Carnegie, I'll be bound!
A most conceited dog, not slow to *go it*
At golf, or anything—a *sort* of poet;
He talks to Wood,—John Wood,—who ranks among
The tip-top hands that to the Club belong;
And Oliphant, the rival of the last,
Whose play, at times, can scarcely be surpass'd.
Who's he that's just arrived?—I know him well;
It is the Cupar Provost, John Dalzell:
When he *does* hit the ball, he swipes like blazes—
It is but *seldom*, and *himself* amazes;
But, when he winds his horn, and leads the chase,
The Laird of Lingo's in his proper place.
It has been *said* that, at the *break of day*,
His golf is better than his evening play:
That must be scandal; for I'm sure that none

First Hole at St. Andrews

Could think of golf before the rise of sun.
He now is talking to his lady's brother,
A man of politics, Sir Ralph Anstruther:
Were he but once in Parliament, methinks,
And working *there* as well as on the *Links*,
The boroughs, I'll be bound, would not repent them
That they had such a man to represent them:
There's *one thing* only, when he's *on the roll*,
He must not lose his *nerve*, as when he's near the hole.
Upon his right is Major Bob Anstruther;
Cobbet's *one* radical—and he's *another*.

    But when we meet, as here, to play at golf,
Whig, Radical, and Tory—all are off—
Off the contested politics I mean—
And fun and harmony illume the scene.
We make our matches from the love of playing,
Without one loathsome feeling but the *paying*.
And that is lessened by the thought, we *borrow*
Only to-day what we shall *win* to-morrow.
Then, here's prosperity to Golf! and long
May those who play be cheerful, fresh, and strong;
When *driving* ceases, may we still be able
To play the *shorts, putt*, and be comfortable!
And, to the latest, may we fondly cherish
The thoughts of Golf—so let St. Andrews flourish!

Golfiana

ANOTHER PEEP AT THE LINKS

*Alter erit tum Tiphys, et altera quæ vehat Argo
Dilectos heroas—erunt etiam altera bella.*
       VIRG. *Ecl.* iv. 34-5.

AWAKE, my slumb'ring Muse, and plume thy wing,
Our former theme—the Game of Golf—to sing!
For, since the subject last inspired my pen,
Ten years have glided by, or nearly ten.
Still the old hands at golf delight to play—
Still new succeed them as they pass away;
Still ginger-beer and parliament are seen
Serv'd out by Houris to the peopled green;
And still the royal game maintains its place,
And will maintain it through each rising race.

 Still Major Playfair shines, a star at golf;
And still the Colonel—though a *little* off:
The former, skill'd in many a curious art,
As chemist, mechanist, can play his part,
And understands, besides the pow'r of swiping,
Electro-Talbot and Daguerreotyping.
Still Colonel Holcroft steady walks the grass,
And still his putting nothing can surpass—
And still he drives, unless the weather's rough,
Not quite so far as *once*, but far enough.

 Still Saddell walks, superb, improved in play,
Though his blue jacket now is turn'd to gray;

Another Peep at the Links

Still are his balls as rife and clean as wont—
Still swears by Ammon, and still bets the *blunt*—
Still plays all matches—still is often beat—
And still, in iced punch, drowns each fresh defeat.

Still on the green Clanranald's chief appears,
As gay as ever, as untouch'd by years;
He laughs at Time, and Time, perhaps through whim,
Respects his nonchalance, and laughs at him;
Just fans him with his wings, but spares his head,
As loth to lose a subject so well bred.

Sir Ralph returns—he has been absent long—
No less renown'd in golfing than in song;
With continental learning richly stored,
Teutonic Bards translated and explored;
A *Literaire*—a German scholar now,
With all *Griselda's* honours on his brow!

The Links have still the pleasure to behold
Messieux, complete in matches as of old;
He, modest, tells you that his day's gone by,
If any think it *is so*—let them try!
Still portly William Wood is to be seen,
As good as ever on the velvet green,
The same unfailing trump; but John, methinks,
Has taken to the *Turf*, and shies the Links.

Whether the *Leger* and the *Derby* pay
As well as *Hope Grant*, I can scarcely say;

Golfiana

But let that be—'tis better, John, old fellow,
To pluck the *rooks*, than *rook* the *violoncello*.

Permit me just a moment to digress—
Friendship would chide me should I venture less—
The poor Chinese, there cannot be a doubt,
Will shortly be demolish'd out and out;
But—O how blest beyond the common line
Of conquer'd nations by the Power divine!—
Saltoun to cut their yellow throats, and then
Hope Grant to play their requiem notes.—Amen.

Still George Moncrieffe appears the crowd before,
Lieutenant-Colonel—Captain now no more;
Improv'd in ev'rything—in looks and life,
And, more than all, the husband of a wife!

As in the olden time, see Craigie Halkett—
Wild strokes and swiping, jest, and fun, and racket;
He leaves us now. But, in three years, I trust,
He will return, and sport his *muzzle dust*,
Play golf again, and patronise all cheer,
From noble *Claret* down to *Bitter Beer*.

Mount-Melville still erect as ever stands,
And plies his club with energetic hands,
Plays short and steady, often is a winner—
A better Captain never graced a dinner.

But where is *Oliphant*, that artist grand?
He scarce appears among the golfing band.

Another Peep at the Links

No doubt he's married; but, when that befalls,
Is there an end to putters, clubs, and balls?
Not so, methinks : *Sir David Baird* can play
With any golfer of the present day ;
The *Laird of Lingo*, Major Bob Anstruther—
Both married, and the one as good's the other.

Dalgleish and Haig, two better men to play
You scarce will meet upon a summer's day ;
Alike correct, whatever may befall,
Swipe, iron, putter, quarter-stroke, and all.

Old Robert Lindsay plays a decent game,
Tho' not a golfer of *enormous* fame.
Well can he fish with minnow as with fly,
Paint, and play *farthing-brag* uncommonly,
Give jolly dinners, justice courts attend,
A good companion, and a steady friend.

But *Cuttlehill*, that wonderful *buffoon*,
We meet him now no more, as wont, at noon ;
No more along the green his jokes are heard,
And some who *dared* not *then*, now take the word.
Farewell ! facetious Jem—too surely gone—
A loss to us—*Joe Miller* to *Boulogne*.

Poor Peter Glass, a worthy soul and *blue*,
Has paid the debt of nature—'tis too true !
Long did his candle flicker with the gout—
One puff, a little stronger, *blew it out*.

Golfiana

And good Patullo! he who drove as none,
Since him, have driven—he is also gone!
And Captain Cheape—who does not mourn the day
That snatch'd so good, so kind a friend away?
One more I name—and only one—but he
Was older far, and lower in degree—
Great Davie Robertson, the eldest cad,
In whom the good was stronger than the bad;
He sleeps in death! and with him sleeps a skill
Which Davie, statesmanlike, could wield at will!
Sound be his slumbers! yet, if he should wake
In worlds where golf is play'd, himself he'd shake,
And look about, and tell each young beginner,
"I'll gie half-ane—nae mair, as I'm a sinner."
He leaves a son, and Allan is his name,
In golfing far beyond his father's fame;
Tho' in diplomacy, I shrewdly guess,
His skill's inferior, and his fame is less.

Now for the *mushrooms*—old, perchance, or new,
But whom my former strain did not review:
I'll name an *old one*, Paton, Tom of Perth,
Short, stout, grey-headed, but of sterling worth;
A golfer perfect—something it may be
The worse for *wear*, but few so true as he;
Good-humour'd when behind as when ahead,
And drinks like blazes till he goes to bed.
His friend is Peddie, not an awful swiper,
But, at the putting, he's a very *viper*;
Give him a man to drive him through the green,

Another Peep at the Links

And he'll be bad to beat, it will be seen—
Paton and Peddie—Peddie and Paton,
Are just the people one should bet upon.

There Keith with Andrew Wauchope works away,
And most respectable the game they play;
The Navy Captain's steadiness and age
Give him, perhaps, the *pull*—but I'll engage,
Ere some few months, or rather weeks, are fled,
Youth and activity will take the lead.

See Gilmour next—and he can drive a ball
As far as any man among them all;
In ev'ry hunting field can lead the van,
And is throughout a perfect gentleman.

Next comes a handsome man, with Roman nose
And whiskers dark—Wolfe Murray, I suppose—
He has begun but lately, still he plays
A fairish game, and therefore merits praise;
Ask him when at his *worst*, and he will say,
"'Tis bad—but, Lord! how I play'd *yesterday!*"

Another man, with whiskers—stout and strong—
A golfer too, who swipes his balls along,
And well he putts, but I should simply say,
His *own opinion's* better than his play;
Dundas can sing a song, or glee, or catch,
I think, far better than he makes a match.

Golfiana

But who is he, whose hairy lips betray
Hussar or Lancer? Muse, oh kindly say!
'Tis Captain Feilden.   Lord, how hard he hits!
'Tis strange he does not knock the ball to bits!
Sometimes he hits it fair, and makes a stroke
Whose distance Saddell's [1] envy might provoke.
But take his *common* play; the worst that ever
Play'd golf might give him *one*, and beat him clever.
Bad tho' he be, the Captain has done more
Than ever man who play'd at golf before.
One thund'ring ball he drove—'twas in despair—
Wide of the hole indeed, but kill'd a *hare!*

Ah! Captain Campbell, old Schiehallion, see!
Most have play'd longer, few so well as he.

[1] Campbell of Glensaddell was a sort of Magnus Apollo with the fashionables of his day. He was a great sporting man, and though a heavy weight rode remarkably well to hounds. He went in a balloon from Heriot's Hospital to Fife, when such a thing was considered a bold feat. He became exceedingly fond of golf, and after his marriage (to a M'Leod of M'Leod) gave up hunting for the sake of it, and settled at St. Andrews. He was a noble-looking man, pompous in his manners, and very irascible. Some good things are told of him. One day playing golf with Captain Campbell (Schiehallion), a well-known golfer, he was getting beat, which did not improve his temper. At the Eden hole, coming home, Schiehallion, in teeing his ball to play off first, put off an unreasonable length of time—he changed his tee several times, pulled up bits of grass to smooth the spot (Saddell fuming), and at length stood to his ball; but in place of making a good stroke, he hit under the ball and it rose high in the air and fell not many yards on. Saddell could control himself no longer, but in his deep voice and grandiloquent style, exclaimed, "He takes more time to tee his ball than any three men, pulls up as much grass as would summer a hunter, and after all he ends in an abortive puff." On one occasion Saddell playing near the hole was much too strong, and his ball was moving slowly towards the bunker on the other side. He was very fearful and very angry; but when he heard the caddie of his opponent in a whisper to the ball saying "hist, hist, hist," he called out in a fury, "By the bones of my ancestors (his usual oath), no man shall hiss my ball."

Another Peep at the Links

A sterling Highlander—and that's no trifle;
So thinks the *Gael*—a workman with a rifle;
Keeps open house—a very proper thing—
And, tho' rheumatic, *fiddles* like a king!

Sir Thomas of Moncrieffe—I cannot doubt
But he will be a golfer out and out;
Tho' now, perhaps, he's off, and careless too—
His misses numerous, his hits are few;
But he is zealous; and the time will be
When few will better play the game than he.
Balbirnie and Makgill will both be good—
Strong, active, lathy fellows; so they should.

But for John Grant, a clever fellow too,
I really fear that golf will never do!
'Tis strange, indeed; for he can paint, and ride,
And hunt the hounds, and many a thing beside;
Amuse his friends with anecdote and fun;
But when he takes his club in hand, he's *done!*
Stay! I retract!—Since writing the above,
I've seen him play a better game, by Jove;
So much beyond what one could have believ'd,
That I confess myself for once deceived;
And, *if* he can go on the season through,
There's still a *chance* that he may really *do*.

I've kept a man in *petto*, for the last—
Not an old golfer, but by few surpassed—
Great Captain Fairlie! When he drives a ball—
One of his *best*—for he don't hit them *all*,

Golfiana

It then requires no common stretch of sight
To watch its progress, and to see it light.

    One moment—I've another to define,
A famous sportsman, and a judge of wine—
Whom faithful Mem'ry offers to my view:
He made the game a study, it is true,
Still many play as well—but, for *position*,
John Buckle fairly beggars competition!

    And now farewell! I am the worse for wear—
Grey is my jacket, growing grey my hair!
And, though my play is pretty much the same,
Mine is, at best, a despicable game.
But still I like it—still delight to sing
Clubs, players, caddies, balls, and everything.
But all that's bright must fade! and we who play,
Like those before us, soon must pass away;
Yet it requires no prophet's skill to trace
The royal game thro' each succeeding race;
While on the tide of generations flows,
It still shall bloom, a never-fading rose;
And still St. Andrews Links, with flags unfurl'd,
Shall peerless reign, and challenge all the world!

THE GOLFER AT HOME[1]

HE following observations and reflections are not written either in praise or explanation of the game of golf. Golf, like cricket, is, as a game, beyond all praise, and none admit its merits more than a really good converted cricketer. It would be insulting, moreover, to the reader to inflict upon him a minute description of the game; if he is a Scotchman, he is probably personally acquainted with it; if he is an Englishman, he knows enough about it from description, or perhaps from having seen it played, not to consider it merely a savage kind of Scotch hocky, in which the players pursue a ball at full speed, the principal object in view being to break each other's shins, and do as much damage as may

---

[1] From *The Cornhill Magazine*, vol. xv. April 1867.

The Golfer at Home

be to their persons, and to their dress, if they happen to have any.

Let us rather note the more peculiar features of the game, and the effect which it has for the time being upon the characters, or rather upon the tempers, of its votaries. Let us inspect the golfer in his golfing home, invade the privacy of his temple, and lay bare the secrets of his eager yet calculating heart. To catch him thoroughly unawares, and too much rapt up in his game to fancy that he is observed, we must seek him in some place consecrated to golf. There is only one place that answers that description, the little town of St. Andrews, in Fife, in which let us imagine ourselves established. Here we breathe an atmosphere of pure golf; in which no living thing that does not play golf, or talk golf, or think golf, or at least thoroughly knock under to golf, can live.

Occasionally some darkened man, to whom the game is unknown, comes here. If he is a distinguished stranger, pains are usually taken to enlighten him; the points of the game are explained to him, and for a day, or may be two or three days, he is looked upon with that interest with which proselytes are usually regarded. But very very soon, unless he really takes to the game, and plays it decently, he sinks out of notice entirely, or is at best regarded with considerable dread, by the very people who have taken such pains to instruct him, lest perchance he should ask them to play with him, and so waste their valuable time and spoil their matches and their tempers. If he is not a distinguished stranger he is of course tabooed at once, and handed over to croquet and the ladies, if they will have him.

The Golfer at Home

When the golfing day is done, and one would fancy he might at length be allowed an innings, he does not find himself much better off; he hears nothing but golf talked at dinner, and the other gentlemen present discuss, stroke by stroke, the matches they have been playing that day. Even if he grovels to them, and affects an interest in the game, he does not find himself listened to, as the company would much rather talk over their own games than listen to any remarks, however theoretically correct, which he may make.

There is a very comfortable little club at St. Andrews, which, like all the other institutions of the town, is subservient to golf. It stands at the end of the links, or downs, upon which the game is played, and from the windows, with a good opera glass, you can rake the first part of the course, and judge from the features and gestures of the players returning, whether they are losing or winning. The parlour of this club will shortly form the scene of some of our observations.

Its members come from all quarters. There is a university at St. Andrews, and not only its students, but also its professors, almost without exception, are keen if not effective players. St. Andrews is a watering place; of the visitors who frequent it, some come with the avowed intention of doing nothing but play golf, while others basely represent to their wives and families that they come for the sake of bracing air and sea bathing. Once, however, let a monster of the latter class safely establish himself, he shakes off all domestic cares, and struts down to the club, in which, from that moment, he is practically lost to his family. If his house lies near the links, he *may* return to lunch, but if

The Golfer at Home

he does, he brings home some other golfer, madder than himself, and the two, when they are not eating, are discussing with more or less acrimony the events of the morning. He pursues the same course at dinner; so it may be imagined how extremely interesting golf as a subject soon becomes to all his relations. If he has children, he propagates the evil by putting into the hands of his boys at an early age the deadly weapons of his craft, which they use indiscriminately on the green and in the drawing-room; this entails a large glazier's account, not to mention considerable bodily risk, to visitors in particular, and the public in general. As for his wife, she must amuse herself as best she can; she cannot even accompany him in his game as a spectator, the presence of ladies being by no means regarded with favour, as we shall see.

Besides the family men, who come for the season, many bachelors come in parties of four or eight, and stay for a week or so; they play golf by day, and whist by night, and very good fun it is for a short time. The air is delightfully keen, and the short intervals left by golf and whist are agreeably filled by eating and drinking voraciously, and sleeping profoundly. In addition to its own attractions, there is no better preparation for the moors than golf. It hardens the muscles, both of arms and legs; and the sportsman who can take his three rounds of St. Andrews links without feeling the worse for it, need not be afraid of knocking up about two o'clock on the 12th of August.

We shall select the first week of August for our inspection, when the regular summer visitors have arrived and the sportsmen not yet departed for the moors. About the 12th

The Golfer at Home

the place will look much thinned, those who have shootings having gone to them, and those who have not being carefully lost to sight for a week, so that their friends may put the most flattering construction upon their absence. It is a strange fact that a man does not like to admit that he is not going to shoot on the 12th. If you put it directly to him, he of course does not assert that he is going to shoot if he is not; but he always qualifies his answer by an explanation that for this year he must wait till the 15th, to his great annoyance and regret, owing to some unforeseen accident, domestic affliction in his host's family, or some such unanswerable reason. This is a degree better than being told by a straightforward friend that poor devils like you and him cannot expect to get grouse-shooting every year.

The golfer, having finished a large and late breakfast, lights a cigar, and turns his steps towards the links and the club; so far there is nothing unusual in his proceedings. Presently he is joined by another, and then another golfer, and about eleven o'clock little knots form in front of the club and in the parlour, and the process of match-making begins. There is only one thing more difficult than getting a good match, and that is, avoiding a bad one. A man must be firm, and sometimes slightly unscrupulous, if he would be spared a match which will make him miserable for the day; for if he once begins a match he is bound in honour to play it all day, and he cannot better his condition. It is therefore a necessary though painful duty to himself always to be engaged till he falls in with a match which he thinks he can play with comfort and amusement. The most handsome and gentlemanly apologies from a bad partner afford no

The Golfer at Home

reparation for a lost day. It is of no use his trying to beguile the time, and soothe your wounded feelings by pleasant remarks and occasional jokes, if you are obliged to spend the day with your heavy iron in your hand, to enable you to dig him out of every sand-hole he puts his and your ball into. It is no substantial consolation to abuse him and his play heartily, as of course you will do, whenever you escape from him. The day has been lost, and probably both temper and money too. Be warned in time, and never, except in peculiar circumstances, be so entrapped. This may seem hard advice, but no one knows till he tries what a painful thing an unequal and uncongenial alliance in golf, as in matrimony, is.

Probably thoughts like these are foremost in the minds of the gentlemen, old and young, whom we see congregating in the parlour. They walk round and round each other with that guarded and cautious air with which a dog receives a stranger canine brother. Some, owing to their superiority, are comparatively safe from solicitations, except from equals; and having probably arranged their matches over night, are finishing their cigars in luxurious ease. But even they are not always safe, as the game is sometimes played in foursomes, as rackets and billiards are. Now there is nothing a certain class of players like better than to get a good powerful driver to help them through the heavy part of the work; while they (they flatter themselves) recompense him by the deadly accuracy with which they approach the hole, and "hole out," as it is called. Every man has, or fancies he has, a distinctive game. There is the "long driver," who hits as far in two strokes as a "short driver" does in three;

The Golfer at Home

but then, says the latter, "he (the long driver) is very wild and unsteady, and not to be depended upon when he gets near the hole." It is amusing to hear the "short driver" applying balm to his soul, as he always does, with a view apparently of deceiving himself into the belief that "short driving" is *better* than "long driving." "Very few holes can be driven in two, and my three shots are quite as good as his; he has two long drives and a short stroke, while I have three moderate 'drives,' and get quite as far, and probably a good deal straighter, as if there is any wind he cannot keep the line." Again, "one good 'putt' is equal to two drives"; or, "the short game is the thing that tells." With such reflections and aphorisms he endeavours to console himself; but all the time there is nothing that annoys him more than being "out driven." Now, if two "short drivers" can get a "long driver" apiece, they are quite happy; they are helped through what is to them the most laborious part of the game, and at the same time have a sort of feeling that they are doing it themselves; and if they have any doubts about this, they have none as to who really wins the game, by his masterly approach to the hole and his deadly "putting." The "long driver" does not always overhear a very flattering account given of him by his "short" colleague; he may perchance hear him telling a friend in confidence that it was all he (the short one) could do to keep him (the long one) straight, and so forth. But it cannot be denied that there are advantages to be derived by the "long driver" from such an alliance, especially if, as is sometimes the case, he is not a good "putter."

Well, the adjustment of "long drivers" and "short drivers"

The Golfer at Home

goes steadily on, and as a rule we may take it for granted that nobody engages himself for a match which he *very* much dislikes. But all is not done when you have got a match which you don't dislike. Perhaps you find three men who, with yourself, will make a good foursome; there remains the question of adjustment, and this is an important one, and betrays what may be considered by a thoughtless looker-on a somewhat depraved side of the golfer's character. Each man wants the best partner, and very naturally; but while each man wants the best partner, each man does not like to admit that he is the worst player, and this gives rise to a slight mental struggle. If a man underrates his play, he may perhaps get a good partner, and win his match, but he wounds his self-conceit; if he overrates it, he loses his match, and makes an enemy of his partner for life: N.B., certain and immediate exposure follows overrating. But, whether it be considered to the credit of golfers, or otherwise, they, as a rule, prefer to overrate their play; and this shows spirit and a certain amount of foresight. The fact is, there are pitfalls on every side, and on the whole the exposure consequent upon overrating is to be preferred. However genuine the modesty may be which leads you to underrate your play, you will not get credit for it from your opponents; if you do so from any other motive, you will not have many chances of doing it again, and serve you right. Still it is mere wantonness to take the worst partner, without being obliged to do so; it shows arrogance and self-sufficiency, and is never supposed to be done from charitable motives. Thus the best feelings of our nature, while they forbid us wilfully to underrate our play, equally forbid us vauntingly to take unto our-

The Golfer at Home

selves inferior partners, unless such burdens are unavoidably thrust upon us.

It is rather dull looking on at this match-making, so we had better take a turn round the links with one of the parties which is just setting out. Instruction and amusement alike may perhaps be derived from it. Colonel Burnett (long driver) and Mr. Greenhill (short driver) play Mr. George Browne (long and wild driver) and Mr. Tom Gurney (medium driver and desperate putter).

A difficulty arises at the very outset. The Colonel resents, though he does not openly object, to Mr. Browne being accompanied by "his women," as the Colonel ungallantly terms Mrs. Browne and her sister Miss Wilkinson. "The links," says the Colonel to his partner, "is not the place for women; they talk incessantly, they never stand still, and if they do, the wind won't allow their dresses to stand still." If the Colonel would admit it, it is not the talking, or the moving, or the fluttering, that interferes with his game, so much as a certain nervousness, inevitable to gallant natures like his, lest he should not appear to the greatest advantage in the presence of ladies. The discomfort experienced by him is not singular. Mr. Tom Gurney, Browne's partner, is also somewhat uneasy; he is not unknown to Miss Wilkinson, he hopes not unfavourably known, and yet he is doomed to appear before her in somewhat scanty garments. The weather being very hot, he has dispensed with waistcoat, collar, and tie, and has endued himself in an alpaca jacket, which, though admirably adapted to the free use of the arms, is more becoming, as far as appearances go, to boys and monkeys than to grown men—especially men desirous of creating a favourable impression

The Golfer at Home

upon the fair sex. Add to this, he knows that if his side loses, the blame will be laid by Browne's female relations upon him, not Browne. They wait their turn at the beginning of the course, and off they go—Greenhill and Gurney striking.

The course is in the shape of a pot-hook, and consists of eighteen holes—nine out to the end of the pot-hook, and nine back again. As we all know, the object of the game is to get from hole to hole in as few strokes as possible. In a "foursome" the partners play alternately, the "long driver" on the one side being pitted against the "long driver" on the other, and the "short" against the "short." Now two things are especially abhorred by the golfer while he is playing—the one is the human voice, the other is any movement of the human body, in his vicinity. The moment a man begins to "address" his ball, as it is called, he expects that, as a matter of course, everybody near him will become dumb and motionless; if they do not, he either refuses to play till they obey, or plays and lays the blame of any bungle he makes upon their heads. It depends, however, upon his position and temper what course he pursues. A man like Colonel Burnett, on hearing anybody near him talking, laughing, or moving, immediately grows hot about the ears, and walks away from his ball, intimating, at the same time, unmistakably to the offender that there will be no sport forthcoming till he desists, and probably adding, that if he does not mean to play the game, the party had better break up before they get too far. Gurney, on the other hand, will play his ball, but if any mishap befall it, will grumble in an audible and plaintive voice about the interruption, not to

The Golfer at Home

the offender, but to the man who carries his clubs, into whose sympathising ear he pours his sorrows; the length of time that the grumbling continues depending upon his success.

To return to our "foursome": everything goes on pretty smoothly till about the third hole, at which point Gurney has sufficiently recovered from the shock which Miss Wilkinson's presence gave him, to button his alpaca jacket about him, and address a remark to her, just as Colonel Burnett is adjusting his "putter" for the sixth and last time. Of course this gives rise to heated ears, and a walk away from the ball, which produces immediate silence on the part of Gurney, but not on the part of the ladies, who are unaware of the offence committed. Accordingly, just as the Colonel after a short walk returns to his ball, Miss Wilkinson answers Gurney's observation; so the Colonel misses his stroke, and much grumbling about the irregularity of females appearing on the links is imperfectly overheard. The ladies are still pleasingly unconscious of the Colonel's wrath, and instead of gracefully withdrawing, begin to take an interest in the game and ask Gurney questions about it, which he answers in a timorous and abrupt manner, justly dreading another outbreak on the part of his irascible opponent. Fortunately for him, that gentleman's attention is diverted by another painful incident, which occurs at the sixth hole.

Both parties have played an equal number of strokes from the fifth hole; the Colonel's partner has put his ball within a foot of the hole, and Gurney has played his to about a couple of yards from it. The Colonel and Browne have now respectively to play, and Browne being farthest from the

The Golfer at Home

hole plays first and goes in; the Colonel, thinking that his ball is so ridiculously near the hole that he will not be called upon to put it in, knocks it away with the back of his club and says "halved hole." But Browne promptly claims the hole, and tells the Colonel that if he wanted half he should have made sure of it by "holing out." This is done more in fun than earnest as the Colonel is known to be a great martinet. But a very dangerous joke it proves; the Colonel deeply resents it, and asks, "What is to become of all the good feeling of the game if a man takes such a dirty advantage as that? Whether Browne thinks that he (the Colonel) would not have holed that ball nine times out of ten?" and so on. However, peace is apparently restored, and the game goes on. At the ninth hole, to the great relief of some of the party at least, the ladies leave them, and make for the beach: Gurney unbuttons his jacket, and the Colonel breathes freely again. The game has been going pretty evenly, and Browne's side turns one hole ahead, an advantage, however, which very soon disappears. The wind having been at his back on the way out, Browne has driven steadily enough; but now the wind meets him, and a good deal of fancy driving ensues. If you hit a ball with what is called the heel of the club, a sort of screw is put upon it, which makes it twist away to the right; if with the toe of the club, it twists to the left. If there is a high wind it exaggerates these erratic tendencies, and the higher a man hits his ball, the more it is affected by the wind. Now Browne always hits his ball high, and usually hits it with either the heel or the toe of the club, with wonderful impartiality, instead of hitting it fairly with the centre, as he

The Golfer at Home

ought to do; the consequence is, that as the course at St. Andrews is too narrow to admit of much deviation from the straight line, Browne's ball is as often in the "bent" and whins which lie at either side of the course as on the course itself. Just as the party are coming round the curve of the "pot hook," Browne hits and heels a terrifically high ball, which is caught by the wind, and whirled miles into the whins. After a protracted search, behold the plaintive Gurney up to his knees in a whin, making frantic endeavours to catch a glimpse of his ball, which is hidden among the roots; suddenly we see the bush convulsed, small pieces of whin flying in every direction before the iron of the furious Gurney, and the ball emerges, not in the direction of the hole, but perpendicularly, and finally lands upon the player's shoulders. According to the stern rules of golf, the ball having touched him, *ipso facto*, the hole is lost. He emerges from the whin, with his legs still tingling and his left wrist slightly sprained, from having had to cut through a root, in order to get at the ball. The next hole is played in solemn silence; but in the course of the one succeeding, Browne varies his partner's entertainment by pulling his ball round with the toe of the club into the whins at the opposite side; another search, another ineffectual uprooting of a whin, and Gurney again emerges, but this time, wonderful to relate, with a comparatively cheerful countenance. He takes out his cigar-case, lights a cigar, and walks along contentedly smoking it, and apparently enjoying the scenery. This is a fatal sign. When a man smokes, he is either winning very easily or has given up all hopes of winning; when a man draws the attention of his companions to lights and shades,

The Golfer at Home

and the beauty of the scenery generally, it is tantamount to his saying, "As mere exercise this is a very pleasant and healthy occupation—plenty of fresh air, a charming day, and St. Andrews looks very well from here; but as to its being golf, to play with a fellow who puts you into a whin or a bunker every other stroke"————

That this is the state of Gurney's mind at present becomes more apparent by his playing his next stroke with one hand, of course losing the hole. Soon, however, he is roused from his apathy by the Colonel also getting into grief, and at the third hole from home makes the match all even by a wriggling, bolting ten yards "putt," which goes in like a rabbit. At the next hole an appalling instance of retributive justice is witnessed; the Colonel's vigilant wrath has merely smouldered for a while, and a fatal opportunity for its explosion presents itself. Browne, in preparing to putt a ball into the hole, and pressing his "putter" against it, moves the ball about half an inch, and follows it up by hitting it. Here the Colonel, with great calmness, claims the hole. "You struck your ball twice, sir. Mr. Gurney should have played. If we are to play the game strictly, that's my hole." Browne is so fairly caught, that he bursts into a laugh, and gracefully yields up the hole. This gives the Colonel's side a hole to the good, which they keep to the end, thus winning a closely contested match by one hole. As they walk towards the club for lunch, the Colonel puts his hand affectionately upon Browne's shoulder, and assures him that he would not have thought of claiming hole No. 16 if Browne had not been rather hard upon him at the sixth hole, and with the exception of a plaintive sigh from Gurney,

The Golfer at Home

as he pays his five-shilling bet to his opponent, all is peace and good-humour. And, notwithstanding the little exhibitions of temper which we have seen, golf is really a good-natured game. During a match some men may be rather over-keen, and from their very keenness lose their temper for the time, but they are the first to regain it when the occasion is past. Perhaps the secret of this is that it is such an invigorating, healthy game, that a man cannot foster ill-nature for such trivial matters as a hole won or lost; accordingly, winners and losers turn voraciously to their lunch.

But it must not be supposed that their game is lost sight of now. They find most of the players who preceded them at lunch, and everybody inquires after everybody else's game. If a man has won, he has of course no objection to say so, and does so curtly, as if it were a matter of certainty that he should win. If he has lost, he does not like to answer directly, unless he has an opportunity of also explaining how it happened. For instance, to watch our friends of the morning: as the Colonel is lighting a cigar, a friend asks how his match ended, and is answered by the monosyllable "won." Gurney is also inquired of, but as the Colonel is sitting at his elbow, finds it convenient to have his mouth full of cold beef at the moment. He, however, avails himself of a subsequent opportunity of putting the inquirer in full possession of the particulars of Browne's evil doings and irregularities and the Colonel's sharp practice. After three-quarters of an hour allowed for lunch and a cigar, the players again take the field, and continue their game till about half-past five. We need not follow them, having seen enough for the present of their manners and customs. We know how

The Golfer at Home

they will all march round and round, wrapt up in their own games; how they will growl and murmur if they are kept an instant waiting by the party in front, and how they will remonstrate indignantly, nay, even ferociously, if a ball from the party behind comes anywhere near them, while, at the same time, they will not scruple to touch up the party in front by sending a ball among them if they conveniently can; how each man will converse almost exclusively with the man who carries his clubs, from whom he will accept any amount of soft sawder and advice, now anxiously inquiring what part of the club he hit the last ball with, and now observing coyly "that ball went away well"; all this we have already seen, and one round may fairly be taken as a sample of the next.

It only remains to take a glance at the golfer when he regains his domestic circle. Having gained a noble appetite by his exertions, he is sufficiently recruited by a bath and dressing for dinner to discourse volubly about his game during that meal. He will probably have some golfing friends dining with him,—but we recommend the uninitiated to take the precaution of furnishing themselves with a manual of the game and a map of the course to enable them to follow intelligently the various addresses on the subject to which they will be compelled to listen, but in which they will not be permitted to take part. For their consolation, however, we may throw out the hint that if any gentleman is fond of female society he will have an uninterrupted innings at St. Andrews. During the hours of golf the young ladies are most shamefully neglected, owing to the conscription levied by the game, and would, no doubt, gladly receive deserters, or those who have not yet been enrolled.

The Golfer at Home

No close observer of the golfer has recorded whether any phenomena are to be observed in him during sleep; whether, like a dreaming greyhound, his limbs move in conformity with the occupations of the day. It is ascertained beyond question that he dreams about golf; dreams how he hit a ball which seemed as if it would never come down, and when it did, fell into the next hole a quarter of a mile away; dreams how he habitually holes out at thirty yards, and how neither "bunkers" nor whins can hold him. All this, and much more, he has been known to dream; but as yet no complaints have been lodged by indignant wives of blows received during the watches of the night from hands wielding imaginary golf clubs; so we must assume that he reclines peacefully, especially as if there existed cause of complaint on this score we should hear of it, the game being by no means regarded with favour by the ladies. Having followed him to his lair, let us bid the golfer good-night; and if any one is inclined to scoff at his untiring zeal and keenness about the game, let him suspend judgment till he too has been exposed to its fascinations. Doubtless after a month's experience, he in his turn will prove an interesting subject of inquiry, and will help to develop some undiscovered vein in the golfer's character.

H. J. M.

THE NINE HOLES OF THE LINKS OF ST. ANDREWS

The First or Bridge Hole
R. C.

SACRED to hope and promise is the spot—
  To Philp's and to the Union Parlour near,
  To every Golfer, every caddie dear—
Where we strike off—oh, ne'er to be forgot,
Although in lands most distant we sojourn.
  But not without its perils is the place;
  Mark the opposing caddie's sly grimace,

Links of St. Andrews

Whispering: "He's on the road!" "He's in the burn!"
   So is it often in the grander game
      Of life, when, eager, hoping for the palm,
Breathing of honour, joy, and love and fame,
      Conscious of nothing like a doubt or qualm,
We start, and cry: "Salute us, muse of fire!"
   And the first footstep lands us in the mire.

The Second or Cartgate Hole
R. C.

FEARFUL to Tyro is thy primal stroke,
   O Cartgate! for behold the bunker opes
      Right to the *teeing*-place its yawning chops,
Hope to engulf ere it is well awoke.
That passed, a Scylla in the form of rushes

The Nine Holes of the

Nods to Charybdis which in ruts appears:
He will be safe who in the middle steers;
One step aside, the ball destruction brushes.
Golf symbols thus again our painful life,
Dangers in front, and pitfalls on each hand:
But see, one glorious cleek-stroke from the sand
Sends Tyro home, and saves all further strife!
He's in at six—old Sandy views the lad
With new respect, remarking: "That's no bad!"

The Third Hole
R. C.

No rest in Golf—still perils in the path:
Here, playing a good ball, perhaps it goes
Gently into the *Principalian Nose*,
Or else *Tam's Coo*, which equally is death.

Links of St. Andrews

Perhaps the wind will catch it in mid-air,
    And take it to *the Whins*—" Look out, look out !
    Tom Morris, be, oh be, a faithful scout ! "
But Tom, though *links-eyed*, finds not anywhere.
Such thy mishaps, O Merit : feeble balls
    Meanwhile roll on, and lie upon the green ;
'Tis well, my friends, if you, when this befalls,
    Can spare yourselves the infamy of spleen.
It only shows the ancient proverb's force,
That you may further go and fare the worse.

The Fourth or Ginger-Beer Hole
P. P. A.

THOUGH thou hast lost this last unlucky hole,
    I prythee, friend, betake thee not to swearing,
    Or other form of speech too wildly daring,

The Nine Holes of the

Though some allege it tendeth to console.
Rather do thou thy swelling griefs control,
    Sagacious that at hand a joy awaits thee
    (Since out of doubt a glass of beer elates thee),
Without that frightful peril to thy soul.
A pot of beer! go dip thine angry beak in it,
    And straight its rage shall melt to soft placidity,
That solace finding thou art wise to seek in it;
    Ah! do not thou on that poor plea reject it,
That in thine inwards it may breed acidity—
One glass of Stewart's[1] brandy will correct it.

The Hell Hole
P. P. A.

WHAT daring genius first did name thee Hell?
    What high, poetic, awe-struck grand old Golfer?
    Misdeem him not, ye pious ones, a scoffer—
Whoe'er he was, the name befits thee well.
"All hope abandon, ye who enter here,"
    Is written awful o'er thy sandy jaws,
    Whose greedy threat may give the boldest pause,
And frequent from within come tones of fear—
Dread sound of cleeks, which ever smite in vain,[2]

---

[1] Stewart, the major-domo of the period, and predecessor of our hospitable friend Paterson, whose brandy is no worse, and has excellent medicinal virtues.

[2] The above seems a little out of date. Hell indeed still exists, but one's ancient awe of it is much mitigated. In the altered condition of the course nobody need go to it unless he likes, and even if the perversity of a drawn

Links of St. Andrews

And—for mere mortal patience is but scanty—
Shriekings thereafter, as of souls in pain,
    Dire gnashings of the teeth, and horrid curses,
    With which I need not decorate my verses,
Because, in fact, you'll find them all in Dante.

The Heather Hole

P. P. A.

AH me! prodigious woes do still environ—
    To quote *verbatim* from some grave old poet—
The man who needs must "meddle with his iron";
    And here, if ever, thou art doomed to know it.
For now behold thee, doubtless for thy sins,
    Tilling some bunker, as if on a lease of it,
    And so, assiduous to make due increase of it;
Or wandering homeless through a world of whins!
And when,—these perils past,—thou seemest *dead*,
    And hop'st a half—O woe! thy ball runs crooked,
Making thy foe just one more hole ahead,
    Surely a consummation all too sad,
Without that sneering devilish "Niver lookit,"
    The closing comment of the opposing cad.

---

ball takes you there, your damnation is by no means so dreadful as it used to be. Time and disuse have, in point of fact, done for this fine old hazard what the labours of the advanced theologians are understood to have done for the other one. Neither is now by any means the terror to evil-doers which I seem to remember it in my youth.

The Nine Holes of the

The High or Eden Hole
R. C. Jr.

The shelly pit is cleared at one fell blow,
    A stroke to be remembered in your dreams!
    But here the Eden on your vision gleams,
Lovely, but treach'rous in its solemn flow.
The hole is perched aloft, too near the tide,
    The green is small, and broken is the ground
    Which doth that little charmed space surround!
Go not too far, and go not to a side;
Take the short spoon to do your second stroke;
    Sandy entreats you will the wind take heed on,
For, oh, it would a very saint provoke,
    If you should let your ball plump in the Eden.
You do your best, but who can fate control?
So here against you is another hole.

Links of St. Andrews

The Short Hole

R. C. Jr.

BRIEF but not easy is the next adventure;
    Legend avers it has been done in *one*,
    Though such long *steals* are now but rarely done—
In *three* 'twere well that you the hole should enter.
Strangely original is this bit of ground,
    For, while at hand the smooth and smiling green,
    One bunker wide and bushy yawns between,
Where Tyro's gutta is too often found.
Nervous your rival strikes and heels his ball—
    From that whin-bush at six he'll scarce extract it:
    Yours, by no blunder this time counteracted,
Is with the grass-club lofted over all.
There goes a hole in your side—how you hug it!
Much as th' Australian digger does a nugget.

The End Hole

R. C. Jr.

THE end, but not the end—the distance-post
    That halves the game—a serious point to thee,
    For if one more thou losest, 'twill be *three:*
Yet even in that case, think not all is lost.
Men four behind have been, on the return,
    So favoured by Olympus, or by care,
    That all their terrors vanished into air,
And caddies cried them *dormy* at the burn!

Links of St. Andrews

I could quote proverbs, did I speak at random:
>Full many a broken ship comes into port,
>Full many a cause is gained at last resort,

But Golf impresses most, *Nil desperandum.*
Turn, then, my son, with two against, nor dread
To gain the winning-post with one ahead.

A Golf Song

AIR—"*The Maiden of Fifty-Three*"

THERE never was a game like the old Scottish game,
    That's play'd 'twixt the hole and the tee;
You may roam the world o'er, but the game at your door
    Is the very best game you'll see.

So I'll sing you a song, 'twill be hearty and not long,
    If kindly you'll listen to me,
Of tees, holes, and clubs—of hazards and of rubs—
    And whatever else in golf may be.

Of the tee, first of all—nor to*tum* nor to*tal*,
    Nor that o'er which old wives agree—
Of earth, clay, or sand, whatever is at hand,
    Come, quickly, and make us our tee.

We get tee from the caddie—not a box but a laddie—
    What though ragged and roguish he be,
The club's face he wipes, we go in for swipes,
    And off fly the balls from the tee.

A Golf Song

Away through the air, in parabolas so rare,
    The balls fly beautifulie;
But, O! woe betide! I've driven mine too wide,
    And now I'm in jeopardie.

And here let me pause while the Muse the moral draws:
    Of hopes that too highflying be,
That dare in the dark, and overshoot the mark,
    Golf teaches the penaltie.

In whins or in sand, in despair now I stand,
    And the cleek swing dubiouslie;
Who would be a funker! I'm clear of the bunker!
    And close to the hole, I see.

But all this time, in love with my rhyme,
    I've forgotten mine enemie;
Alike now we lie, but how nettled am I—
    The villain! he is dead, I see.

The putter in my hand, around me many stand,
    The end of the game to see;
I borrow, and I steal, my way I slowly feel—
    Hurrah! the first half for me!

"Halved hole," says the foe; but "No"—I say—"No;
    Putt it out, mine enemie!
You're dead, but not buried." He's shaky and flurried!
    O! a terrible miss makes he.

A Golf Song

And here I stop again, for the Muse I find is fain
    To do more moralitie;
"There's many a slip, but ne'er withdraw the lip,
    For nowhere is certaintie."

I wish that were true; but 'tis certain I and you
    With "short holes" won't well agree;
That soon, without a doubt, we'll all be holed out,
    And life's round finished shall be.

But still while we may, let us keep to the play,
    That our days in the land long may be;
For headache, cold, or cough, there is nothing like golf—
    So here's to it, three times three!

J. F. M‘L.

"Putt it out, mine enemie!"

"He was horsed amid the smiles of passengers and onlookers."

A Tale of Golf [1]

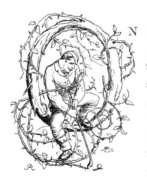

ON the morning of the 17th August 183—, two native golfers of the famous Dubbieside, in Fife, were seen resting on the brow of the links, and anxiously casting their eyes in the direction of Methill, as if expecting the smoking funnel of the ever-restless "St. George." Their coats of business were donned, their caps were drawn resolutely over their brows, and they examined with more than common care the knitting of their clubs, the insertion of the lead, and the indentation of the bone.

---

[1] From *Lectures, Sketches, etc.* By William Graham, LL.D. Edinburgh : Seton and Mackenzie, 1873.

A Tale of Golf

From their capacious pockets they turned out ball after ball with mysterious care,[1] and the names of the makers were interchanged with reverential whispers, as they peered into one or two of the most select. At their feet reclined their caddies, grasping each a complete establishment of clubs, and listening with deep respect to the conversation of their masters. At last a towering column of smoke announced that the steamer was at hand, while from the end of the bank the florry[2] boat was plying its way to receive the passengers for Leven. The sportsmen leaped to their feet as the passengers descended the side of the steamer, and an exclamation of "He's come!" burst from them as they saw a large package of clubs lowered down into the boat. They hastened to the sands to welcome the arrival of the stranger sportsman, who had been sent to dim the glory of Dubbieside; and there in the stern of the boat, with his arm encircling his instruments of play, did they behold the doughty champion, who was backed against the rustic players by some discomfited metropolitans, and who was destined to open the eyes of Dubbieside to its ignorance and vanity in assuming an equality with the clubs south of the Forth.

He was a short, stout-made, sandy-whiskered man; his spectacles not altogether concealing his ferretty eyes; his nose short, and ever ready to curl; and his lip compressing itself, as if it were bridling up under some slight or insult. He was the ideal of small pomposity, set off with a finical

---

[1] The balls were then made of leather, stuffed so full of feathers as to be at once hard and elastic.

[2] The boat which conveyed passengers ashore from the steamer at places where there was no pier, or when the tide would not allow the landing at the pier.

A Tale of Golf

attention to dress; rings clasped his little fat fingers, and a diamond pin shone in his puffy breast. He surveyed his new brothers on the shore with an air of loftiness, although he must have known them for his intended associates and opponents, and cast on the country round a vexed look, as if his friends had compromised his dignity by sending him to a place that appeared so questionable. His stateliness, however, gave way to rage and abuse, when he found that to get ashore he must mount on the back of one of the boatmen. This mode of landing is seldom resorted to now—to ladies it was a torturing thought to be obliged to submit to be carried like babies through the breakers by some staggering boatmen who resented their fidgety movements by muttered threats of committing them to the deep, or of pinching them unceremoniously. No less torture was felt by our indignant golfer, but there was no alternative. He was horsed amid the smiles of passengers and onlookers—his legs drawn up most ungracefully to save his boots from the brine, and his face, over the shoulder of his carrier, suggesting the appearance of the man of the moon in a state of excitement. Arrived at the shore, he was set down with little ceremony, when unluckily, his first contact with the county of Fife was a sudden seat on the cold wet sand. He was soon put on his legs by his brother sportsmen, whose mixed condolence and banter were ill-calculated to soothe his ruffled feelings; but with a tremendous effort the high pressure gentleman readjusted his spectacles, and did assume enough of calmness to look contempt on all around, and discharge an execration at the county of Fife and the disgraceful incommodiousness of its conveyances.

A Tale of Golf

The party now moved to the hole from which they were to strike off, the stranger receiving the proposal of a short pause at the public-house of the village with a look of horror. They were here joined by a number of second-rate golf men, and old lovers of the game who could yet, in despite of rheumatism, follow the rounds—besides a whole troop of ordinary villagers, inspired, if not with a love of golf, at least with an interest in the honour of Dubbieside. The stranger having undone his clubs, round which his red coat was tightly roped—having renounced his handsome green one with gilt anchor buttons, and relinquished it with a sigh, and a shrink of composure to his fate, to a Dubbieside caddie, whom he looked on as a second Caliban, addressed himself to the business of the day. He cast on the ground a "Gourlay," white as snow, hard as lead, and elastic as whalebone ; and the trembling caddie having, amid the whizz of a shower of novel oaths, teed it at last to his satisfaction, he seized a club which, like Cuttie Sark in Tam o' Shanter, was a "supple jaud and strong," and gave it a few preparatory vibrations—then assuming the honour of precedence, he addressed his body to his ball, raised his club, and came round with a determined sweep. The missile sped right into a sandy brae, which the generality of players clear with the first stroke ; but such a thing will occasionally happen with the best player. So little was thought of it, though the testy stranger glowed like a red herring ; and his humour was by no means restored when he saw his partners, after "licking their looves," make their balls fly like sky-rockets over the place where he was earthed. Away, however, the crowd moved—principals, caddies, amateurs, club-makers, weavers,

A Tale of Golf

and hecklers—the last class of gentlemen having at this time struck for an advance of wages, and being glad of anything about which to occupy themselves. The whole formed a ring round the stranger gentleman, who was now to dig his ball out of its firm lodgment of sand. The occasion, the company, the awkwardness of his position, and the consciousness of the want of sympathy in all around, contributed to heighten the angry feelings of the champion; so, darting a glance of fire at one of the hecklers, who remarked with tipsy gravity, and most offensive familiarity, in allusion to the hopeless situation of the ball, that it would require spectacles to find it out, he gave it such an ill-natured and ill-directed whack, that it sank completely into the regions of night. The hurras of the hecklers, the yells of the boys, the placid laughter of the paralytic old players, who shook upon their sticks, and the condolence of the rival players, which was given in all the offensiveness of Scotch diminutives, now nearly threw the mortified stranger into a fit of apoplexy. The ball, however, was declared not playable; and being dug out by the fingers of the caddie was thrown back on the green, at the loss of a stroke in counting to its owner. So, reconcentrating his energy, and assuming as much calmness as could be collected in a composition so formed, he aimed a well-directed stroke. Unfortunately, at the very instant, a prophetic groan or hem from one of the flax-tearing fraternity gave a wrong turn to the blow, and swept the ill-destined ball into a bunker or sand hole. Another cheer for Dubbieside was about to be raised, when the enraged stranger grappled with the obnoxious heckler, and lustily called for a constable. This produced a rush from his companions, who in an instant released him

A Tale of Golf

from the clutch of the indignant golfer, around whom the released heckler began dancing and sparring, with his jacket and paper cap doffed, demanding a ring and fair play. But the honour of the links being at stake, the Dubbieside players laid hands on the shoulders of the rioters, and awed them into civility; so, after a few grumblings, the Dubbieside men having taken their second strokes which sent their balls far into safe and beautiful ground, the troop once more moved on. The metropolitan champion was now to strike his fifth stroke, or three more, and the perspiration stood in beads on his brow when he came up and beheld his infatuated Gourlay sitting as if in an egg-cup of sand. The more civilised of the idlers felt something like sympathy, and a feeling of commiseration was beginning to steal over the multitude, when the caddie, having given the *cleek* instead of the *iron*, which the gentleman swore was the proper instrument, the said caddie was unceremoniously deposed with a cuff in the neck that sent him sprawling in the sand, and the clubs were at the same time wrenched from him by his irate master, who swore he would carry them himself. This event did not make the player more cool, or the spectators more indulgent; so when the ball was jerked from its position, it went slant over the bank to the firm bed of sand on the beach, when it rolled as on an iron floor till it cooled itself in the sea. The flaxmen, swinging arm-in-arm to the top of the bank, now burst out with a chorus of—

> The sea—the sea—the open sea,
> I am where I would ever be, etc.

This was too much. For a moment a sort of stupor seemed to fall on the devoted stranger; but an unearthly

A Tale of Golf

calmness and paleness succeeded, as he moved leisurely to the sea, picked up his ball, and put it into his pocket. He had observed the steamer on its return from Largo, and walking leisurely to the florry boat which was just going out, he arrived in time to secure his passage. His exit might have been dignified—for even the hecklers remarked that there was something "no cannie in his look" when he left the ground, and they did not even venture to cheer—but just as the boat was shoving off, a frenzied-looking woman, running along the beach, made signs for the boat to stop, and in an instant the mother of the dismissed caddie was in the boat demanding his pay, and reparation for the damage done to her bit laddie. The approach of the obnoxious hecklers to witness this new scene, operated more on the discomfited golfer than the woman's clamour—and a bonus, most disproportionate to the damage, was slipped into the horny fist of the outraged mother, who, suddenly lowering her tone, stood upon the beach his only friend. Yet could she not, as the boat moved off, prevent the flaxmen sending after him their chorus of "The sea, the sea," until he was seen to ascend the steamboat and suddenly disappear below.

Who or what he was remains a mystery; his backers never gave his name, or a hint of his profession. Some imagined him to be a principal Edinburgh clerk; others, a half-pay resident in Musselburgh; but who or what he really was, could not be discovered by the most curious inquirer.

The Links o' Innerleven

By William Graham, LL.D.

Sung at the Autumn Meeting of the Innerleven
Golfing Club, 1841

Wha wad be free from doctor's bills—
From trash o' powders and o' pills—
Will find a cure for a' his ills
    On the Links o' Innerleven.
For there, whar lassies bleach their claes,
And bairnies toddle doun the braes,
The merry Golfer daily plays
    On the Links o' Innerleven.

Sae hie ye to the Golfer's ha',
And there, arranged alang the wa',
O' presses ye will see a raw,
    At the Club o' Innerleven.
There from some friendly box ye'll draw
A club and second-handed ba',—
A Gourlay pill's the best o' a',
    For health at Innerleven.

And though the Golfer's sport be keen,
Yet oft upon the putting-green
He'll rest to gaze upon the scene
    That lies round Innerleven—
To trace the steamboat's crumpled way

The Links o' Innerleven

Through Largo's loch-like silvery bay,
Or to hear the hushing breakers play
    On the beach o' Innerleven.

When in the evening of my days,
I wish I could a cottage raise
Beneath the snugly-sheltering braes
    O'erhanging Innerleven.
There in the plot before the door
I'd raise my vegetable store,
Or tug for supper at the oar
    In the bay near Innerleven.

But daily on thy matchless ground
I and my caddie would be found,
Describing still another round
    On thy Links, sweet Innerleven!
Would I care then for fortune's rubs,
And a' their Kirk and State hubbubs,
While I could stump and swing my clubs
    On the Links o' Innerleven?

And when the e'ening grey sat doun,
I'd cast aside my tacket shoon,
And crack o' putter, cleek, and spoon,
    Wi' a friend at Innerleven.
Syne ow'r a glass o' Cameron Brig,[1]
A nightcap we would doucely swig,
Laughing at Conservative and Whig,
    By the Links o' Innerleven.

---

[1] The name of a noted distillery.

In Praise of Gutta Percha

By William Graham, LL.D.

Sung at the Meeting of the Innerleven Golf Club,
1st September 1848

Of a' the changes that of late
Have shaken Europe's social state,[1]
Let wondering politicians prate,
    And 'bout them mak a wark a'.
A subject mair congenial here,
And dearer to a Golfer's ear,
I sing—the change brought round this year
    By balls of Gutta Percha!

Though Gouf be of our games most rare,
Yet, truth to speak, the tear and wear
O' balls was felt to be severe,
    And source o' great vexation;
When Gourlay balls cost half-a-croun,
And Allan's no a farthing doun,
The feck o's wad been harried soon
    In this era of taxation.

Right fain we were to be content
Wi' used-up balls new lickt wi' paint,
That ill concealed baith scar and rent—
    Balls scarcely fit for younkers.

---

[1] The year of the expulsion of Louis Philippe from the throne of France.

In Praise of Gutta Percha

And though our best wi' them we tried,
And nicely every club applied,
They whirred and fuffed, and dooked and shied,
    And sklentit into bunkers.

But times are changed—we dinna care
Though we may ne'er drive leather mair,
Be't stuffed wi' feathers or wi' hair—
    For noo we're independent.
At last a substance we hae got,
Frae which for scarce mair than a groat,
A ba' comes that can row and stot—
    A ba' the most transcendent.

They say it comes frae yont the sea,
The concrete juice o' some rare tree—
And hard and horny though it be,
    Just steep it in het water—
As saft as potty soon 'twill grow,
Then 'tween your loofs a portion row—
When cool, a ba' ye'll get, I trow,
    That ye for years may batter.

Hail, GUTTA PERCHA! precious gum!
O'er Scotland's links lang may ye bum;
Some purse-proud billies haw and hum,
    And say ye're douf at fleein';
But let them try ye fairly out,
Wi' ony balls for days about,
Your merits they will loudly tout,
    And own they hae been leein'.

In Praise of Gutta Percha

'Tis true—at first ye seem to hing,
And try the air wi' timid wing—
But firmer grown, a sweep ye'll fling
    Wi' ony ba' o' leather.
Ye're keen and certain at a putt—
Nae weet your sides e'er opens up—
And though for years your ribs they whup,
    Ye'll never mout a feather.

But noo that a' your praise is spent,
Ye'll listen to a friend's comment,
And kindlier tak on the paint,
    Then ye wad be perfection.[1]
And sure some scientific loon
On Golfing will bestow a boon,
And gie ye a cosmetic soon,
    And brighten your complexion.

---

[1] The first gutta percha balls were dark in colour.

"FAR AND SURE!"

BY THE LATE SHERIFF LOGAN

"FAR AND SURE! Far and Sure!" 'twas the cry of our fathers,
    'Twas a cry which their forefathers heard;
'Tis the cry of their sons when the mustering gathers:
    When we're gone may it still be the word.

"Far and Sure!" there is honour and hope in the sound;
    Long over these Links may it roll!
It will—O it will! for each face around
    Shows its magic is felt in each soul.

Let it guide us in life; at the desk or the bar,
    It will shield us from folly's gay lure;
Then, tho' rough be the course, and the winning-post *far*,
    We will carry the stakes—O be *sure!*

Let it guide us in Golf, whether "Burgess" or "Star";
    At the last round let none look demure!
All Golfers are brothers when *driving* is *far*,
    When putting is canny and *sure*.

Far and Sure

"Far and Sure! Far and Sure!" fill the bumper and drain it,
    May our motto for ever endure;
May time never maim it, nor dishonour stain it;
    Then drink, brothers, drink, "Far and Sure!"

A Chapter on Golf [1]

SIX o'clock has rung, and groups of artisans are sauntering along to their daily toil; we pass them and the busy housemaids, who are at work dusting carpets and cleaning bell-handles, and in fifteen minutes we are on the links, and then we look around for one minute on the glorious prospect. There is the sky festooned overhead with blue and fleecy clouds, and the choristers of heaven flapping their glittering plumage in the golden sunbeams; there is the sea, calm as a silver mirror, and dotted with ships and fishing boats, the measured sounds of whose oars boom solemnly along the face of the deep; there is the town itself, with its white towers and steeples, and the smoke of breakfast fires, your own among the rest, curling up like incense; there are the fields of yellow corn ripening for the harvest; there is the greensward underneath your feet, literally sparkling with floral jewels—the white gowans, the sheep gowans, the yellow butter-cups, the sea-pinks, and the blue-bells, all appealing in turn to different senses; and last, and not least, there is yourself in health and vigour; and in all this happy world there is nothing more

---

[1] From *Fraser's Magazine*, August 1854.

A Chapter on Golf

poetical, although to dull mortals it may seem prosaic, than the firm tread and buoyant bearing of genuine physical vigour.

But we are on the links to play and not to moralise. Very well then, to work. Thomson takes a handful of brown sand from a hole, excavated for the purpose, and, forming a small pyramid, the ball is carefully placed on the apex. The club is then taken in hand, and, after two or three trial-aims, the implement is swung round with full radius, and the ball takes an upward flight of some hundred feet and disappears behind a small hill. Forthwith, an attendant urchin, y'clept a *caddie*, darts off in pursuit, and has its whereabouts fixed before the party come forward. Smith has his ball ready, but by this time a boy with a fleet of cows, or a couple of nymphs with washing baskets, are seen hovering in the locality where Smith, from long experience, knows that his ordnance is likely to fall, and he has to pause. The delay is needful, because a blow with a golf-ball may be fatal, and in no circumstances is pleasant; and so much is this understood and acted on, that in some districts the authorities are Vandalistic enough to prohibit the sport entirely.

"Hollo, you there!" shouts the remaining caddie, "cut your stick, will you! and look sharp about it!"

The parties admonished, knowing from experience that golfers do not brook delays, immediately act on the polite hint given by the youth, and there now being a clear field, Smith in turn proceeds to send off his ball. But instead of causing it to describe a brilliant parabolic curve like his antagonist, his shot produces a low horizontal movement, which carries the ball to a greater distance. Both having played, it is time that the party should move off, but you are

A Chapter on Golf

a stranger, and as there are spare clubs and balls, you are courteously invited to try your hand; and, sooth to say, inasmuch as Messrs. Thomson and Smith struck their balls with so much ease, you do not think that there can be any great difficulty in the matter, and you grasp the proffered implement without any hesitation. But, tyro, beware! When one looks at a gardener mowing grass, there does not in all the world appear to be a more simple operation. Well, friend, try it, sweep first, and you bury the point of the scythe in mother earth; sweep second, and you innocently brush the tip of the grass-blades; sweep third, and you cut the grass in some places, but not in others; sweep fourth, you feel the perspiration running down your forehead, and your shoulders aching, and you give up the operation in despair. It is the same with Golf. Your friends advise you not to attempt a heavy stroke, but you are determined to do something brilliant, and you draw full force, but as you have struck nothing, you swing round on one foot, and narrowly escape falling on your nose. Of course you are certain that by striking lower next time you will do the business—but this time the club comes thump upon the ground, and a tingling pain runs from the wrist to the elbow. Messrs. Thomson and Smith are too polite to interfere—indeed, you do not give them time, for you are anxious to retrieve the blots on your escutcheon, and in fury you strike again. All at once you are taken back by a sharp crack, and a feeling of lightness comes over your grasp. *You have broken the club.* The head nearly paid its compliments to Thomson's encephalon, and as for the ball it is at Smith's feet, having positively not been dispatched, notwithstanding your Herculean effort, one yard

A Chapter on Golf

from your standing point. You gaze at the shattered shaft in your hand, and have to admit with shame and confusion, that golf, like everything else, cannot be mastered without experience, and that the ease and dexterity of veterans in the art is not the result of chance, but of long and continued practice. Now at last we move off in earnest.

Thomson's ball lies in an advantageous position, and a red flag denoting the goal is seen fluttering in the distance. His next stroke sends the ball within a yard of the staff, and this is by all pronounced to be a good shot. Smith has not been so fortunate, his ball lies in a sand-rut, whilst some ungainly whins are in close vicinity, and he calls despairingly for the *iron*. The ball is driven from its lair, but the awkwardness of its site has prevented an effective blow, and it has not been propelled onwards to its destination farther than some ten feet, and this turns the scale in Thomson's favour, who tries to hole his ball with the third shot, but the touch given is homœopathically too strong, and it provokingly bounds over the hole. Smith now comes up within a foot. Thomson holes, but Smith is also entitled to play, in order that the shot may be equalised, and as he also holes with the fourth shot, the first hole is a draw between the two players.

This, then, is golf, consisting of pedestrianism round the margin of the links, two or three powerful blows, and two or three delicate manipulations. No game that yet has been invented affords more gentle and equable exercise, and if, at first sight, it seems to the players of more active sports to be too tame for general acceptance, we must refer in proof of contrary experience to the antiquity of golf, and to the numbers, distinction, and enthusiasm of its votaries.

A Chapter on Golf

We have now to refer to some singular feats in golfing, properly so called, as well as to some wonderful performances, which, although achieved by golfers, are not legitimately within the sphere of the game. Of the first class may be mentioned the dexterity of a northern player, who was in the habit of striking off three balls from one hole to another (the distance being nearly five hundred yards) with such precision, that giving a uniform number of strokes to each ball, the three would so cluster round the second hole that the player could touch them all with his club. To the uninitiated other kinds of feats had a greater appearance of the marvellous. When striking a ball on a large common, the vertical or horizontal distance traversed cannot be accurately judged, except by a practised eye; hence, to send a ball up to the top of a mountain, or over the apex of a public building, confers on the golfer laurels which could not be accorded to him on his own proper field. Some daring spirit, having evidently steeplechases in his eye, conceived the bold idea of driving a ball from Bruntsfield Links to the top of Arthur's Seat, near Edinburgh—a performance which appeared so extravagant to a local historian who flourished in the middle of last century, that, like the steam navigation of the Atlantic, it was dogmatically asserted to be an utter impossibility. It has, however, been accomplished, affording another instance, among many, of the danger of rash assumption of the prophetic office.[1] The feat has not been tried latterly,

---

[1] This feat was performed in 1815 by Mr. Brown of the Edinburgh Burgess Golfing Society, who backed himself to drive a ball from the Golf House, Bruntsfield Links, over Arthur's Seat, at 45 strokes. Mr. Brown accomplished the task in 44 strokes.—See p. 112.

A Chapter on Golf

as the number of houses and streets that intervene would render it a tedious, although, having duly the fear of our own warning before our eyes, we shall not add—an impracticable operation.

The next enterprises that deserve notice are the driving of balls over public buildings; and the first of these was a bet, taken in 1798, that no two members of the Burgess Golfing Society of Edinburgh could be found capable of driving a ball over the spire of St. Giles's church. The late Mr. Sceales of Leith, and Mr. Smellie, printer, were selected to perform this formidable undertaking, and they were allowed to use six balls each. The required elevation was obtained by a barrel stave, suitably fixed. The balls carried considerably higher than the weather-cock, and were found nearly opposite the Advocates' Close. The bet was decided early in the morning, in order to prevent accident and interruption, and the balls were struck from the south-east corner of Parliament Square. For greater precision an erection for the judges was placed near the weather-cock. The height, including base distance, is a hundred and sixty-one feet. After-experiment demonstrated that the undertaking was not up to the average stroke of formidable players.

The next match of the kind was to surmount the Melville Monument, situated in the New Town of Edinburgh—a bet which the challengers could not have proposed had they been aware of the St. Giles's affair, as the monument is only a hundred and fifty feet high, although it is possible that the parties in this second business, which took place many years after the other, may have thought that golfing had so much degenerated in modern times, that the chivalry of the last

A Chapter on Golf

century could not be maintained. The wager was, however, duly won by a Writer to the Signet, *Anglicè*, an attorney.[1]

One word more and we end our chapter on golfing. If in selecting a pastime permanence be any recommendation, the golf is evidently deserving of consideration. When the arm loses its vigour, cricket must be given up, feeble knees will not suit for football, and the archer must cease to string his bow when the eye grows dim. But golf outlives all—for as it does not heavily tax the bodily powers, that gentle-paced old age which Shakspeare says comes on us "frosty but kindly," is not incompatible with its moderate indulgence.

---

[1] Mr. Donald M'Lean, W.S.

SPIRE OF ST. GILES'S CATHEDRAL

Ballade of the Royal Game of Golf

THERE are laddies will drive ye a ba'
   To the burn frae the farthermost tee,
But ye mauna think driving is a',
   Ye may heel her, and send her ajee,
Ye may land in the sand or the sea;
   And ye're dune, sir, ye're no worth a preen,
Tak' the word that an auld man 'll gie,
   Tak' aye tent to be up on the green!

The auld folk are crouse, and they craw
   That their putting is pawky and slee;
In a bunker they're nae guid ava',
   But to girn, and to gar the sand flee.
And a lassie can putt—ony she—
   Be she Maggy, or Bessie, or Jean,
But a cleek-shot's the billy for me,
   Tak' aye tent to be up on the green!

I hae play'd in the frost and the thaw,
   I hae play'd since the year thirty-three,
I hae play'd in the rain and the snaw,
   And I trust I may play till I dee;
And I tell ye the truth and nae lee,
   For I speak o' the thing I hae seen—
Tam Morris, I ken, will agree—
   Tak' aye tent to be up on the green!

ENVOY.

Prince, faith you're improving a wee,
   And, Lord, man, they tell me you're keen;
Tak' the best o' advice that can be—
   Tak' aye tent to be up on the green!

                      A. L.

A HUNDRED GOLFERS

Air—"*A Hundred Pipers*"

Wi' a hundred golfers an' a', an' a',—
The club, the cleek, an' the ba', the ba',
O, Bruntsfield Links look braw, look braw,—
Wi' a hundred golfers an' a', an' a'.

The *Burgess* are auldest of a', of a'—
Wi' Robertson, Martin, an' Shaw, an' Shaw—
Fresh laurels they gain, which weel they maintain,
Though their vet'rans are wearin' awa', awa'.
The *Bruntsfield* comes next in the raw, the raw,
Wi' the *Burgess* they've oft a *fracas, fracas;*
To add to their honours most gallantly Chambers
Frae St. Andrew a prize brought awa', awa'.

    Wi' a hundred golfers an' a', an' a',—
    The club, the cleek, an' the ba', the ba',
    O, Bruntsfield Links look braw, look braw,—
    Wi' a hundred golfers an' a', an' a'.

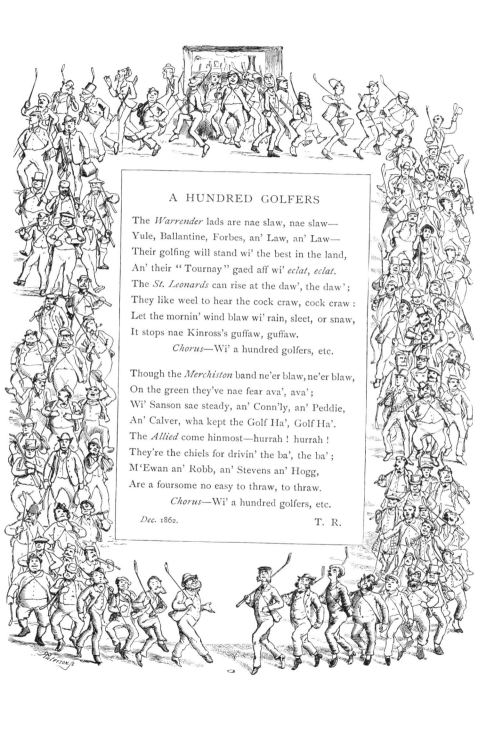

A HUNDRED GOLFERS

The *Warrender* lads are nae slaw, nae slaw—
Yule, Ballantine, Forbes, an' Law, an' Law—
Their golfing will stand wi' the best in the land,
An' their "Tournay" gaed aff wi' *eclat, eclat.*
The *St. Leonards* can rise at the daw', the daw';
They like weel to hear the cock craw, cock craw:
Let the mornin' wind blaw wi' rain, sleet, or snaw,
It stops nae Kinross's guffaw, guffaw.
      Chorus—Wi' a hundred golfers, etc.

Though the *Merchiston* band ne'er blaw, ne'er blaw,
On the green they've nae fear ava', ava';
Wi' Sanson sae steady, an' Conn'ly, an' Peddie,
An' Calver, wha kept the Golf Ha', Golf Ha'.
The *Allied* come hinmost—hurrah ! hurrah !
They're the chiels for drivin' the ba', the ba';
M'Ewan an' Robb, an' Stevens an' Hogg,
Are a foursome no easy to thraw, to thraw.
      Chorus—Wi' a hundred golfers, etc.

Dec. 1862.   T. R.

A GOLFING SONG

By James Ballantine

Air—"*Let Haughty Gaul*"

Come leave your dingy desks and shops,
    Ye sons of ancient Reekie,
And by green fields and sunny slopes,
    For healthy pastimes seek ye.
Don't bounce about your "*dogs of war*,"
    Nor at our *shinties* scoff, boys,
But learn our motto, "*Sure and Far*,"
    Then come and play at golf, boys.
Chorus—Three rounds of Bruntsfield Links will chase
        All murky vapours off, boys;
    And nothing can your sinews brace
        Like the glorious game of golf, boys.

Above our head the clear blue sky,
    We bound the gowan'd sward o'er,
And as our balls fly far and high,
    Our bosoms glow with ardour.

Golfing Song

While dear Edina, Scotland's Queen,
   Her misty cap lifts off, boys,
And smiles serenely on the Green,
   Graced by the game of golf, boys.
            Chorus—Three rounds, etc.

We putt, we drive, we laugh, we chat,
   Our strokes and jokes aye clinking,
We banish all extraneous fat,
   And all extraneous thinking.
We'll cure you of a summer cold,
   Or of a winter cough, boys,
We'll make you young, even when you're old,
   So come and play at golf, boys.
            Chorus—Three rounds, etc.

When in the dumps with mulligrubs,
   Or doyte with barley bree, boys,
Go get you off the green three rubs,
   'Twill set you on the " *Tee*," boys.
There's no disease we cannot cure,
   No care we cannot doff, boys;
Our aim is ever "*far and sure*"—
   So come and play at golf, boys.
            Chorus—Three rounds, etc.

O, blessings on pure cauler air,
   And every healthy sport, boys,
That makes sweet Nature seem more fair,
   And makes long life seem short, boys;

Golfing Song

That warms your hearts with genial glow,
 And makes you halve your loaf, boys,
With every needy child of woe—
 So bless the game of golf, boys.
  Chorus—Three rounds, etc.

Then don your brilliant scarlet coats,
 With your bright blue velvet caps, boys,
And some shall play the *rocket shots*,
 And some the *putting paps*, boys.
No son of Scotland, man or boy,
 Shall e'er become an oaf, boys,
Who gathers friendship, health, and joy,
 In playing at the golf, boys.
  Chorus—Three rounds, etc.

SONG FOR THE FIRST MUSICAL MEETING OF THE
WARRENDER GOLF CLUB, January 1870

BY JAMES BALLANTINE

AIR—"*A Man's a Man for a' that*"

TEN jolly years awa' hae fled,
 Since first our Club was founded;
And oh what happy lives we've led,
 By healthy sport surrounded.

Golfing Song

We've raxed our arms wi' richt gude will,
    And pluck baith sharp and keen, boys,
Till now for Golfing power and skill
    We rival a' the Green, boys.
Chorus—We're blythe without, we're blythe within,
        And now 'mid winter snell, boys,
    We strive in harmony to win
        Aboon a' clubs the bell, boys.

Oh, when a hard day's darg is done,
    How pleasant 'tis to meet, boys,
And listen to an auld Scotch croon,
    Frae voices low and sweet, boys.
And 'neath our genial Captain's sway—
    A chield to a' sae dear, boys—
Each singing night, like golfing day,
    Our joyous hearts shall cheer, boys.
        Chorus—We're blythe without, etc.

Then Tenor, Bass, and Treble join,
    And swell the happy lay, boys;
For Music is the Art divine
    That drives all woe away, boys.
And 'neath this roof so snug and bien,
    Wi' sangsters in galore, boys,
There's money joyous nights, I ween,
    And canty songs in store, boys.
        Chorus—We're blythe without, etc.

Happy Thought!

Unhappy Result!

DUFFERS YET

A PARODY

By Two "Long Spoons"

AFTER years of play together,
After fair and stormy weather,
After rounds of every green,
From Westward Ho to Aberdeen—
Why did e'er we buy a set,
If we must be duffers yet?
    Duffers yet! Duffers yet!

Duffers yet

After singles, foursomes—all,
Fractured club and cloven ball;
After grief in sand and whin,
Foozled drives, and "putts" not in—
Ev'n our caddies scarce regret,
When we part as duffers yet.
    Duffers yet! Duffers yet!

After days of frugal fare,
Still we spend our force in air;
After nips to give us nerve,
Not the less our drivers swerve;
Friends may back, and foes may bet,
And ourselves be duffers yet.
    Duffers yet! Duffers yet!

Must it ever then be thus?
Failure most mysterious!
Shall we never fairly stand,
Eye on ball as club in hand?
Are the bounds eternal set
To retain us duffers yet?
    Duffers yet! Duffers yet!

      M. T. S. D.

RUINS OF BLACKFRIARS' ABBEY

St. Andrews

THERE is no single spot in Scotland equally full of historical interest. A foreigner who reads the Annals of Scotland, and sees in every page the important position which this place occupied in the literary, the political, and the ecclesiastical transactions of the country, would naturally imagine the modern St. Andrews, though amerced perhaps of its ancient greatness, to be a large and influential city. On approaching it, he sees, across an almost treeless plain, a few spires standing on a point of rock, on the edge of the ocean; and, on entering,

---

[1] From *Journal of Henry Cockburn.* 8vo, 1874.

St. Andrews

he finds himself in a dead village, without the slightest importance or attraction except what it derives from the tales these spires recall. There is no place in this country over which the genius of antiquity lingers so impressively. The architectural wrecks that have been spared are, in themselves, too far gone. They are ruins, or rather the ruins of ruins. Few of them have left even their outlines more than discoverable. But this improves the mysteriousness of the fragments; some of which, moreover, dignify parts of otherwise paltry streets, in which they appear to have been left for no other purpose but that of protesting against modern encroachment. And they are all of a civil character. Even what is called the Castle was less of a castle than of a palace. It was a strong place, but not chiefly for military defence. They all breathe of literary and ecclesiastical events, and of such political transactions as were anciently involved in the Church. There is no feeling here of mere feudal war.

The associations of ancient venerableness which belong so peculiarly to St. Andrews are less disturbed by the repugnances of later ages than in any place I can think of, where the claims of antiquity are opposed to those of living convenience. The colleges, which, though young in comparison with the cathedral, the tower, and the castle, are coeval with the age of the Reformation, instead of interfering with the sentiment of the place, bring down the evidence of its learning into a nearer period, and prolong the appropriate feeling. The taste of some of their modern additions may be doubted, but the old academic edifices are in excellent keeping with the still older ruins. These colleges display many most interesting remains, especially the University Library.

St. Andrews

The Town itself—though I would rather have no town at all, is less offensive than might at first be conceived possible. I don't speak of that detestable Bell Street, nor of a few villa things which have set themselves down on the edges of the city, and have too often been allowed to steal bits of ancient walls and gardens. But the proper town—the true St. Andrews—is in good character. It is still surrounded by its ancient wall, and is said never to have been larger than it is now—a statement which the absence of all vestiges of ancient buildings beyond the wall makes probable. Its only three considerable streets all radiate, at an acute angle, from the cathedral westward. There has never been attempt at decoration on the houses, which are singularly plain, though often dignified by a bit of sculpture or scarcely legible inscription, a defaced coat of arms, or some other vestige of the olden time. There are few shops, and—how thankful they should be!—no trade or manufactures. I could not detect a single steam-engine; and their navy consisted of three coal sloops, which lay within a small pier composed of large stones laid rudely though strongly together upon a natural quay of rock. The gentry of the place consists of professors, retired Indians, saving lairds, old ladies and gentlemen with humble purses, families resorting there for golf, education, economy, or sea-bathing. No one comes for what is called business. Woe to the ignorant wight who did! He would die in a week.

For all this produces a silent, calm place. The streets on Saturday evening and on Sunday were utterly quiet. The steps of a passenger struck me, sitting in the Black Bull parlour, as if it had been a person moving in a cloister, or crossing some still college quadrangle, amid the subdued noises of a

St. Andrews

hot forenoon. I remember when I was in Dr. Ferguson's, long ago, observing a young man on the street, in the month

ST. ANDREWS CATHEDRAL: WEST FRONT

of August, with a grand blue coat, a pair of bright yellow leather breeches, and glorious boots. I asked who he was; and was told "O, that's *the boarder.*" He was an English

St. Andrews

Lord Somebody, who had been at the college in winter, and was sentenced by his friends to remain there till the classes met again. He was the only visible student. I felt for *the* boarder.

It is the asylum of repose—a city of refuge for those who can't live in the country, but wish for as little town as possible. All is in unison with the ruins, the still surviving edifices, the academical institutions, and the past history of the place. On the whole, it is the best Pompeii in Scotland. If the professors and the youths be not learned and studious, it is their own fault. They have everything to excite ambition—books, tranquillity, and old inspiration. If anything more were needed, they have it in their extensive links, their singular rocks, their miles of the most admirable hard dry sand. There cannot be better sea walks. The prospects are not very good, except perhaps in such a day as I had—a day of absolute calmness and brightness; when every distant object glitters; and the horizon of the ocean, in its landless quarter, trembles in light; and white sea-birds stand on one leg on the warm rocks; and the water lays itself out in long unbroken waves, as if it was playing with the beautiful bays. The water, however, though clear enough for the east coast, is no match for the liquid crystal that laves our western shores.

But though tranquillity is deeply impressed on the whole place, the inhabitants are not solitary. On the contrary, among themselves they are very social. Except those who choose to study, they are all idle; and having all a competency, they are exactly the sort of people who can be gregarious without remorse, and are allured into parties by the necessity of keeping awake. They have a local pleasure

St. Andrews

of their own, which is as much the staple of St. Andrews as old colleges and churches. This is golfing, which is there not a mere pastime, but a business and a passion, and has for ages been so. This pursuit draws many a middle-aged gentleman, whose stomach requires exercise and his purse cheap pleasure, to reside there with his family. It is the established recreation of all the learning and all the dignity of the town. There is a pretty large set who do nothing else. They begin in the morning, and stop only to eat; and after playing all day in the sea breeze, they discuss it all night. Their talk is of *holes*. The intermixture of these men, or rather the intermixture of this occupation, with its interests, hazards, and matches, considerably whets the social appetite. However, all is done innocently and respectably, in so much that even the recreation of St. Andrews partakes of what is and ought to be its peculiar character and avocation.

THE PENDS, ST. ANDREWS

To St. Andrew[1]

ODE III. OF BOOK IV.

THAT man upon whose natal hour,
    Thy beaming eye has smiled,
Inspiring with a Golfer's power,
    Dear Saint, thy favoured child,

Ne'er shall the Turf's blue ribbon grace,
    Victorious on the course,
His the first favourite for the race,
    Or his the winning horse.

'Tis not for him, a Golfer born,
    The warrior's pæan rings;
Nor his the laurel rudely torn
    From the brow of conquered kings.

But the sunlit seas that, laughing, lave
    Bright Eden's sandy shore,
Shall whisper his name in each rippling wave
    Till time shall be no more.

And the deep green seas, with their billowy dash
    And their stern triumphant roar,
Shall bellow his name, as they thundering crash
    On old St. Andrews' shore—

---

[1] Horatian Lyrics, No. II. From *Blackwood's Magazine*, Oct. 1872.

To St. Andrew

In Royal Ancient records placed
    Amidst the sons of fame,
With never-ending medals graced,
    Great master of The Game.

Sweet Saint! whose spirit haunts the Course,
    And broods o'er every Hole,
And gives the Driver vital force,
    And calms the Putter's soul,

Thou giv'st me, to the world's last hour,
    A Golfer's fame divine;
I boast—thy gift—a Driver's power;
    If I can Putt—'tis thine.

                KNAPDALE.[1]

[1] The nom-de-plume of W. A. Campbell of Ormsary.

"As they thundering crash on old St. Andrews' shore.

AMONG THE ST. ANDREWS GOLFERS[1]

Y friend Mr. Reginald Potts—indeed I may say my respected nephew Mr. Reginald Potts — one of the best known of its inhabitants, has at last prevailed on me to visit St. Andrews. The railway from Edinburgh to St. Andrews for worry and delays is an indescribable abomination; and I had finished one or two after-dinner cigars, and had disposed of a bottle of Mr. Potts' Château Margaux, before my sweeping adjectives for the torment of the ride ceased to flow, and ere my habitual calm stole over my ruffled nervous system. It was then I realised that I was in a city I had not seen for thirty years, and that as the probabilities were against my return to it, it was only proper I should make the most of my present sojourn. I remembered the place had no woods to wander in—had not even a decent tree to show—and though of illustrious historical descent and full of interesting ruins, was, apart from the "melancholy ocean," not dowered with objects for

---

[1] From the *Glasgow News*, September 21, 1874.

Among the St. Andrews Golfers

the tourist to spend much time over. I inquired of Mr. Potts his designs for the morrow. He began about a Club he wished me to see, and talked in a lively manner about a "foursome" at golf he had arranged for me. "Your happiness," said he, "will be complete, if, so long, dear uncle, as you are here, you only be passive." I suspect that is the key to more happiness than can be scraped up in St. Andrews, capable as it is, now that I have seen its Club and its Links, of furnishing it in no stinted measure.

In the bright morning sunlight I found the Club-house come up to my expectations. It has no architectural pretensions to speak of, and clearly was built for comfort rather than display. It has a bow-window looking west—the window of a large room used for luncheon, for the weed, and the annual dinners. This is flanked by a billiard and a reading room, and is covered in the rear by lavatories and the steward's apartments. I don't know what is above, for I never go upstairs if I can help it, and there was no pressure of necessity in this instance. Innumerable names stare at you from the inside walls of the rooms and corridors, and on inquiry you are told that they are those of members who, inside the framework of wood below, have their clubs locked and their variegated *togæ* enclosed. The *togæ* are made up of shoes and boots, new and old, with hobnails, and of coats of all fashions, and ages, and colours, which, when worn on the Links, as is the custom, give that picturesqueness to golf which no other pastime can rival. The lavatories abound with this kind of gear. You are just on the eve of thinking that you are in an old-clothes shop when you realise that these coats would not easily be made saleable, and that next

Among the St. Andrews Golfers

door are the plentiful evidences of wealthy *abandon*. One little snuggery to the right of the entrance-door displays in a glass case the disused implements of the game, and they look like the monitory flintlocks in curious armouries, which tell of new devices. A step or two further on, and you are at the kindly steward's bar, in the principal hall, where, as in all club-houses, you get what you want, and sometimes more than is good for you. Overlooking this scene of luxury and leisure are two oil portraits—one that of the courtly Mr. Whyte-Melville (convener of the county of Fife, and absolutely the oldest member of this charming institution), by Sir Francis Grant, the other that of Sir Hugh Playfair. As you master the details and accessories of the building, the numbers and the rank in life of those who frequent it, you conclude that if ever the existing political representation is to be changed, the Royal and Ancient Golf Club of St. Andrews —that, if I remember, is the title of it—must in all fairness have the right by itself to return a member to the Collective Wisdom. I frankly said so to Mr. Potts, who, using lawful familiarities, clapped me on the shoulder with the remark, " Dear old Jonathan, you never will drop your old-fashioned sentiments "; and saying so he produced a not unwelcome flask of cognac and fresh cigars.

But I am soon made conscious that I am in the company of famed *literati* and men of note, no less than of golfers. That man, for instance, who has just entered, with the comely face and the frank bearing, is Principal Tulloch, whose studious ways and thousand preoccupations are not, I happen to know, incompatible with the most genial hospitality. That cigar over there which escapes from under the scoop of a

Among the St. Andrews Golfers

shepherd tartan bonnet, set awry on the head, is ministering its soothing balms to the editor of *Blackwood*, who is fresh from the revised proofs of the September Ebony, and the unconcerned-looking inheritor of some of the brightest of Scotch literary traditions. Down the steps in front of the building, and towards the breezy bents, with a bundle of books under his arm, walks a fragile man, with a meek white face, who is interesting with the interest of distinguished authorship —and he is Professor Flint. Coming the other way, you notice a taller figure, but equally far from portly, with also a tendency to stoop: he is Principal Shairp—the vigilant authority on Ossian, the tender poet, the subtle essayist, and the staunch Conservative. To hear him read Michael Bruce's *Ode to the Cuckoo* is to be made acquainted with the music of the human voice when burdened with sympathetic emotion, while the mind's eye has a sight of things which are far away. My interlocutor with the fine forehead is Patrick Proctor Alexander, the loving biographer of Alexander Smith, and the biting critic of the late Stuart Mill. There goes Dr. Spencer Baynes, energetically after a brisk "constitutional," seeking variety and relief in the white autumn day from the bad manuscripts of the new "Encyclopædia" he is editing for the Messrs. Black. If you will step into the reading-room you will see, partly concealed behind the open pages of the *Pall Mall Gazette*, the anxious features of the "Country Parson," and the demigod of many readers of *Fraser*, when, as "A. K. H. B.," he writes "concerning" something or another in the most piquant and elegant English. Over at the other hearthstone is a mighty Senior Wrangler, who has just suppressed me in a conversation in which I had joined

Among the St. Andrews Golfers

for gratitude's sake. I was gently praising Mr. Alfred Wallace's history of Spiritualism in *The Fortnightly Review*, when, with delightful holiday dogmatism, I was put down with the remark, "Tuts! a parcel of lunatics altogether!" But, nevertheless, he is an eminent man who uttered these thoughtless words. That venerable form, with the long iron-grey hair, who enters our clouds of smoke, is the pet of the Senatus for the years he has to carry and the "infant treble" of his social ways; and he fulfils in the professorial economy here the function of telling the end of all merely intellectual activity. Arm-in-arm go seawards two other erudite divinities of the place—namely, Drs. Crombie and Roberts—whose presence, stalking across this classical scene, suggests the reflection that St. Andrews University has a singular wealth of means for setting up as a theological school. Nor is this group of *literati* unusual here, or even just now at its best. Into it occasionally walks "Shirley," freed from the commonplaces of Supervision in Edinburgh; and mightier than the mightiest of her sex, there is just about this time of the year to be seen hereabouts the biographer of Irving and the Chronicler of Carlingford. How unpardonable it would be were I to omit noticing that that man on the gravel-path outside, with the agile gait and the inquiring features, is the author of *The Gladiators*, *The Queen's Maries*, and *Bones and I*—Whyte-Melville, to wit, the best rider to hounds, and the best teller of how it is done, of any man I know! He is in the company of his estimable father, though which looks oldest I do not undertake to say, and the St. Andrews people, I am told, decline to decide. Of both the city is honestly and garrulously proud. It was away along that expanse of grass and whin westwards

Among the St. Andrews Golfers

where the remarkable author of the *Book of Days*, Dr. Robert Chambers, sought to make his declining hours happy with the champagne of the breezy downs, the good cheer of genial human intercourse, and the innocent pastimes and frolics of laughing youths and dutiful men, and where it is still believed he found what he so gently sought. But luncheon is set, and " tucking into " some hot potatoes and cold beef, you observe an individual of an easy, reserved presence, and with great glistening eyes. He is in golfing deshabille, like all the rest of them, with a brown towering wideawake. That is the Lord Justice-General of Scotland, who has just had his forenoon's round, and is now coaxing the inner man to have another. How well the ease in this inn becomes the character of a judge so distinguished, and the leisure of an orator who has shone in the past in the strife of public life! Entering towards us is a man with wistful features, a nasal twang, and a stoop from the shoulders. He clamantly wants to be drilled. He is Sir George Campbell of Edenwood, just home from India, where, as Lieutenant-Governor of Bengal, he has been making a page or two bright in the thronging history of that great British possession.

It was at this point in the day's conversations and inquiries that Mr. Potts informed me that the hour for the foursome was come; and so behold me on the Links of St. Andrews in a tawny scarlet coat and a bonnet which crowned, I may say, the figure of a guy! It were superfluous to tell what the origin of golf is. I have just time before striking off to state that what of it is not lost in the mists of antiquity came over with William the Conqueror. That is what my caddie tells me, and he is no less an authority than Tom Morris, who was

Among the St. Andrews Golfers

born in the purple of equable temper and courteous habits. Well, I began my game by missing what is called "the globe" altogether, and (to anticipate events just a little) I finished it by breaking a club. I early acquired an inexplicable, undefinable, interest in my ball. I heeled it and topped it; I went under it and over it; I stood behind it and stood in advance of it; and in my multifarious endeavours, I exhausted the entire armoury of Tom's implements. Play-club and spoon, niblick and cleek, putter and heavy iron, were in constant requisition in order to get that ball to go. I followed it into the Swilcan Burn; I thrashed it out of numerous sandy bunkers; I fought with it in whinny covers; I drove it forth from grassy tufts with a zeal which, I was constantly told, was beyond all praise. At what is called "the hole across" I was extremely warm, and no doubt looked far from myself; whereupon Tom offered the polite remark—"Ye wid be nane the waur o' a black strap, sir." "Certainly, Tom," I rejoined; "my performances are so miserable that I feel you cannot chastise me enough with any sort of strap." "You mistake me, sir," responded Tom; "I didn't mean that; I mean, ye wid be nane the waur o' a pint o' porter." As when the acid joins the soda there instantly arises the effervescence, so at this juncture at "the hole across" I exploded with laughter. It only wanted Tom's calling porter by the name of "black strap" to fill in, to myself, the comicality of the scene in which I was the central figure; and so, casting myself on the ground, I struck work like any miner. But it was of no use. I was compelled to resume, with the ultimate result of the club breaking, as aforesaid, and with the intimation that we had won the foursome! It seems that odds were allowed to

Among the St. Andrews Golfers

me, a half or a whole or something—I never inquired what, seeing the issue was obtained through a conspiracy of flatterers. This conclusion was deepened in my mind at dinner—a meal in St. Andrews at which the day's games are gone over again hole by hole and stroke by stroke. Mr. Potts let fall a sentence or two then which showed me that his main object was to egg me on to that degree of fascination with the game when all self-restraint is lost, and when the enthralled novice becomes, in the choice between work and golf, quite unable to resist golf when there is a doubt existing. My nephew has so far succeeded that I have had three more rounds since; and as the October Meeting is coming—to the dinner of the members of which I have received a courteous invitation —I am resolved at this writing to practise away.

The Links themselves for a walk are most enjoyable. You play, as it were, in a path of beautiful greensward, which in form is like a shepherd's crook, with the stem notched and twisted, on whose brecks of heather the bees are humming, and above which the song-birds are gyrating among the flight of balls. Than my present situation nothing could be more agreeable or desirable; and then Mr. Potts has given me quite a ministry of useful introductions besides that to the game of golf. Among these I highly rank my introductions to the Provost and Magistrates of the city, whose privilege it is to rule in so famous a place. I have been shown by the Provost the keys of the city, with his expressions of regret that they cannot be formally presented, and I have nothing to regret at our pleasing intercourse save that he has just beaten me at billiards. I do not know whether I shall ever fulfil the expectations Mr. Potts has formed of me as a golfer

Among the St. Andrews Golfers

—most likely not, even short of the grace of the St. Andrews "swing"; but I can most sincerely say that I have unbounded delight in being among—in having formed the acquaintance of many of—the St. Andrews players.

JONATHAN OLDBUCK.

ADDRESS

By the Captain—a.d. 1871—of the Royal and Ancient Golf Club of St. Andrews to his Crew, on the Eve of setting out, after the Autumn Campaign, for his Winter Quarters in Edinburgh.

Imitated from *Horace*, Ode vii. of Book I.

"*Laudabunt alii claram Rhodon, aut Mitylenen.*"

Some praise the Isles of Greece, or hieroglyphic
    Egypt—connecting link 'twixt two great seas;
Some love the palmy isles of the Pacific—
    Tahiti, Owhyhee, and the Fijis.

One loves the impregnable, sun-smitten Malta—
    Her dresses and her tongues of every land;
Another vaunts the Rock of strong Gibraltar—
    The friend of nations, in Great Britain's hand.

One spends his time and talents in describing
    The Modern Athens and her castled Crag:—
Swears she's the Queen of Cities; that ascribing
    Such praise to others were an empty brag.

Address

To me St. Andrews far beyond them all is;
   Her bright Links satisfy my every want;
For true enjoyment she's the only "Πολις"—
   The love of all men justifies my vaunt.

I love Strathtyrum and its leafy grove;
   I love the Links with their smooth, velvet Greens;
The sandy Bunkers and the Club I love;
   I love the Ladies' Links and sunny denes.

Alas! the time has come now for our parting,
   And I must hie me to a southern clime;
The thought, though, keeps my heart from over-smarting,
   That I shall come again some other time.

As Teucer once addressed his hardy crew,
   When seeking a new home beyond the sea;
As he to *his* friends, I address to you
   These words, with which I know your sympathy:—

Never despair. Where'er your Captain leads
   The true Apollo promises new Links:
Old Musselburgh now must serve our needs,
   With dear "Auld Reekie" and her curling rinks.

Brave partners in The Game, who oft have passed
   Along with me through darker times than these,
Enjoy your dinner, for it is the last
   Before we tempt the perils of the seas;
Drown all your cares in wine, and let's be merry,
To-morrow we must cross the stormy Ferry.

                              ANONYMOUS.

SUTHERLANDIA

AS the traveller approaches St. Andrews, everything indicates that Golf is the business of the place. The railway winds alongside of the Links—"The Happy Golfing Grounds" as they are called by the votaries of the game. Parties of golfers are sure to be seen all over the green, and sympathisers in the train stretch their necks out of the carriage-windows to see who the players are, and to guess how the matches are going.

The first building at the head of the Links nearest the sea is the Club-House, where golfers muster and refresh themselves after the labours of the day. The house does not possess architectural beauty, to use a very mild phrase, and the architect is, happily for himself, unknown; but it is comfortably adapted for its purpose, and lined throughout with boxes containing the clubs of the members.

On the corner of the wall outside there is an inscription which has often puzzled strangers,—"All players are requested not to tee their balls on the putting-green." One

Sutherlandia

day William Story, the great American sculptor, called to us for assistance. He was staring at the writing on the wall, and said, "Help! I am afraid to move lest I should be doing this forbidden but unknown thing." On another occasion we saw a foreign-looking seaman gaping at the inscription, and evidently in difficulties. We went forward to explain, and he turned out to be a Dutch skipper who had traded all his life with Dundee, and naturally prided himself on his knowledge of English. On telling these stories, and pointing out the warning to an eminent but non-golfing Scot (the late Sir W. Stirling-Maxwell), he laughed, and said, "I am ashamed to confess that I am in the same boat with Story and the Dutchman." He asked if the words were to be found in any dictionary; we were in turn ashamed to confess that we thought not, but promised that the defect should be remedied in any dictionaries over which we had influence.

The great golfers are the heroes of the place, and St. Andrews still remembers Allan Robertson, the champion golfer of his day, who died in the year 1859. Along with many others, we attended his funeral in the churchyard at the old Cathedral. After laying poor Allan in his grave, we walked down the Scores to the Club with a dear old golfing friend, the late Mr. Sutherland, who suddenly broke his melancholy reverie by exclaiming,—"They may toll the bells and shut up their shops in St. Andrews, for their greatest is gone." We told this at dinner shortly afterwards, when some of the professors of St. Andrews College were present—then, as now, many of them very eminent men—and Allan's memory was drunk and recognised with

Sutherlandia

all due solemnity. "Old" Sutherland, whom we have mentioned above, was for some twenty years about the most familiar figure on the Links at Musselburgh in winter, and St. Andrews in summer. He was about five feet nine inches, very upright, with singularly square shoulders, and a grey head surmounted by a peculiar Scotch bonnet, which all golfers will recollect. He made Golf more thoroughly the business of his life than any man we ever knew. On a Saturday he asked us to make a match for the Monday. We were reluctantly obliged to say that the month was getting on and we must work. He exclaimed, "God bless me! are you going to *waste* a Monday?" We had to think some time before we discovered the meaning of the peculiar value of the Monday, until, with fits of laughter, we reflected that after the Sunday's rest his old sinews must be fresher on Monday than on any other day of the week.

His attention to promising young golfers was like that of a father to a son. One day playing the last hole in, our friendly antagonist, Mr. Kinloch, was about to strike off, when a boy appeared upon the bridge over the burn. Old Sutherland shouted out, "Stop! stop! don't play upon him; he is a fine young golfer." The warning came too late to stop Kinloch's club, but in a convulsion of laughter over this consideration, not for a boy but for a fine young golfer, he nearly *missed the globe*.

One of the best young players in these days—perhaps the best—was Captain John Stewart, and when he was ordered out to India with his regiment, old Sutherland sorrowed in this wise,—"It is a shame for a man with such powers (golfing) to go out to India." He always looked upon the game

Sutherlandia

as a very serious business, and we were once the subject of one of his severest rebukes. We had been playing a foursome, in which the other two players were quite young men, and there was an undue amount of laughing and joking. After the match was over he was stalking gloomily about the Links, and met a friend, just arrived from Edinburgh, to whom he unbosomed himself. "There was too much *levity* about our match to-day—I was not surprised at the others, but your brother John was as bad as any of them." We need not say that the old gentleman had *lost his match*, and having been his antagonist we felt the rebuke.

Sutherland's mind was completely imbued with golf, and one day at the head of the Links he upset us utterly, as, when introduced to a lady, instead of the ordinary greetings, he exclaimed, without a word of preface,—"Well, ma'am, you never saw such a game as George Condie was playing to-day."

He was in great force when an important match was going on, and reprehended anything like *levity* in the sternest manner. One day a very big match was starting, and an excursion train from Dundee arrived, when the people, not unnaturally, streamed over the Links at the first hole out. He strode forward, cleek in hand, waving the people off, and having frightened them back a bit, he turned to us and said, —"It is disgraceful of the railway people bringing a parcel of uneducated brutes down here when they knew a real match was going on." Uneducated, with him, meant not knowing golf. He delighted to describe the chances and changes of the match he had been playing—a weakness in which all golfers more or less share. There was often a kind of

Sutherlandia

Malapropism or big-wordedness about his language which was irresistibly laughable. There is a vulgar phrase, in common use, that a thing is devilish good, but old Sutherland got quite beyond that. Describing with great minuteness the vicissitudes of a match, he wound up by saying, "And we would have lost it, but by the damndest providence Blackwood holed his putt." There was no irreverence in the good old man, and how this strange contradiction of terms got into his head we have no knowledge. In spite of his devotion to golf he had a strong sense that carrying clubs was not a career likely to produce success in life, and in more than one case we have known him fit out lads, "caddies," albeit "fine young golfers,"—to get a chance of more permanent employment in life at sea or elsewhere.

He took an immense pride in the rapid extension of golf in England. Many years ago, an English friend, Mr. Delane, was one day walking round with us, and Sutherland expatiated largely on the spread of his favourite amusement in England, adding, as a finish, that an English clergyman had taken it down to Westward Ho.[1] To Delane saying he knew the ground and its perfect adaptability for golf, but the difficulty would be to get golfers—"He will teach them," said Sutherland emphatically. "Oh! then," said Delane, "he is a Golfing Missionary?" Sutherland looked rather stern at a joke on such a theme, but smiled a grim assent.

Dear old Sutherland! many a good match we have played with him, arguing almost as solemnly as himself over the

---

[1] Since become one of the best and most popular of golfing grounds.

Sutherlandia

respective merits of the players, ourselves included; and we think all golfers who knew his game will agree with us that a steadier or more straightforward player according to his powers never lifted club.

J. B.

GROUP OF CADDIES

THE MORNING ROUND (6–8 A.M.)

By "The Glutton"

Air—"*Beautiful Star*"

BEAUTIFUL ROUND! superbly played—
Round where never mistake is made;
Who with enchantment would not bound
For the Round of the Morning, Beautiful Round?

Never a duffer is out of bed;
None but the choicest of bricks instead
On the links, at *six*, can ever be found;
Round of the Morning, Beautiful Round!

There they lie in a hideous doze
Different quite from a golfer's repose—
That from which he starts with a bound
For the Round of the Morning, Beautiful Round!

The Morning Round

Agile and light, each tendon strung,
With healthy play of each active lung,
He strides along o'er the dewy ground
In the Round of the Morning, Beautiful Round!

Beautiful Round! most cleverly won
Under the gaze of the rising sun,
And hailed with a pleasant chuckling sound;
Round of the Morning, Beautiful Round!

Beautiful Round! vain duffers try
Thy manifold virtues to deny:—
They!!! mere specimens of a hound!
Round of the Morning, Beautiful Round!

Beautiful Round! in thee is health,
The choicest gem of earthly wealth:—
Hands and face most thoroughly browned,
Round of the Morning, Beautiful Round!

Beautiful Round! to thee is due
All the work I am fit to do:—
Therefore in fancy stand thou crowned
Queen of the Morning, Beautiful Round!

Beautiful Round! I think of thee
Through months of labour and misery:—
Round thee the strings of my heart are wound,
Round of the Morning, Beautiful Round!

Impromptu by the Glutton.

MEDAL DAY AT ST. ANDREWS [1]

THIS is the season of Congresses, and many have been in session lately, but few, we venture to think, have excited more enthusiasm among those who attended them than one that met last week at St. Andrews—we suppose we must hardly say in session. On the last day of September the "Royal and Ancient Golf Club" of that Royal and ancient burgh assembled by the shores of their sad-resounding sea, in the weather-beaten district known as the "East Nuik of Fife," to hold their annual autumnal meeting. Students of Scottish history remember the decaying city of the Scottish patron saint as the seat of an archiepiscopal see whose metropolitans played a conspicuous part in the religious troubles that convulsed the kingdom. Archæologists may have made pilgrimages to the ruins of its venerable shrines, or to the fragments of the famous castle that witnessed the burning of Wishart, the murder of the Cardinal who martyred him, and the fervid ministrations of the Scottish Apostle when the

---

[1] From the *Times*, October 5, 1874.

Medal Day at St. Andrews

Reformers were being blockaded by the avengers of blood. But we fear that modern Scotchmen set but small store by those stirring memories, ecclesiastical or political. In Scotland St. Andrews is best known as the capital and headquarters of Golf, and golf is pre-eminently the national game. Curling alone can pretend to vie with it in popularity, but curling depends on the caprices of the weather. It can only be enjoyed in an iron frost, whereas you may indulge in golf any day or all days; and in point of antiquity even the venerable St. Andrews itself, with its musty memories, need not be ashamed of its profitable foster child.

Golf has been played by the Scots literally from time immemorial, and we have little doubt that there were golf holes to be filled on the North Inch of Perth on the memorable day when the ground was cleared for the combat between the Clan Chattan and the Clan Quhele. We know, at all events, that His Majesty James II., nephew of that Earl of Rothsay who perished miserably in the tower of Falkland, found himself constrained to promulgate a statute against the game, setting forth that its too universal popularity interfered with the training for the national defence. The Scots of our own time are more peaceably disposed than their ancestors; but we venture to say that even a Liberal Ministry that advocated any such measure nowadays would have small chance in Scotch constituencies when they sent down candidates to contest the seats.

There are districts and burghs where every second inhabitant is a golfer. It is the game of the country gentry, of the busy professional men, of the *bourgeoisie* of flourishing centres of trade, of many of the artisans, and even of the tag-

Medal Day at St. Andrews

rag and bobtail. People who never took a golf club in their hands have a high regard for it as a game which is eminently respectable. It is the one amusement which any "douce" man may pursue, irrespective of his calling, and risk neither respect nor social consideration. Read the list of the champions who paired off for the round of the course at last Thursday's contest, and we believe you will actually find gentlemen in Orders—and those, Scottish Orders—figuring among them. The fact speaks volumes to those who are familiar with local prejudices, for it is an unwritten canon of the Church that the consecrated caste of the Levites should avoid giving even a shadow of offence. This we know, that rising young barristers may take rank as golfers without resigning the hope of briefs, while they might as well sign a self-denying ordinance as go out fox-hunting even once in a way, or be detected indulging in the frivolity of dancing. On the other hand, the most ardent fox-hunters, salmon-fishers, deer-stalkers,—the men who are most devoted to the sports which make the pulses throb with the most irrepressible excitement, are among the very keenest patrons of the game. Once a golfer you are always a golfer; you find besides that *bon chien chasse de race* and the hereditary taste will break out in successive generations.

Wherever the golfer settles, or wherever he colonises, he prospects the neighbourhood with both eyes wide open. One he naturally rivets on the main chance—on the farming, grazing, mining, or whatever may be his special object; but with the other he glances at the capabilities of the ground for his favourite game. We hear of golf in Canada, in Australia, in New Zealand, in all the colonies that are most affected by

Medal Day at St. Andrews

Scotchmen. There are towns in France where the Scotch settlers have inoculated the natives with the love of it; while in England it has been acclimatised from the bleak coasts of Northumberland to the sunny shores of Devon, and reports of matches are regularly forwarded to our sporting contemporaries from Crookham and Wimbledon, Blackheath and Westward Ho.

We own that at first sight it is difficult for the uninitiated looker-on to sympathise with the evident enthusiasm of the players. There does not seem to be anything very stimulating in grinding round a barren stretch of ground, impelling a gutta-percha ball before you, striving to land it in a succession of small holes in fewer strokes than your companion and opponent. But as to the reality of the excitement, you are soon compelled to take that for granted. You see gentlemen of all ages, often of the most self-indulgent or sedentary habits, turning out in every kind of weather, persevering to the dusk of a winter day, in spite of bitter wind and driving showers; or dragging about their cumbrous weight of flesh in hot defiance of the most sultry summer temperature. The truth is, that, appearances notwithstanding, experience proves it to be one of the most fascinating of pursuits; nor can there be any question that it is among the most invigorating. You play it on some stretch of ground by the sea, generally sheltered more or less by rows of hummocky sand-hills which break the force of the breeze without intercepting its freshness. You keep moving for the most part, although there is no need for moving faster than is necessary to set the blood in healthy circulation. In a tournament like that which ended on Wednesday at St. Andrews you select your own

Medal Day at St. Andrews

partner. The deep-chested, strapping young fellows in their prime, with the reach of arm and strength of shoulder that make their swing so tremendous in driving the ball, pair off together. The obese and elderly gentlemen, touched in the wind by time, and doubtful subjects for insurance offices, may jog round placidly at their own pace. When the players are fairly handicapped as they ought to be, the excitement lasts from the beginning to the finish of the game—each separate stroke has its visible result; ill-luck may balk you when you least expect it, and a trivial mistake may land you in some fatal difficulty. Strength will tell no doubt, but it is skill that lands the winner. Be cautious as you will even when playing over the flat, it is seldom that your ball will be lying on the level, leaving you nothing to do but to take a free sweep at it with a sharp eye and a steady wrist. The variety of the clubs that your "caddie" staggers under behind you is eloquent of the extreme niceties of the play. The club proper or the driver is a long shaft of seasoned hickory, tapering to a tough and narrow neck, before it swells into the broad flattened head, faced with horn or loaded with lead, which is intended to come in contact with the ball. But you have the shafts of others shortened to a variety of lengths, and the heads scooped out and bevelled away at all conceivable angles. This one is to be used when the ball lies embedded in a tuft of grass; that other when the ball must be "skied" or lifted over some swell of the ground that looms awkwardly full in front of you. Then, again, there are clubs headed with iron instead of wood, with which you may lay on with less fear of breakages, when the ball has to be excavated by knack and force from some ugly pitfall it has

Medal Day at St. Andrews

chosen to settle into. Finally, there are the putting clubs, and in their judicious use is embodied the perfection of golfing science. It is comparatively easy getting your ball near to the hole; a combination of fair luck with average skill will carry most people over the long distances at a reasonable pace. But it is quite another thing succeeding in "holing yourself." Around each of the small circular orifices is a tolerably smooth bit of turf, termed the putting green, and once landed on the green or near to it, you settle down to a sort of lawn billiards. It is then the cool and wary old players have the advantage over their more athletic adversaries. It is then that nervousness will come out if you are any way given to it, and many a fine player will show himself flurried when a ring of scientific amateurs with money on the match are closing round and watching him breathlessly. He singles out the short stiff club he is to strike with, draws back and stoops to let his eye travel over the bit of ground that lies between his ball and the hole. All may look pretty level in a bird's-eye view, but there are endless minute inequalities and obstacles; the stump of a green blade may divert the ball at the moderate pace at which he must set it rolling. Nothing but long experience and cool reflection will indicate the line the ball should be directed by, or train him to regulate the precise strength of his stroke. Let him lay on his hands half an ounce too heavily, and he sees the ball glide past the edge. Let him rest then a feather weight too lightly, and as it trickles down the imperceptible slope, it takes a faint bias to the side and balances itself tremblingly upon the lip instead of tumbling over the edge. There is exhilaration in the brisk walk round

Medal Day at St. Andrews

the links in the fresh sea air, but it is the culminating excitement of the critical moments on the putting greens which gives the national game its universal zest.

Not that you may not have had excitement in plenty, and in the way of play too, in the course of that same brisk round. The links, as we said, are stretches of short sandy grass by the sea shore, although occasionally they rise into steep downs, or sometimes, as with the Inches at Perth, are meadows on the banks of a river. Flat they are, and ought to be, in their general character, but if they were level like a lawn over all their surface, half the pleasures of Golf would be gone. The charm of the "going" game lies in the excitement of the "hazards"—a variety of malignant natural obstacles which are set like so many traps for the ball. Often skill may be trusted to clear these; sometimes skill will avail nothing, as when a sudden gust of wind curls your ball aside; not unfrequently a somewhat indifferent stroke will meet with punishment beyond its demerits. You meant to send your ball up the straight course, full in front of you, clearing the Scylla of a furze thicket on the one side, the Charybdis of a yawning sand-pit on the other. Your ball has made a turn to the right hand or to the left. In the former case it has fallen among the furze roots, and extrication is probably hopeless. You may as well lift it at once and submit to the penalty. In the latter you betake yourself to the most weighty of your irons, and labour to disengage yourself with more or less success. But hazards of the kind, though disagreeable, are indispensable, and on their quantity and character depend the merits of a golf ground. Thus the most famous gathering-places in Scotland, St. Andrews—

Medal Day at St. Andrews

which claims precedence over all—and North Berwick, Prestwick, and Gullane, come very nearly to perfection in their several ways. But there are others nearly as good, although less notorious. Often, however, the hazards are wanting in a country where there is plenty of elbow-room with other conditions in your favour, and it is to that fact, coupled with ignorance, that we may attribute the comparatively circumscribed popularity of Golf. It certainly has the merit of being one of the healthiest, cheapest, and most innocent of recreations, and considering the ubiquity of Scotchmen who have delighted in it in their boyhood, it is a marvel that it has not been more generally acclimated all over the world.

A Voice from the Rhine

On Board the Steamer "Prinz Von Preussen,"
between Mayence and Cologne,
17th *September* 1875.

In the heart of the Rhineland! afloat on the Rhine!
Ho! Kellner, schnell kommen! gleich bringen sie Wein!
What? Look at the scenery? Let it go hang!
I leave that to Herr Cook and his Cockneyfied gang.
Bring the hock to the cabin and leave me alone
Till we're moored to the jetty at fragrant Cologne.
But eight solid hours! I can't drown them in drink:
No, I've pens in my bag—also paper and ink;
And what can I better than score off a few
Correspondents at home, to whom letters are due?
Strathtyrum stands first for a missive in prose;
But since I'm in verse, I'll continue. Here goes.
I was dreaming, dear Editor, fondly last night
Of this festival season of Scottish delight;
And its whole panorama of pleasure seemed spread
In a luminous ether enclosing my bed;
So that whithersoever my eyes chanced to move,—
Right, left, or in front—or below or above,—
They met something—some vision—suggestive to me
Of joys that have been, and of joys that might be.
Here a well-driven grouse-pack swept level and low
O'er a bright bit of moorland, and blotted its glow;

A Voice from the Rhine

Here, huge on the sky-line, a stag sniffed the breeze ;
There a stalker crept, cat-like, on hands and on knees.
Here "Fan" in the turnips stood firm as a rock ;
There "Flo" through the covert went bustling the cock.
In a stream to the right trout and salmon arose ;
Overhead pheasants rocketed thicker than crows.
To the left, o'er blue waters—all glitter and gleam—
Danced a tight little yacht with the wind on her beam.
And what was that orb, of elliptical flight,
That flashed like a meteor and whizzed out of sight?
It recalled an occasion when multitudes yelled
O'er a ball by thy biceps, Tom Morris, propelled.
And what was that flash? By my oath, 'twas the gun
Which announced to St. Andrews the meeting begun.
And there, to be sure, was the usual array
Which greets one each year on the opening day.
Fair bevies of ladies awaiting the start,
And couples "tee'd up," and in haste to depart.
Looking on, Tom and Tommie, Kidd, Jamie, and Strath,
And all the professional children of wrath,
And armies of caddies in quest of a job—
Except, of course, swells like "The Daw" or old Bob,
The apple-faced sage, with his nostrum for all,
"Dinna hurry the swing ! keep your e'e on the ball !"
But the gun it went off, and the fun it began,
And off to the "high hole" in vision I ran ;
And there, where the critics and "ring-men" were massed,
I watched the quiet tide of the game as it passed.
And first, with a cleek-shot, the Editor stole,
Like a thief in the night, to the edge of the hole ;

A Voice from the Rhine

So that gallant Mount-Melville (whom Time touches not)
Clapped his hands in applause and cried, "Capital shot!"
Then himself played a "*putt*" which brought life to the eye
Of the mummified "Ancient," who hiccupped hard by.
And next came the *flyers* to show them the way—
Brave Innes and Boothby, and lithe Robert Hay;
And Hodge and a man who's too free with his damns—
(I don't know his name)—and a couple of Lambs.
Then Kinloch who's rather a one-er to slog,
And with him Bob Bethune caressing a dog.
Then stout Willie Mure with his muscular grace;
And wild Davie Wauchope, all over the place;
And Ormsary—lyrical son of the Gael—
With his whirligig spoon swung aloft like a flail.
And then the *hoi polloi*,—some better, some worse—
Delving and sawing through sand and through gorse,
Interspersed, to be sure, with some heroes of fame—
M'Whannel whom Rarey himself couldn't tame,
And Elliot the ardent, in peace as in war,
And Morton "that bright and particular star."
Last, a couple of greybeards came "*papping* along"
Who with whin-bush and bunker the fun did prolong,
Till two fat men in rear, cried, "With anger we rave!
By the Lord, they've been hours, sir, in 'Walkinshaw's grave'!"
'Twas the "Beefer" and "Burnhouse" whose anger thus rose,
Till it blazed in their cheeks with the tints of their hose;
And so fierce was the glare that the dreamer awoke,
And the phantasmagoria vanished like smoke.
But again, half asleep, at the close of the night,
As I dreamed of St. Andrews and Scottish delight,

A Voice from the Rhine

I sat up in my bed and proclaimed with a shout,
I was sick of this kingdom of beer and sauer-kraut;
And that in the first train—this I swore by the Rood—
I'd be off to the land of the mountain and flood.
Brave words! But some objects took shape in the dawn,
Which but now on the table lay shapeless and wan.
These were mountains of foolscap, still virgin and white,
Which sent forth a voice that said, "Write, villain, write!"
And a mean little hillock of "copy" hard by,
Which could only re-echo the sinister cry.
My portmanteaus, 'tis true—taking voice from despair—
Whined, "Pack us, old fellow, we pine for home air."
But the hungry portfolio which held 'Fair to See'
Yelled, "Pack you! Then, damn it! pray, who's to pack me?"
The portfolio was right, though its language was strong,
And it cuts short a yarn that's already too long;
For in its fierce words the sad moral I hear,
"For me there's no fun, no Strathtyrum this year."

L. W. M. L.

MEDAL DAY AT BLACKHEATH

IS an ill wind that blows nobody good. The grey skies and east winds of yesterday were bad for Ascot; but they were appropriate enough over the bleak and sandy undulations of Blackheath, where the golfers had come to compete for their summer medal. Many of the hardy Scotchmen who came out in their scarlet jackets and white breeches must have fancied they were at home again—that they were playing on the famous links of St. Andrews, or by the Fair City of Perth, or within sight of Salisbury Crags. Might they not, with a little imagination, have changed the scene, taking the distant slopes of Shooter's-hill for a sort of reduced Arthur's Seat, the windings of the Thames at Greenwich for the windings of the Forth, and recognising all around that prevailing mist that comes in from the sea to tone down

From the *Daily News*, June 1874.

MEDAL DAY AT BLACKHEATH

Medal Day at Blackheath

the colours of Scotland's capital? But perhaps in the excitement of "teeing" they

> Forgot the clouded Forth,
> The gloom that saddens Heaven and Earth,
> The bitter east, and misty summer,
> And grey metropolis of the North,

and proceeded with their accustomed ardour to show their southern rivals how to go safely and boldly round a "course." It was possible, indeed, in many cases to apportion the nationality of the combatants, even though no explanatory music heralded their approach.

Here, for example, are two players who have just come on to the green plain of the Heath from the Dover road—that Dover road on which, we have been informed by good authority, mile-stones are to be found. One is a man of sixty-five or so, six feet in height, broad-shouldered, with a majestic white beard and keen grey eyes looking out from under shaggy eyebrows. Those eyes, one may well imagine, have watched for the first appearance of the red deer as dawn broke over the mists of the Jura mountains, and then woe to the first stag that came along the rocks in advance of the herd! In addition to the scarlet jacket, and instead of the orthodox white trousers, he wears rough and serviceable knickerbockers: they may have brushed the heather on the moorlands of Ross or in the moist valleys of the far island of Lewis. The other is a handsome young man of a thoroughly English type, slender in make and soft in feature, with fair hair, light grey eyes, and sun-tanned face. They are preceded by a scout, who carries a red flag. The scout is not a tall

Medal Day at Blackheath

and stalwart gillie in kilts, but a short, stout, in-kneed youth, who seems to have just left his barrow round the corner, and who would probably prove an ugly customer in a rush along the Strand on a Lord Mayor's Day. They are attended by two other persons, also apparently costermongers out of work, each of whom carries an armful of the implements used in the game, and who is supposed to hand the necessary club, spoon, or putter when his master requires it. There are few people on the Heath. The spectators are chiefly boys, who take their position at critical points, and soon get to acquire a sufficient knowledge of this occult game to calculate the chances of the players, although they might not be able to estimate accurately the value of "one off three." For the rest, there is little picturesqueness about the scene—except for these bits of scarlet colour scattered over the dull green of the Heath. It is a sombre day. The houses and trees about shut out the grey river and its masts. Shooter's-hill looks distant in the thin fog; there is not a break in the low-toned sky; and the gallant golfer is not the less inclined to consider himself back in Scotland again when he overhears his companion suddenly say to a dilatory attendant, "Whut the deevil ur ye daein' here? Get on, man!" It is thus that they sing the songs of Zion in a strange land.

Now at the beginning of the game a little law is allowed; and if the player chooses he may place the small white ball on a tiny heap of sand in order to deliver the first blow more effectually. Shall we calculate the chances of the new comers by this "teeing"? MacCallum-Mhor, having carefully placed the ball, kicks aside a twig here or there to clear the way, grasps his club, straightens up his shoulders, and has a look

Medal Day at Blackheath

across the broad and shallow sand-pit near him, on the farther side of which stands the scout with his red flag. Up goes the club over his shoulder, there is a moment's deliberation, and then the rapid blow is delivered—sending the ball whistling through the air some hundred and fifty yards or so before it drops, while we see it thereafter go bounding on to within a dozen yards of the red flag. The younger man also carefully places his ball; he too measures his distance, and delivers a heavy blow—but, somehow, the ball flies off at an angle, it drops short of the opposite crest, and comes rolling down into the hollow. By the time the small crowd of people has walked round to the other side of this little valley, the players have already crossed, and each is doing his utmost to get his ball, with the fewest possible number of strokes, into a certain small hole dug in the ground. But then MacCallum-Mhor has it all his own way; for at the very first stroke he came within a few yards of this particular spot. At present his ball is within three-quarters of a yard of the small black hole. He chooses a particular club; measures distance and direction carefully; gives the ball a tap, and as straight as a line can go it trundles along and disappears. He picks it out; tosses it to an attendant to be sponged; and takes another to continue the game. If there were any betting going on, the small crowd would be inclined to back the elder of these two players.

And what is the opinion which the unexcited Southron forms of this imported pastime? Well, it is obviously one that involves a good deal of physical effort, as well as the exercise of trained skill of various kinds. In the case of long courses, the holes or goals are sometimes a quarter of a mile

Medal Day at Blackheath

apart; and a good player must be prepared to put all his strength into the blow which he then deals at the ball. Then he must be able to judge distances accurately; he must be capable of taking sure aim and sending the ball in a straight line; and he must have experience of the various chances which may befall him on uneven ground. The golf-player does not desire a smooth plain. His best ground lies near the sea, where the sand has been washed in bygone ages into all sorts of gentle hills and dales; and failing that, an occasional gravel-pit offers the best obstruction he can get. When one of the longed-for holes lies close by the brink of some abrupt hollow, the manœuvring with which a skilful player will get his ball over the hollow, and yet not too far on the other side, is beautiful to witness. There is not, certainly, the nicety of billiard playing in the performance; but there is a vast deal more of exercise in the game, and the air that one breathes—even when the east winds are blowing—is preferable to the gas-smoke of a billiard-room. Indeed, there is so much exercise in the game that one can observe our hardy mountaineers who hail from the north puffing and blowing at times in a fashion which suggests that they are not quite in condition to go "chasing the wild deer and following the roe." Perhaps our southern fashions have corrupted them. City dinners are not a good preparation for work of this sort. The mountaineer's legs may keep firm enough, but heavy luncheons begin to alter his figure somewhat and keep him scant of breath. Ought the corpulent golfer to "Bant," or trust to his favourite exercise to restore to him his wonted length of wind? The latter is the more natural method, certainly, although we are in these times so given

Medal Day at Blackheath

over to the teachings of physiology that one can scarcely understand how Shakspeare managed to get through such an enormous amount of intellectual labour, considering that he was probably unaware of the fact that there is phosphorus in fish, and that Greek wines are good for the exhausted brain.

THE GOLFER'S GARLAND [1]

OF rural diversions too long has the Chace
All the honours usurp'd, and assum'd the chief place;
But truth bids the Muse from henceforward proclaim,
That GOFF, first of sports, shall stand foremost in fame.

O'er the Heath, see our heroes in uniform clad,
In parties well match'd, how they gracefully spread;
While with long strokes and short strokes they tend
    to the goal,
And with putt well directed plump into the hole.

---

[1] Composed for the Blackheath Golf Club, and often sung with great spirit at the celebration of the Ludi Apollinares of Edinburgh. This Song must have been written previous to 1793, as it is printed in the Appendix to the Third Edition of Mathison's Poem of *The Goff*, published in that year.

The Golfer's Garland

At Goff we contend without rancour or spleen,
And bloodless the laurels we reap on the green;
From vig'rous exertions our raptures arise,
And to crown our delights no poor fugitive dies.

From exercise keen, from strength active and bold,
We'll traverse the green, and forget we grow old;
Blue Devils, diseases, dull sorrow and care,
Knock'd down by our Balls as they whizz thro' the air.

Health, happiness, harmony, friendship, and fame,
Are the fruits and rewards of our favourite game.
A sport so distinguish'd the Fair must approve:
Then to Goff give the day, and the ev'ning to love.

Our first standing toast we'll to Goffing assign,
No other amusement's so truly divine;
It has charms for the aged, as well as the young,
Then as first of field sports let its praises be sung.

The next we shall drink to our friends far and near,
And the mem'ry of those who no longer appear;
Who have play'd their last round, and pass'd over that
    bourne
From which the best Goffer can never return.

Allan Robertson

ALLAN ROBERTSON, the greatest golf-player that ever lived, of whom alone in the annals of the pastime it can be said that he never was beaten, was born at St. Andrews on the 11th September 1815. He came of a golfing race. His grandfather, Peter Robertson, who died in 1803, was a ball-maker and professional golfer. His father, too, David Robertson, who lived till 1836, followed the same trade, and was moreover a good player in his day—nay, few were better on the golfing green. As might be expected from such a generation of golfers, ALLAN took naturally to the Links. It is a fact that his very playthings as a child were golf clubs. As he grew up, this natural tendency, joined to a natural desire of his father that his son should continue the business of ball-maker, decided ALLAN'S profession, and in due course of time he likewise took up the awl and the feathers to learn the manufacture of golf-balls.

At that period golfing was quite another thing from what it is now, or at least its accessories were. Gutta percha was unknown, and golf-balls were composed of stout leather cases stuffed hard with boiled feathers. Their manufacture, indeed, was both a difficult and an arduous matter; and their expense when finished was such as to restrict the practice of the game, as a rule, to the more wealthy of the community. The Links of St. Andrews, in consequence, were less frequented than now; the course was rougher; the sport had an aristocratic and portly mien; and the matches of professionals were as pregnant with interest as any public event. It is not so now; the St. Andrews Links are crowded with careless multitudes luxuriating in the pastime cheapened to them by the discovery of gutta percha; and the game is popularised at the expense of its stately traditions.

ALLAN, however, commenced his golfing career in what, despite the

---

From the *Dundee Advertiser,* Sept. 1859.

Allan Robertson

dearness of leather and the paucity of players, we must still call the palmy days of golf. His entire nature was bent on being a golfer. It is yet told on the Links, how ALLAN would rise betimes, and with shirt sleeves rolled up for better muscular play, start alone for practice across the deserted Links still wet with early dew. His success was abundant. ALLAN has improved in his day on the old theories of golf, and to him are owing many of the improved methods and styles of the present game. Some of these we will afterwards more particularly allude to.

In the spring of 1848, Mr. Campbell, of Saddell (we believe), brought a few experimental gutta percha balls from London to St. Andrews. They were not very first-rate, to be sure; were not hammered, and flew heavily. Still the material was unquestionably good, and adaptable; and consternation stood on every face, ALLAN'S included. And no wonder. The leather ball trade was the only one St. Andrews could boast, and it was considerable, extending to exports to the colonies as well as home consumption. In ALLAN'S shop alone there were made, for example, in 1840, 1021 balls; in 1841, 1392; in 1844, 2456; and so on. The introduction of gutta percha, which anybody could mould into a sphere, was a dreadful prospect for ALLAN and his brethren, and dire was their alarm. It is even related that ALLAN would gladly buy up all the gutta percha balls found among the whins, etc., and actually attempted to destroy the obnoxious interlopers with fire!

However, the influx was too great for this system to be pursued any longer, and about 1850 ALLAN entered regularly into golf-ball making from gutta percha; and we are glad to know that his labour, whilst it was easier to himself, was not a whit less rewarded than in the old monopoly days of feathers.

The life of a professional golfer, like ALLAN'S, is so composed of continuous matches and a certain recurring sameness of incident, that we have found it impossible to trace in anything like a consecutive story the incidents of ALLAN'S life. All we can do is to recall a few memories here and there, and give a selection in chronological order of his more important matches and feats.

Who will ever forget ALLAN, having once seen him? What Sir Hugh Lyon Playfair has been to the city proper, has ALLAN been to the Links of St. Andrews. They have unwittingly been in close partnership. Sir Hugh renovated a rough ruined street; ALLAN had an eye the while to the improvement of the Links. Sir Hugh attracted citizens, ALLAN, golfers; ah! it was a magnificent partnership, and has done wonders. The analogy holds good between the two in other respects also. Who could

Allan Robertson

do the honours of the Links like ALLAN? He was as perfectly at home with a descendant of William the Conqueror as with one of the caddies. Without the least tinge of servility, ALLAN could accommodate himself to everybody, and arranged everything on the golfing links with the politeness of a Brummel and the policy of a Talleyrand.

We have asked, Who that has once seen the champion golfer can ever forget him? Let us try to help the picture which every player will oft in fancy draw. Our scene is the St. Andrews Links on a genial summer's day. ALLAN's house crowns the summit of the slope; down towards the sea—the blue, beautiful sea—lies the white Club-House, with its gravelled terrace. It is not yet eleven, that great hour of cause on the Links. Groups of caddies are prowling about; a clash and rattle of clubs are heard as you pass the club-makers' shops. One or two golfers are putting idly at the starting hole with their burnished cleeks, trying some impossible *putt*, which, if they had only done but yesterday, would have put a very different finish on to a certain match. Suddenly a golfer appears at the Club-House door; he looks about for somebody who is evidently lacking; "Where's ALLAN?"—the cry is repeated by telegraphic caddies right up to the champion's little garden. A minute elapses, and down comes the champion in hot haste to the Club-House. He is, you will recollect, oh! golfer, not of much stature, compact, rather robust indeed, with a short stoop, and short-necked. His face is pleasant to look at—rather Hibernian, indeed, with its habitual expression of drollery, which has almost given the stalwart golfer one or two dimples. He is dressed, as you must well remember, in his favourite red jacket, and carries a cleek (a pet weapon) in his hand. But now the match is arranged. ALLAN has evidently got to nurse an elementary golfer. It is a foursome; ALLAN and his *protégé* against two rather good hands. Remark how pleasant the little man is; no miss of his partner causes a shade to his habitual good nature, and, ten to one, when the match comes in from their round, but the new player swears by ALLAN, and gives in his adhesion to golf for once and all.

But it was in a grand match that the figure of ALLAN should live in the memory of all. Who shall describe his elegant and beautifully correct style of play? The champion was remarkable for his *easy* style, depending on a long cool swing, and never on sheer strength. His clubs were of the *toy* description, as the slang of the Links hath it, possessing no weight or misproportion of wood. Indeed, in a word, ALLAN's game throughout was pure unadulterated science. No man, perhaps, so well united in his play all the bits of the game. Pretty driver as he was, we will stake our belief on ALLAN's short game, especially in quarter shots. And this was

Allan Robertson

an important point in ALLAN'S practice. He it was that introduced the deadly use of the cleek in playing up to the hole. Previous to about 1848 or 1849, short wooden clubs, the baffing or short-spoons, were used for this important stroke—both difficult, and frequently inaccurate. But ALLAN employed the cleek to jerk up his ball; however badly it might lie, it was all the same; and this killing game, destructive to a certain extent to the green, is now all but universal.

To return to ALLAN'S great matches. His coolness was unique, and almost miraculous. He was never known to *funk* or indeed change his off-hand manner in the least. He was never beaten—proud epitaph. It is something to be the best in anything, of all the world, and ALLAN stood confessed the model player. But it is not only as a golfer that ALLAN is to be deeply deplored. He was possessed of the best heart and kindliest feelings in the world. In the intricate dealings of the Links, in the formation and playing of great matches, ALLAN was honourable, just, and gentlemanly, from first to last.

ALLAN did much for golfing both in and out of St. Andrews. He has laid out capital Links in various districts, and played thereon himself to the incitement of beginners.

A new era is about to dawn on the golfing links; the old stars are paling; when will others arise? Hugh Philp, who knew how to make a club, is gone; gone too, fine ALLAN, who knew how to handle one.

Up to the spring of the present year, ALLAN was a hale, stout little man, with scarcely the memory of an hour's illness. Temperate too, in an uncommon degree, regular in his habits, and enjoying daily exercise on the Links; no one could reasonably foretell the rapid change that has taken him from us. In the spring, ALLAN had an attack of jaundice, proceeding, we believe, from an abnormal state of the liver. He never rallied; and after six months' weakness, he gradually sunk, and died on the 1st of September. God rest him, noble golfer, excellent companion—we will not easily see his like again.

We have already noticed how impossible it is, especially with imperfect means of information, to give a consecutive or full account of the champion's feats, but we subjoin a few, in hopes that this meagre outline may testify, in some small way, to the merit, as a man and a golfer, of ALLAN ROBERTSON.

1840. Allan played a grand match with Tom Alexander, ballmaker, Musselburgh, over the St. Andrews Links, in October, and beat him by 4 holes, doing the round at 95.

Allan Robertson

1842. Allan and Sandy Herd played in a double against Tom Morris and Jamie Herd, beating them by 2 holes. Strokes, 91 and 94.

1842. Allan played a match in December with Tom Morris, beating him by 2 holes, and holing the Links at 93.

1843. Allan played during the month of June, over the St. Andrews Links, a great match of twenty rounds, two each day, against William Dunn of Musselburgh. Allan gained on the tenth, or last day, by two rounds and one to play.

1843. Allan played a great match of 36 holes with William Dunn of Musselburgh, beating him by 8 holes, and holing the second round at 88 strokes.

1844. Allan played a match with William Dunn, over three links: 1st, on Musselburgh Links, where Dunn gained; 2nd, at North Berwick Links, where Allan was victorious; and 3rd, at St. Andrews, where he also won, thus gaining the match also.

1846. In April, Allan played another of his matches with W. Dunn: 1st, at Musselburgh, where Dunn beat Allan by 7 ahead and 5 to play; 2nd, at St. Andrews, where Allan won by 5 and 3; and 3rd, at Leven, where he also was victor by 6 and 4 to play, thus winning the match.

1846. Allan played with a single driving club against Captain Broughton, and holed the round of the St. Andrews Links at 95.

1848. Allan played a threesome with William Dunn and Tom Morris over Dubbieside Links. Allan holed 18 holes (two rounds), at 80; Tom Morris, at 89; and Dunn, at 91 strokes.

1849. A great match for £400 was played in the summer between Allan and Tom Morris against the two Dunns of Musselburgh, on three links, Musselburgh, St. Andrews, and North Berwick. At Musselburgh the Dunns won at a canter, winning by 13 holes and 12 to play. At St. Andrews, however, Allan and Tom won their rounds, and retrieved some two or three holes. North Berwick was the deciding place, and at the commencement of the *last round of all*, the Dunns had four holes ahead, and only eight to play. However, Allan and Tom, by a magnificent game, gained the first hole, then the second, halved the third, gained the fourth, halved the fifth, and gained the sixth, thus making the poll *all even!* and two to play. These two holes Allan and Tom also won, thus obtaining the match, one of the most brilliant and extraordinary in the whole annals of golfing.

1850. In October Allan and Tom Morris played over the St. Andrews Links a foursome against the two Dunns for £50 a-side. Allan and his partner finished at the burn hole by 2 and 1 to play, holing at 88.

Allan Robertson

1852. In October, over the St. Andrews Links, Allan and Tom Morris played a great match of 36 holes with Robert Hay, Esq., and William Dunn, Blackheath, for £100 a-side. Allan and his partner won by 6 holes ahead and 5 to play.

1853. In October, over the St. Andrews Links, Allan played a round with Captain John Campbell Stewart, 72nd Highlanders, winner at that meeting of the Royal Medal. This round was halved, though Allan was 3 ahead and 4 to play, and dormy at the burn.

At this time, also, Sir Thomas Moncrieffe and Allan played Tom Morris and Captain Fairlie. The first round was won by Allan and his partner, at 3 and 1 to play; and the second by their adversaries, at 4 and 3 to play. This foursome was played repeatedly, and on the whole play it may be said to have formed one of the closest matches on record.

1857. Allan and Andrew Strath, in May, over the St. Andrews Links, played a round against Tom Morris and Park junior, winning by 6 holes. Strokes, 84 and 90.

1858. On the 15th September, Allan, in a round with Mr. Bethune of Blebo, accomplished the round of the St. Andrews Links at 79 strokes, a number altogether unparalleled, and likely to remain so. The following are the particulars of this superb score:—Going out—1 in 4; 2 in 4; 3 in 4; 4 in 5; 5 in 5; 6 in 6; 7 in 4; 8 in 4; 9 in 4. Total going out, 40. Coming in—10 in 4; 11 in 3; 12 in 5; 13 in 6; 14 in 4; 15 in 5; 16 in 5; 17 in 4; 18 in 3. Total coming in, 39.

At various times Allan has holed the St. Andrews Links at the following numbers, selecting his best holes:—Going out—1 in 3 strokes; 2 in 3; 3 in 3; 4 in 3; 5 in 4; 6 in 4; 7 in 3; 8 in 1; 9 in 3. Total, 27. Coming in—10 in 3; 11 in 2; 12 in 3; 13 in 4; 14 in 4; 15 in 3; 16 in 3; 17 in 4; 18 in 3. Total, 29. Number of strokes to this selected round, 56.

In comparing the above scores, it must be kept in mind that the St. Andrews Links are now not nearly so difficult to play as they were in Allan's time.

Tom Morris Jun.

A PAINFUL feeling of surprise was experienced in the city and elsewhere on Christmas, when the report spread that one so well known and respected, both on his own account and that of his father, had died suddenly that morning. The deceased had returned home on Thursday, after two days' absence, in his usual health. The following evening—Christmas eve—he supped at a private party with a few friends, and was in his accustomed cheerful spirits. On returning home at eleven he sat and conversed for some time with his mother, who is an invalid. After retiring to bed in an adjoining room, his father, according to custom, went and bade him good-night. The following morning his parents heard his usual movements, and about an hour after, upon his being called for breakfast, and no answer being obtained, the sad fact then became apparent that he had passed away, and so quietly that he did not appear to have been awakened out of sleep. The cause of so sudden and peaceful an end appeared, from a minute medical examination, to have been the sudden bursting of an artery under the right lung.

"Tommy," by which name he was so universally known, was born at St. Andrews, and not at Prestwick as has been incorrectly stated. He was therefore a native of the place with which he had been so long associated, and will be long remembered. He was twenty-four years of age. Shortly after his birth he removed with his father to Prestwick, and returned with him in 1864, when, shortly afterwards, he began to display those wonderful golfing powers of which mention will presently be made.

A little more than a year ago he was married—a union of the strongest mutual affection, which promised to be both long and happy. It will be in the recollection of our readers that at the close of a victorious golf match in September between his father and himself against the brothers Park, at North Berwick, he received intelligence of the sudden illness of his wife, and ere he had time to leave for St. Andrews in a yacht kindly put at his disposal by a gentleman, a second telegram announced her death, and also that of his child, which had just been born.

To all who knew Tommy and his fine sensitive nature, it will not be difficult to understand that he received a blow from which he never recovered.

His next public appearance was after the October meeting, when he played with his father against Strath and Martin, and after bringing it

Tom Morris Jun.

so near a successful close as to be four holes up, and five to play, he unexpectedly and so completely broke down as to lose the five holes and consequently the match. After this he became seriously unwell, and no effort availed to rouse him from the recollection of her with whom all his interest in life had passed away.

On the challenge of the late match with Mr. Molesworth being given, Tommy's friends readily entered into it with the view that it might happily rouse him and do him good, although it was manifest he was far out of condition for such a match, and those who witnessed it could not fail to observe a strange want of that spirit and determination which characterised all his previous performances on the green; and, indeed, he more than once observed to the writer of these lines that but for the interests of his friends and backers he would not have continued it.

As to his professional career, which commenced at the early age of sixteen, it is interesting to notice how the aptitude for athletic games runs in and descends through certain families. As in cricket we have the names of the Walkers, the Lyttletons, and the Graces, so in golf we have those of the Morrises, Straths, and Parks.

Young Tom was first brought into public notice at a golf tournament at Carnoustie in 1867, where he defeated all comers, professionals and amateurs. On the back of it he played and beat Willie Park. He seems after this to have been victorious at every green on which he appeared. This led to the most brilliant display of golf ever known, and which constituted him, not only by the result, but by the performance, "The Champion."

The Prestwick Club in 1860 instituted a challenge belt to be played for annually there, and to be held by the winner until won from him; but in the event of it being won in three consecutive years by the same player —which was considered almost impossible—it was then to become his absolute property. It will not be uninteresting to state the history of the playing for the belt :—

	Strokes.
1860, won by W. Park, Musselburgh	174
1861, won by T. Morris, Prestwick	163
1862, won by T. Morris, Prestwick	163
1863, won by W. Park, Musselburgh	168
1864, won by T. Morris, Prestwick	167
1865, won by A. Strath, Prestwick	162
1866, won by W. Park, Musselburgh	169
1867, won by T. Morris, St. Andrews	170

Tom Morris Jun.

	Strokes.
1868, won by Tom Morris, jun., St. Andrews	154
1869, won by Tom Morris, jun., do.	157
1870, won by Tom Morris, jun., do.	149

So the trophy, which consists of red morocco, and is an exquisite piece of workmanship, richly ornamented with massive silver plates, bearing appropriate devices, and produced at the cost of thirty guineas, became the property of Young Tom, and remains an heirloom in his family. After an interval of a year a challenge cup was substituted, to be played for annually in turn on the three greens, Prestwick, St. Andrews, and Musselburgh, when Tommy again was victorious at Prestwick, with a score of 166—thus winning the distinction four consecutive times.

As an instance of the smallness of his scores, when playing for professional prizes in 1869, after tieing twice with Bob Fergusson, they went out a third time, when he won with the smallest score ever known to be made on St. Andrews Links, viz.—

$$\begin{aligned} \text{Out,} & \quad 4\ 4\ 4\ 5\ 6\ 4\ 4\ 3\ 3 — 37 \\ \text{In,} & \quad 3\ 3\ 4\ 6\ 5\ 4\ 5\ 5\ 5 — 40 \\ & \qquad\qquad\qquad\qquad\quad —77 \end{aligned}$$

It would be endless to enumerate the many great professional matches in which he distinguished himself; but it cannot be doubted that the only one of his brother professionals who could claim to enter the lists with him was his old and firm friend Davie Strath. They acted towards each other as professional adviser, whenever and wherever a common foe was to be met. Many were the matches which they had against one another, the last two of which, played in 1873, resulted in very narrow majorities— one in favour of each. They continually met in foursome play, which so largely distinguishes the St. Andrews Links.

From his amiable temperament and obliging disposition, his gentlemanly appearance and manly bearing, combined with that undaunted determination which so marked his play, Young Tom became a great favourite with every one with whom he played; and these lines cannot better be concluded than with the remark of one, writing since his death, who played often with him, and was a good judge of the game—"Tommy," says he, "was the best player who ever addressed himself to a ball."

A memorial has been erected to his memory, funds having been collected for the purpose.

J. G. D.

January 1876.

Rules for the Game of Golf

AS IT IS PLAYED BY

THE ROYAL & ANCIENT GOLF CLUB OF ST. ANDREWS

1. The Game of Golf is played by two or more sides, each playing its own ball. A side may consist of one or more persons.

2. The game consists in each side playing a ball from a tee into a hole by successive strokes, and the hole is won by the side holing its ball in the fewest strokes, except as otherwise provided for in the rules. If two sides hole out in the same number of strokes, the hole is halved.

3. The teeing ground shall be indicated by two marks placed in a line at right angles to the course, and the player shall not tee in front of, nor on either side of, these marks, nor more than two club lengths behind them. A ball played from outside the limits of the teeing ground, as thus defined, may be recalled by the opposite side.

The hole shall be $4\frac{1}{4}$ inches in diameter, and at least 4 inches deep.

4. The ball must be fairly struck at, and not pushed, scraped, or spooned, under penalty of the loss of the hole. Any movement of the club which is intended to strike the ball is a stroke.

5. The game commences by each side playing a ball from the first teeing ground. In a match with two or more on a side, the partners shall strike off alternately from the tees, and shall strike alternately during the play of the hole.

The players who are to strike against each other shall be named at starting, and shall continue in the same order during the match.

The player who shall play first on each side shall be named by his own side.

In case of failure to agree, it shall be settled by lot or toss which side shall have the option of leading.

6. If a player shall play when his partner should have done so, his side shall lose the hole, except in the case of the tee shot, when the stroke may be recalled at the option of the opponents.

Rules for the Game of Golf

7. The side winning a hole shall lead in starting for the next hole, and may recall the opponent's stroke should he play out of order. This privilege is called the "honour." On starting for a new match, the winner of the long match in the previous round is entitled to the "honour." Should the first match have been halved, the winner of the last hole gained is entitled to the "honour."

8. One round of the Links—generally 18 holes—is a match, unless otherwise agreed upon. The match is won by the side which gets more holes ahead than there remain holes to be played, or by the side winning the last hole when the match was all even at the second last hole. If both sides have won the same number, it is a halved match.

9. After the balls are struck from the tee, the ball furthest from the hole to which the parties are playing shall be played first, except as otherwise provided for in the rules. Should the wrong side play first, the opponent may recall the stroke before his side has played.

10. Unless with the opponent's consent, a ball struck from the tee shall not be changed, touched, or moved before the hole is played out, under the penalty of one stroke, except as otherwise provided for in the rules.

11. In playing through the green, all *loose* impediments, within a club length of a ball which is not lying in or touching a hazard, may be removed, but loose impediments which are more than a club length from the ball shall not be removed under the penalty of one stroke.

12. Before striking at the ball, the player shall not move, bend, or break anything fixed or growing near the ball, except in the act of placing his feet on the ground for the purpose of addressing the ball, and in soling his club to address the ball, under the penalty of the loss of the hole, except as provided for in Rule 18.

13. A ball stuck fast in wet ground or sand may be taken out and replaced loosely in the hole which it has made.

14. When a ball lies in or touches a hazard, the club shall not touch the ground, nor shall anything be touched or moved before the player strikes at the ball, except that the player may place his feet firmly on the ground for the purpose of addressing the ball, under the penalty of the loss of the hole.

15. A "hazard" shall be any bunker of whatever nature :—water, sand, loose earth, mole hills, paths, roads or railways, whins, bushes, rushes, rabbit scrapes, fences, ditches, or anything which is not the

Rules for the Game of Golf

ordinary green of the course, except sand blown on to the grass by wind, or sprinkled on grass for the preservation of the Links, or snow or ice, or bare patches on the course.

16. A player or a player's caddie shall not press down or remove any irregularities of surface near the ball, except at the teeing ground, under the penalty of the loss of the hole.

17. If any vessel, wheel-barrow, tool, roller, grass-cutter, box, or other similar obstruction has been placed upon the course, such obstruction may be removed. A ball lying on or touching such obstruction, or on clothes, or nets, or on ground under repair or temporarily covered up or opened, may be lifted and dropped at the nearest point of the course, but a ball lifted in a hazard shall be dropped in the hazard. A ball lying in a golf hole or flag hole, may be lifted and dropped not more than a club length behind such hole.

18. When a ball is completely covered with fog, bent, whins, etc., only so much thereof shall be set aside as that the player shall have a view of his ball before he plays, whether in a line with the hole or otherwise.

19. When a ball is to be dropped, the player shall drop it. He shall front the hole, stand erect behind the hazard, keep the spot from which the ball was lifted (or in the case of running water, the spot at which it entered) in a line between him and the hole, and drop the ball behind him from his head, standing as far behind the hazard as he may please.

20. When the balls in play lie within six inches of each other—measured from their nearest points—the ball nearer the hole shall be lifted until the other is played, and shall then be replaced as nearly as possible in its original position. Should the ball further from the hole be accidentally moved in so doing, it shall be replaced. Should the lie of the lifted ball be altered by the opponent in playing, it may be placed in a lie near to, and as nearly as possible similar to, that from which it was lifted.

21. If the ball lie or be lost in water, the player may drop a ball, under the penalty of one stroke.

22. Whatever happens by accident to a ball *in motion*, such as its being deflected or stopped by any agency outside the match, or by the fore-caddie, is a "rub of the green," and the ball shall be played from where it lies. Should a ball lodge in anything moving, such ball, or if it cannot be recovered, another ball shall be dropped as nearly as possible at the spot where the object was when the ball lodged in it. But if a ball *at*

Rules for the Game of Golf

rest be displaced by any agency outside the match, the player shall drop it or another ball as nearly as possible at the spot where it lay. On the Putting Green the ball may be replaced by hand.

23. If the player's ball strike, or be accidentally moved by an opponent or an opponent's caddie or clubs, the opponent loses the hole.

24. If the player's ball strike, or be stopped by himself or his partner, or either of their caddies or clubs, or if, while in the act of playing, the player strike the ball twice, his side loses the hole.

25. If the player when not making a stroke, or his partner or either of their caddies touch their side's ball, except at the tee, so as to move it, or by touching anything cause it to move, the penalty is one stroke.

26. A ball is considered to have been moved if it leave its original position in the least degree and stop in another ; but if a player touch his ball and thereby cause it to oscillate, without causing it to leave its original position, it is not moved in the sense of Rule 25.

27. A player's side loses a stroke if he play the opponent's ball, unless (1) the opponent then play the player's ball, whereby the penalty is cancelled, and the hole must be played out with the balls thus exchanged, or (2) the mistake occur through wrong information given by the opponent, in which case the mistake, if discovered before the opponent has played, must be rectified by placing a ball as nearly as possible where the opponent's ball lay.

If it be discovered before either side has struck off at the tee that one side has played out the previous hole with the ball of a party not engaged in the match, that side loses that hole.

28. If a ball be lost, the player's side loses the hole. A ball shall be held as lost if it be not found within five minutes after the search is begun.

29. A ball must be played wherever it lies, or the hole be given up, except as otherwise provided for in the Rules.

30. The term " Putting Green " shall mean the ground within 20 yards of the hole, excepting hazards.

31. All loose impediments may be removed from the Putting Green, except the opponent's ball when at a greater distance from the player's than six inches.

32. In a match of three or more sides, a ball in any degree lying between the player and the hole must be lifted, or, if on the Putting Green, holed out.

Rules for the Game of Golf

33. When the ball is on the Putting Green, no mark shall be placed, nor line drawn as a guide. The line to the hole may be pointed out, but the person doing so may not touch the ground with the hand or club.

The player may have his own or his partner's caddie to stand at the hole, but none of the players or their caddies may move so as to shield the ball from, or expose it to, the wind.

The penalty for any breach of this rule is the loss of the hole.

34. The player or his caddie may remove (but not press down) sand, earth, worm casts or snow lying around the hole or on the line of his putt. This shall be done by brushing lightly with the hand only, across the putt and not along it. Dung may be removed to a side by an iron club, but the club must not be laid with more than its own weight upon the ground. The putting line must not be touched by club, hand, or foot, except as above authorised, or immediately in front of the ball in the act of addressing it, under the penalty of the loss of the hole.

35. Either side is entitled to have the flag-stick removed when approaching the hole. If the ball rest against the flag-stick when in the hole, the player shall be entitled to remove the stick, and, if the ball fall in, it shall be considered as holed out in the previous stroke.

36. A player shall not play until the opponent's ball shall have ceased to roll, under the penalty of one stroke. Should the player's ball knock in the opponent's ball, the latter shall be counted as holed out in the previous stroke. If, in playing, the player's ball displace the opponent's ball, the opponent shall have the option of replacing it.

37. A player shall not ask for advice, nor be knowingly advised about the game by word, look, or gesture from any one except his own caddie, or his partner or partner's caddie, under the penalty of the loss of the hole.

38. If a ball split into separate pieces, another ball may be put down where the largest portion lies, or if two pieces are apparently of equal size, it may be put where either piece lies, at the option of the player. If a ball crack or become unplayable, the player may change it, on intimating to his opponent his intention to do so.

39. A penalty stroke shall not be counted the stroke of a player, and shall not affect the rotation of play.

40. Should any dispute arise on any point, the players have the right of determining the party or parties to whom the dispute shall be referred, but should they not agree, either party may refer it to the Green Committee

Rules for the Game of Golf

of the Green where the dispute occurs, and their decision shall be final. Should the dispute not be covered by the Rules of Golf, the arbiters must decide it by equity.

SPECIAL RULES FOR MEDAL PLAY

(1) In Club competitions, the competitor doing the stipulated course in fewest strokes shall be the winner.

(2) If the lowest score be made by two or more competitors, the ties shall be decided by another round to be played either on the same or on any other day as the Captain, or, in his absence, the Secretary shall direct.

(3) New holes shall be made for the Medal Round, and thereafter no member shall play any stroke on a Putting Green before competing.

(4) The scores shall be kept by a special marker, or by the competitors noting each other's scores. The scores marked shall be checked at the finish of each hole. On completion of the course, the score of the player shall be signed by the person keeping the score and handed to the Secretary.

(5) If a ball be lost, the player shall return as nearly as possible to the spot where the ball was struck, tee another ball, and lose a stroke. If the lost ball be found before he has struck the other ball, the first shall continue in play.

(6) If the player's ball strike himself, or his clubs or caddie, or if, in the act of playing, the player strike the ball twice, the penalty shall be one stroke.

(7) If a competitor's ball strike the other player, or his clubs or caddie, it is a "rub of the green," and the ball shall be played from where it lies.

(8) A ball may, under a penalty of two strokes, be lifted out of a difficulty of any description, and be teed behind same.

(9) All balls shall be holed out, and when play is on the Putting Green, the flag shall be removed, and the competitor whose ball is nearest the hole shall have the option of holing out first, or of lifting his ball, if it be in such a position that it might, if left, give an advantage to the other competitor. Throughout the green a competitor can have the other competitor's ball lifted, if he find that it interferes with his stroke.

(10) A competitor may not play with a professional, and he may not receive advice from any one but his caddie.

A fore-caddie may be employed.

Rules for the Game of Golf

(11) Competitors may not discontinue play because of bad weather.

(12) The penalty for a breach of any rule shall be disqualification.

(13) Any dispute regarding the play shall be determined by the Green Committee.

(14) The ordinary Rules of Golf, so far as they are not at variance with these special rules, shall apply to medal play.

ETIQUETTE OF GOLF

The following customs belong to the established Etiquette of Golf and should be observed by all Golfers.

1. No player, caddie, or onlooker should move or talk during a stroke.

2. No player should play from the tee until the party in front have played their second strokes and are out of range, nor play to the Putting Green till the party in front have holed out and moved away.

3. The player who leads from the tee should be allowed to play before his opponent tees his ball.

4. Players who have holed out should not try their putts over again when other players are following them.

5. Players looking for a lost ball must allow any other match coming up to pass them.

6. A party playing three or more balls must allow a two ball match to pass them.

7. A party playing a shorter round must allow a two ball match playing the whole round to pass them.

8. A player should not putt at the hole when the flag is in it.

9. The reckoning of the strokes is kept by the terms "the odd," "two more," "three more," etc., and "one off three," "one off two," "the like." The reckoning of the holes is kept by the terms—so many "holes up"—or "all even"—and so many "to play."

10. Turf cut or displaced by a stroke in playing should be at once replaced.

ACT of Council and regulations to be observed in playing for the City of Edinburgh's Silver Club, 41

Allan, David, elected an honorary member of the Honourable Company of Golfers, 51

Anecdote of Campbell of Glensaddell, 174 *note*

Anecdote of Prince Henry, eldest son of James I., 9

Anecdotes of Charles I. and James II., 12, 13

Arthur's Seat, ball driven over, from Club House, Bruntsfield Links, 112, 224

'A solemn match at golf' played on Leith Links between Captain Porteous and Hon. Alexander Elphinstone, 18 *note*

A Tale of Golf, 206

BALFOUR, James, Secretary of the Honourable Company, notice of his death, 52; portrait of, by Raeburn, to be engraved, 53; anecdotes of, 54

Ball, first, given by the Golf Club of St. Andrews, 66

Blackheath, medal day at, 275

Boy appointed to summon members of the Edinburgh Burgess Club to dinner on Saturdays, 110

Bruntsfield Links Golf Club, Captain of, to have a person in uniform to carry his clubs, 99

'By the la' Harry, this won't go for nothing,' 137

CARLYLE, Rev. Dr., of Inveresk, gained the silver cup of the Musselburgh Golf Club, 88

Carnegie, George Fullerton, 155

Centenary of the Bruntsfield Links Golf Club, 106

Chalmers, Sir George, painter of William St. Clair's portrait, 48

Chambers, Robert, admitted a member of the Musselburgh Golf Club, 92

Chambers, Robert, jun., champion golfer of Great Britain, 106

Champagne first introduced at the Bruntsfield Links Golf Club dinners, 101

Chaplain, the Honourable Company elects Rev. Dr. John Dun as, 46

Cock o' the Green, 137

DECLARATION concerning sports, 118

Dinner Bill of the Honourable Company of Golfers in 1801, 63

Dinner, charge for, in 1785, 89; in 1800, 91

Dinner given by the Honourable Company to Henry Sanderson, Esq., Surgeon, R.N., 59

Index

Dinners of Musselburgh Golf Club, charge for, in 1785, 89; in 1800, 91

Drummore, Lord, portrait to be painted and hung up in the Golf House, Leith, 47

Dubbieside Links, Fife, 206

Duel between Hon. Alexander Elphinstone and Lieutenant Swift, 18 *note*

Duke of York, afterwards James II., a keen golfer, 13 ; story of an important match at golf played by him and two English noblemen, 15

Durham, James, Esq., of Largo, won the St. Andrews Silver Club in 94 strokes, 71

EARLY notices of Golf, 123

Elphinstone, Hon. Alexander, 18

Erskine, Hon. Henry, admitted a member of the Honourable Company, 51

Etymology of the word Golf, 2

Excerpt from Act of Council of the Lord Provost and Magistrates altering condition on which Silver Club is to be played for, 45

Extracts from—
 Accounts of the Lords High Treasurers of Scotland, 135
 Blackwood's Magazine, 142, 242
 Burgh and Parish Records, etc.—
  Archbishop Hamilton's acknowledgment of license granted him to plant rabbits on St. Andrews Links, 123
  Calderwood's *History*, 125
  Kirk Session of St. Andrews, 125 *et seq.* ; Perth, 126 *et seq.* ; North Leith, 128 ; Stirling, 129; Cullen, 129; Humbie, 129
  Letters from William Cramond, LL.D., to *Banffshire Journal*, 130 *et seq.*

Extracts from—
 Chambers's *Domestic Annals of Scotland*, 17-19 *note*
 Chambers's *Traditions of Edinburgh*, 19, 54
 Cornhill Magazine, 177
 Dundee Advertiser, 285
 Fraser's Magazine, 220
 Glasgow News, 244
 Journal of Henry Cockburn, 236
 Kay's *Portraits*, 137
 Macmillan's Magazine, 144
 Note-books of Sir John Foulis, Bart., of Ravelstoun, 133
 Strutt's *Sports and Pastimes of the People of England*, 4
 The Times, 263

FORBES, Duncan, Lord President of the Court of Session, anecdote of, 19 *note*

'Fute-ball and golfe utterly cryed downe' by statute of James II., 116

GLENNIE, George, Esq., in 1855, holed the round of St. Andrews Green in 88 strokes, 78

Golf, a chapter on, 220

Golf a fashionable game among the nobility at the beginning of the 17th century, 9

Golf, a tale of, 206

Golf ball driven over the spire of St. Giles's Cathedral, Edinburgh, 225

Golf Clubs, history of, and extracts from Minute Books—
 Bruntsfield Links Golf Club, 95
 Edinburgh Burgess Golfing Society, 109
 Honourable the Edinburgh Company of Golfers, 39
 Musselburgh Golf Club, 88
 Royal and Ancient Golf Club, 64

Index

Golf, early notices of, 123
Golfer at home, the, 177
Golfers, among the St. Andrews, 244
Golfer's Land, Canongate, 14
Golf, etymology of the word, 2
Golf, game of, very general during the reign of James II., 3
Golf, historical account of the game of, 1
Golf, scrap relative to, 135
Golf, Smollett's description of the game of, 46 *note*
Golfiana, or niceties connected with the game of golf, 155
Golfing, wonderful feats in, 224, 225
Gows to supply music at St. Andrews Golf Club Ball, 1796, 73
Grace, Charles, Esq., plate presented to, 75
Grace, Mr. Stuart, retirement of, 81
Gutta percha balls first given as prizes, 104

HISTORICAL account of the game of golf, 1
Holyrood, Palace of, 12, 13
Honourable Company of Golfers, presented with a Silver Club by the Magistrates of Edinburgh, 39, 41; used to meet in Luckie Clephan's until 1768, 40; each member shall have a diploma, 50; private green acquired at Muirfield, 40, 62; new Silver Club (the third) presented, 61
Hope, Sir Archibald, Bart., re-elected President of the Musselburgh Golf Club, 93

JAMES II., statute of, decrees and ordains 'that the fute-ball and golfe be utterly cryed downe,' 116

KING Charles I. extremely fond of golf, 12; while playing golf on the Links of Leith received the first account of the rebellion in Ireland, 12
King William IV. patron of the Royal and Ancient Golf Club of St. Andrews, 66; medal of, list of winners, 84
Knowles, James Sheridan, Esq., admitted honorary member of the Edinburgh Burgess Club, 113

LADIES' Green at St. Andrews, 69
Leith Links the resort of the golfers of the 'olden time,' 17
Logan, Halbert, of Restalrig, anecdote of, 19 *note*

M'KELLAR, Alexander, the Cock o' the Green, 137
M'Millan, Thomas, Esq., of Shorthope, Cup presented to Musselburgh Club by, 88
Magistrates of Edinburgh present Silver Clubs to the Honourable Company of Golfers, 39, 41, 61
Mansfield, James, Recorder of the Honourable Company, 61
Mathison, Thomas, author of *The Goff*, 23
Mayne, William, appointed clubmaker, etc., by James VI., 20
Medal day at Blackheath, 275
Medal day at St. Andrews, 263
Melvill, James, appointed golf-ball maker to James VI., 21
Melville, J. Whyte, Esq., 67, 81
Melville Monument, Edinburgh, golf ball driven over the top of, 225
Montrose, the Marquis of, xviii
Morris, Tom, appointed keeper of St. Andrews Links, 68

Index

Muirfield, private green of the Honourable Company, acquired, 40, 62

NASMYTH, Alexander, landscape-painter, admitted a member of the Edinburgh Burgess Golf Club, 111

PALACE of Holyrood, 12, 13
Parliament (XIV.) of King James II., 1457, cries down golf, 116
Patersone, John, partner to the Duke of York in a match at golf on Leith Links, 15
Petition by the Honourable Company of Golfers to the Town Council of Edinburgh for a seal of cause, 1800, 56
Plate presented to Charles Grace, Esq., by the Royal and Ancient Golf Club of St. Andrews, 75
Playfair, Sir Hugh, prime mover in New Club House, St. Andrews, 67
POEMS AND SONGS—
 Address by the Captain of the Royal and Ancient Golf Club, 253
 Address to St. Andrews, 157
 A Golf Song, 203
 A Golfing Song, 230
 A Hundred Golfers, 228
 Another Peep at the Links, 168
 A Voice from the Rhine, 271
 Ballade of the Royal Game of Golf, 227
 Duffers Yet! a Parody, 234
 Far and Sure, 218
 In Praise of Gutta Percha, 215
 Sanctandrews, 142
 Song for the first Musical Meeting of the Warrender Golf Club, 232
 The First Hole at St. Andrews on a crowded day, 163
 The Golfer's Garland, 282

Poems and Songs—
 The Goff, an heroi-comical poem, 23
 The Golfiad, 158
 The Links o' Innerleven, 213
 The Morning Round, 261
 The Nine Holes of the Links of St. Andrews—
  First or Bridge Hole, 194
  Second or Cartgate Hole, 195
  Third Hole, 196
  Fourth or Ginger-Beer Hole, 197
  Hell Hole, 198
  Heather Hole, 199
  High or Eden Hole, 200
  Short Hole, 201
  End Hole, 201
 To St. Andrew, 242
Prince Henry (eldest son of James I.) and his schoolmaster, 9
Prince of Wales becomes patron of the Royal and Ancient Golf Club of St. Andrews, and elected captain, 66
Porteous, John, Captain of the Edinburgh City Guard, 18 *note*

QUEEN Adelaide (Dowager), patroness of the Royal and Ancient Golf Club of St. Andrews, presents a gold medal, 66

RAEBURN, Henry, admitted a member of the Honourable Company, 52
Registrum secreti sigilli, 20
Regulations to be observed by members of the Honourable Company in playing for the Silver Club, 41
Robertson, Allan, keeper of St. Andrews Links, 67; account of his life, 285

SABBATH, profanation of, by golf, 126

Index

St. Andrews, 236

St. Andrews Royal and Ancient Golf Club, Dowager Queen Adelaide, patroness, presents a gold medal to, 66 ; His Royal Highness the Prince of Wales, patron, 66 ; King William IV., patron, presents a handsome gold medal to, 66

St. Clair, William, portrait of, to be hung up in large room of Honourable Company's Club House, Leith, 48 ; Sir Walter Scott's description of, 48 *note* ; laid foundation-stone of Club House for the Gentlemen Golfers on Leith Links, 47

St. Giles's Cathedral, Edinburgh, golf ball driven over the spire of, 225

St. Rule, the Links of, 144

Sanderson, Henry, dinner given to, by the Honourable Company, 59

Seal of cause granted to the Edinburgh Burgess Club, 111

Silver Cross of St. Andrew, list of winners of, 86

Silver Club presented to the Honourable Company by the Magistrates of Edinburgh in 1744, 39, 41 ; intimation by tuck of drum when to be played for, 42 ; new club (the third) presented, 61

Silver Club of St. Andrews, 45, 70

Smollett's description of the game of golf, 46 *note*

Statutes prohibiting the exercise of golf, 116-118

Sutherlandia, 255

TABLET on the wall of a house in Canongate, 17

Tom Morris, jun., account of his life, 291

Tulloch, Principal, 81

Tytler, Mr., of Woodhouselee, reminiscences of, 13

UNION Club and the Royal and Ancient Golf Club of St. Andrews amalgamated, 1854, 66

'Union Parlour,' first Club House of the St. Andrews Golf Club, 67

WHYTE-MELVILLE, J., Esq., 67, 81

Wine, price paid for at Club dinners in 1788, 90

Winners of the Silver Club of the Honourable Company to attach a gold or silver piece thereto, 42

Winners of King William the Fourth Medal, 84 ; of the Silver Cross of St. Andrew, 86

THE END

Printed by R. & R. CLARK, *Edinburgh.*